From Chant to Script

From Chant to Script

Winand M. Callewaert

DK PRINTWORLD
Publishers of Indian Traditions

Cataloging in Publication Data — DK
[Courtesy: D.K. Agencies (P) Ltd. <docinfo@dkagencies.com>]

Callewaert, Winand M.
From chant to script / Winand M. Callewaert.
p. cm.
Includes verses in Braj.
Includes bibliographical references (p.).
ISBN 9788124606957

1. Devotional literature, Hindi–History and criticism.
2. Sikh literature–History and criticism. 3. Bhakti in literature. I. Title.

DDC 891.4309 23

ISBN 13: 978-81-246-0695-7 ISBN 10: 81-246-0695-1
First published in India in 2013

Printed and published by:
D.K. Printworld (P) Ltd.
Regd. Office : '*Vedaśrī*', F-395, Sudarshan Park
(Metro Station: Ramesh Nagar)
New Delhi - 110 015
Phones : (011) 2545 3975; 2546 6019; *Fax* : (011) 2546 5926
e-mail : indology@dkprintworld.com
Web : www.dkprintworld.com

Preface

In 1965 I arrived in India and under the guidance of the Belgian Jesuit Father Camille Bulcke (कामिल बुल्के) I started my studies of Hindī and Sanskrit at St Xavier's, Ranchi. He was then working on his *English-Hindī Dictionary* (1968), writing with a pen and revising the typeset proofs and he told me repeatedly: "Winand, never start a dictionary. It is so hard." After studying at three different Indian universities, till 1971, I went to Paris to study with the great *bhakti* scholar Charlotte Vaudeville. Along with her enthusiasm she gave me the suggestion to work on *nirguṇa bhakti* literature in Rajasthan: "work on manuscripts, that will make your research worthwhile". I followed her advice and enjoy my research on *bhakti* literature till today. With all my admiration for the great Father Bulcke, I ignored his advice and in 1996 I started my last great project: *Dictionary of Bhakti: North-Indian Bhakti Texts into Kharī Bolī and English*, to be completed in four years. It took me thirteen years.

In 1971 I came back from India, after six years of study, and had a clear picture of what my research would consist of: the copying of manuscripts and preparation of critical editions of original texts, and translation. I also saw that my work would necessarily include going to far away places in Rajasthan and to important institutions in the cities. On the basis of the manuscripts found, I would *reconstruct*, I thought, the archetype of the *pad*s I wanted to edit. Scribes committed errors, intentionally or unknowingly, and obviously these variant readings should enable a researcher to establish the relationship between the manuscripts. On the basis of these relationships the stemma should allow one to reconstruct the "critical" text: a classical, scholarly approach to manuscripts leading to the Archetype! It all looked very simple and easy but wrong, and it became an even more exciting adventure, when I started to discover the singers in the manuscripts.

If I could start again, would I do what I have been doing? The answer is definitely yes, for several reasons. That research has given me some good friends, all over the globe, it has given me the opportunity — when I was young — to make adventurous tours all over Rajasthan, using all available diplomatic skill in order to have access to the manuscripts. Most importantly with that research I have contributed to the preservation and critical text-editions of old texts threatened with destruction.

After a long period of preparation I started to publish in 1973[1] and in this book I give a survey of my research, with

(1) a selection of revised articles (1973-98),

(2) a summary of some published books (1989-2009), and

(3) a summary of some published articles (1996-2011)[2].

1 For the complete list of my publications, which includes 35 books and 139 articles, I refer to my website http://mill.arts.kuleuven.be/caies/wcal.htm.

2 All dates are of the Common Era (CE; AD), except when specified as VS (Vikram Saṁvat, beginning shortly before CE 57).

Contents

Part III
Summaries of Published Articles (from 1996 to 2011)

Part I
Revised Articles
(from 1973 to 1998)

1

Life and Works of the Dādūpanthī Rajab
(North India Sixteenth-Seventeenth Century)

[1973][1]

The poets and saints of the so-called *nirguṇa-sādhanā* in the fifteenth-seventeenth centuries in northern India are not less important than the contemporary Saguṇa Vaiṣṇav Bhaktas. Although some detailed critical studies have been devoted to Guru Nānak, Kabīr and, to a lesser extent, to Dādū Dayāl, nevertheless only recently are orientalists becoming aware of the immense richness of literature and mysticism further to be explored in the field of Hindu-Muslim devotion during the Mughal period.

Unlike Kabīr, who is immense but solitary in his own tradition, the Dādūpanth of Rajasthan has brought forth a very vast literature. Tradition says that Dādū (1544-1603) had 152 disciples; fifty-two of them are said to have founded Dādū-centres (*dvārā*s). V. Varma[2] lists 77 disciples and their followers (*śiṣya*s and *praśiṣya*s) in the Dādū sect who have produced some literary work or other.

1. In: *Orientalia Lovaniensia Periodica*, 4, 1973, 141-53.
2. V. Varma, *संत कवि रज्जब*, Jodhpur, 1965, p. 170-74. [Printed Hindi editions and studies often spell "रज्जब", although in all the early manuscripts which I consulted of the *Rajab-vāṇī*, the *Rajab Sarvāṅgī*, and even the *Dādūjanmalīlā* I read everywhere रजब. For a discussion on this issue, see B.K. Singhal, *रज्जब की सरबंगी*, pp. 63ff.; Singhal gives in this text-edition everywhere रज्जब, although the manuscripts give consistently रजब. Interestingly, even when quoting the *Dādūjanmalīlā* in his Introduction, Singhal writes there, too, रज्जब, although all the manuscripts give रजब.]

Some of these works have been printed (e.g. of Garībdās, Jangopāl, Rajab and Sundardās), but the greater part is still to be found only in manuscripts. Traill[3] was one of the first[4] to draw the attention of Western orientalists to the "Bhāṣā literature", especially mentioning the writings of the Dādū Sampradāy. Referring to a manuscript in his possession he writes that in the *Dādū-vāṇī* there are 20,000 lines; actually there are only about 7,500. Relying on local informers he believes that "Rajab ji is said to have written 72,000 lines". The *Rajab-vāṇī*, however, contains only about 15,000 lines. Could it be that his estimates were on the high side in order to receive a bigger grant?

Life of Rajab

Rajab(dās), probably[5] surnamed Alī Khān, was with Sundardās, the most influential of Dādū's disciples. His father was a Muslim Paṭhān, serving in the Rājpūt forces of Rājā Bhagavantdās (one of the first Rajput allies of Akbar) and living in Sanganer, *c.* 15 km south-west of Jaipur, Rajasthan.[6] No written record is at hand mentioning the dates of Rajab's birth or death. The legend[7] popular among Rajab's disciples (*Rajabāvat*) that their master lived for 122 years makes him as worthy a saint as Kabīr but is not necessarily based on historical data. The traditional birthdate of Rajab is 1567. In the *Bhaktamāl* (or Garland of the Faithful) of Rāghavdās[8] we

3. John Traill, *Memo. on Bhasha Literature*, Jeypore, 1884 (India Office Library, London, manuscript B 28a).

4. The first translation into English of a few couplets of Dādū was made by G.R. Siddons in the *Journal of the Asiatic Society of Bengal*, 6, 1837, pp. 480-87 and 750-56.

5. See P. Chaturvedi: 1964, p. 503.

6. See V. Varma, *संत कवि रज्जब*, pp. 8f. For Sanganer, see *The Imperial Gazetteer of India*, rev. edn., Oxford, 1931, vol. XXVI, plate 36, D 2. An inscription recently discovered shows that the name of the son of Bharmal of Amber was Bhagavantdās and not Bhagavāntdās, Cf. *Indian Archaeology: A Review*, 1959, p. 59.

7. For more information see महात्मा रजब, in: *Rājasthān* (Calcutta), 1, 1935, *aṅka* 3 and 4, and *संत-वाणी*, Jaipur, 1, 1948, *aṅka* 1.

8. Narayandas:1975b, p. 687. *'rajjaba ajjaba rājasthāna āmbānerī āye, guru ke*

→

read that Rajab met Dādū in Amber and became his disciple there. This event, with the details of Rajab's wearing the bridegroom's attire, is not related in the earlier account, *The Life Story of Dādū* (*Dādūjanmalīlā*) by Jangopāl. The first meeting between Rajab and Dādū, related by Jangopāl, was apparently years later, when Rajab already had disciples of his own. The absence in the *Janmalīlā* of earlier details about Rajab's meeting Dādū is, however, not yet a guarantee of historicity. Only after the incident with Mān Singh and Dādū's departure from Amber does Jangopāl start mentioning Rajab as one of Dādū's disciples. Dādū came to Amber in 1579, resided there for 14 years and left the place in 1593, after a dispute with the governing Mān Singh. If Rajab met Dādū for the first time in Amber, this must have happened before 1593. On the other hand, Rajab's initiation may have taken place after 1585, the year in which Dādū with some disciples is supposed to have met emperor Akbar in Fatehpur Sikri and stayed with him for forty days.

Among the seven disciples accompanying Dādū on this journey, Rajab's name is not mentioned by Jangopāl.[9] We can presume, however, that Rajab may have been quite young[10] at the moment of his marriage and of his vocation, and that he could have met Dādū in the year of the latter's departure from Amber. To sum

---

→ *sabada triyā byāha saṅga tyāgo hai'*, i.e. "when Rajab came to Āmbanerī in Rajasthan, he (heard) the word of the guru, and left behind his wife and the marriage party". One Āmbanerī is situated in the Warora tahsil of Chanda district, in the south-east part of Maharastra, more than 500 km from Jaipur. See *Indian Archaeology: A Review*, 1960, p. 24. The Āmbanerī of the inscription seems to refer to Amber, about 8 km north-east of Jaipur, also spelled as Amer; see Bhandarkar, *A List of the Inscriptions of Northern India*, No. 70.

9. The seven disciples are Cāndā, Ṭilā, Jag Jivan, Śyāmdās, Jagadīś, Gunadās, Dharmadās, cited in the 16th *viśrām* of the *Janmalīlā*. See H. Mahesvari, *राजस्थानी भाषा और साहित्य*, 1960, p. 288. Again, the absence of Rajab's name does not give complete certainty. Incidentally, 1585 is also the year when Akbar left Fatehpur Sikri never to go back, after having resided there for 15 years.

10. Sundardās (c. 1596–1689) became Dādū's disciple at the age of six. Cf. P. Chaturvedi: 1964, p. 507.

up, till further proofs add more certainty to one particular date, we may place Rajab's year of birth between 1567 and 1580.[11]

In connection with Rajab's death we only know for certain that he died before the year 1689. In his Introduction to the *Sundargranthāvalī*[12] Sharma accepts 1689 as the year of death of Sundardās, referring to the inscription[13] "in Saṁvat 1746, on the eighth day of the bright half of the month Kārttik, in the third *pahar* of Bṛhaspativāra, Sundardās went to heaven", i.e. Sundardās died on a Thursday afternoon at the end of October 1689 CE. Sundardās had gone to visit his old friend Rajab in Sanganer and on hearing that Rajab had died, he had an attack and died a few months later. Of course, Rajab could well have died a long time before 1689.

Works of Rajab

Rajab occupies a special place in the Dādū tradition, not only on account of his own high religious standing but also because he grouped the couplets of his master together into thematic chapters. Mohandās, sometimes referred to as Mohandās Daftarī (secretary), most probably wrote Dādū's *pad*s "as the guru uttered them"[14] and Rajab arranged them in the order we also find in the other contemporary *vāṇī*s. The work was also called *Aṅgabandho* or *Aṅgabandhu*[15] and is now known as *Dādū-vāṇī.*

Two works are attributed to Rajab himself: the *Rajab-vāṇī* and the *Sarvāṅgī*, also called *Sarvāṅga-yoga*. The *Vāṇī*, which is a collection of Rajab's own compositions, was for the first time printed by Sadhu Sevādās and others, in the Gyansagar Press, Bombay, 1918; a commentary was given to the *chhappai* section,

---

11. See B.K. Singhal, op. cit., pp. 67ff.
12. Sharma:1936, pp. 59 and 118.
13. This inscription was written on the tombstone of Sundardās' grave at Sanganer. The canopy above the tomb has now disappeared but the inscription on the stone was recorded by P.H. Sharma: op. cit., p. 119.
14. See Narayandas: 1975b, p. 692.
15. V. Varma, संत कवि रज्जब, p. 175.

along with a short vocabulary. Varma writes about this work: "The editors, not well acquainted with the Rajab literature, have made it quite a different text. Many words, sentences and metres have been distorted."[16] A second edition with Hindī translation was prepared by Kaviratna Svami Narayandas, Pushkar, and published by Narayan Singh Shekhavan, Ajmer (not dated). Only one manuscript, found at the Dādū Mahāvidyālaya in Jaipur, was used for that edition.

Vrajalal Varma provided another edition of the *Vāṇī* text, which in fact is merely a reprint of the above-mentioned manuscript, without the intention to produce a critical edition. He added a vocabulary of about 1,400 words with Hindī equivalents. The words in the vocabulary cannot be easily found because they do not always appear in the order in which they occur in the text, and there is no alphabetical list.[17] In his introduction to the *Vāṇī* text Varma states that "the manuscripts of the *Rajab-vāṇī* have nearly disappeared". This statement is as vague as the list of manuscripts Varma then adds is incorrect.

> During my search for manuscripts in Rajasthan I discovered a copy of the *Rajab-vāṇī* in the Vidyā Bhūṣan Saṅgrah, Prācya Vidyā Pratiṣṭhān, Jaipur, vol. 13, pp. 1-151 (dated CE 1675-86) and one copy in the Pothī Khānā of the City Palace, Jaipur, vol. 1933 (dated CE 1703). Other copies are in Narainā, Dādū Dvārā: big vol. pp. 285-348 and in the Dādū Mahāvidyālaya, Jaipur: ms. 1, pp. 247-344; 7B, pp. 1-149, 1-56; 34B, pp. 1-138; 7, pp. 129ff.; 19B; 7C and 18B. The most ancient selection of the *kavitta*s was found in the above-mentioned Saṁgraha, vol. 34/253, pp. 570-75 (dated 1653) and in the Dādū Mahāvidyālaya collection, vol. 2, p. 424 (1676), besides many more selections in other volumes. The most ancient selection of *sākhī*s I found in the same Saṁgraha, vol. 34/95 (1658) and vol. 12/46, pp. 272-90 (1684).

---

16. Vrajalal Varma, *रज्जब वाणी*, p. 9.
17. After the words of the *sākhī* chapters 1 to 125 are given the words of the *kavitta* chapters 1 to 33 and then again those of the *sākhī* chapters 127-92.

The *Rajab-vāṇī* consists of mainly *sākhīs*, *pads* and *kavittas*. The 5,352 couplets (*sākhīs* or testimonies), thematically grouped in 193 chapters (*aṅga*),[18] constitute the main bulk of the *Vāṇī* (372 of the 514 pages in Varma's edition). This *sākhī* collection has 24 titles of chapters in common, more or less in the same order as in the *Kabīr-Granthāvalī*, which is a selection of Kabīr's *sākhīs* made and piously preserved by the followers of the Dādū sect in Rajasthan. The *pad* section (pp. 373-430) is a collection of 200 short poems on different topics, composed in as many as 30 different *rāgs*. The *kavitta* section (pp. 494-514) contains 40 chapters with concise spiritual guidelines, very popular among the *sadhus* of the sect. In the remaining pages (pp. 431-93) containing poems in praise of Dādū or of Rajab, a considerable number of verses are to be attributed to Rajab's disciples Caindās, Rāmdās, Khemdās, Mohandās and Kalyāndās.

Rajab's second work, the *Sarvāṅgī*, lists 146[19] titles of *sākhī* chapters, in order generally agreeing with the *Rajab-vāṇī*. In this work Rajab has grouped thematically in chapters couplets of his own *Vāṇī* and of more than 50 *nirguṇa* and Vaiṣṇav poets, Sanskrit authors and Sufis.[20] About 102 titles are identical with titles of chapters in the *Rajab-vāṇī*; 20 titles in the *Sarvāṅgī* list, however, do not figure in the *Rajab-vāṇī*. One can hardly overestimate the effect such a gigantic compilation must have had on the Dādūpanth followers, broadening their religious and literary knowledge and

18. The *Dādū-vāṇī* (ed. Svami Mangaldas, Jaipur 1951) has, in comparison, only about 2,500 couplets in the 37 *sākhī*-chapters. This text is a reprint of the Ajmer edition of 1917, by C.P. Tripathi, "along with the mistakes of the Tripathi-text", Introd., p. 3.

19. V.Varma, *संत कवि रज्जब*, pp. 181-86, lists 146 titles. W.G. Orr speaks of 142 chapters of the *Sarvāṅgī*, the book "taking the form of an elaborate commentary on the sayings and hymns of Dādū, with parallel passages cited from Rajab's own poems and those of a large number of other writers". See *A Sixteenth-Century Indian Mystic*, London, 1947, pp. 40ff.

20. Of the 2790 *sākhīs* and 890 *pads*, about 200 *sākhīs* and 170 *pads* were identified to be of Kabīr, 360 *sākhīs* and 100 *pads* of Dādū, 55 *pads* of Sūr(dās), 40 *pads* of Nāmdev; of Hardās and Raidās 25 *pads* each, and 10 *pads* of Gorakh.

providing them with an inexhaustible source of inspiration. On the other hand, it makes a critical study of the dependence and the originality of the Dādū-school and of Rajab more imperative. Similarly, a study of the earliest Dādū-inspiration would be welcome. The "five manuscripts on which the Ajmer text (of the *Dādū-vāṇī*) is based are all comparatively recent, the oldest being dated CE 1779". "In view of indubitable traces of the redactor's hand in the other early literature of the *panth*", it would be recommendable to make a careful scrutiny of the earliest text; Orr here refers especially to "the temple of Nārāiṇā, where is believed to repose a very ancient manuscript, to which however the visitor is denied access".[21]

V. Varma proposes the hypothesis that Guru Arjan was influenced by the structure of the *Sarvāṅgī* to compose in a similar style the *Gurugranth*.[22] He quotes G.E. Sen, *Cultural Unity of India*: "A few years before Guru Arjan compiled the sacred scriptures of the Sikhs, Dādū requested his disciples to gather songs and hymns from Hindu, Islamic and Sufi sources, which could help the devotee in his search for the universal God. This was perhaps the first collection of its kind in the world". This hypothesis raises some difficulties. Since W.H. McLeod[23] dates the compilation of the Sikh canonical scriptures by Guru Arjan in the years 1603-04, we can hardly admit that the compilation work in the Dādūpanth could, before 1603, have been much beyond the initial stage. Moreover, V. Varma "takes it for granted (*yah nirvivād hai*) that the *Sarvāṅgī* anthology was composed by Rajab after his own *Vāṇī*, because in the *Sarvāṅgī* Rajab incorporated the couplets of his own *Vāṇī*."[24] Even if we, e.g. accept 1590 as the year of Rajab's initiation

21. Orr: 1947, pp. 79-80 *passim*. The four most ancient copies of the *Dādū-vāṇī* which I discovered are in the Vidyā Bhūṣan Saṁgrah, Jaipur, dated CE 1661 and 1684 and in the Dādū Mahāvidyālaya, Jaipur, dated CE 1636 and 1676. [All were by me copied on microfilm and are now in the University of Heidelberg; Digitization and cataloguing in progress.

22. V.Varma, *संत कवि रज्जब* pp. 40-41.

23. McLeod:1968, p. 1.

24. Vrajlal Varma, *रजब वाणी*, p. 10.

with Dādū in Amber, at the age of fifteen, Rajab could hardly have finished his own *Vāṇī* and a good deal of the *Sarvāṅgī* before 1603, as an example for Guru Arjan.

No critical edition[25] of this immense anthology has been prepared so far, although this would be valuable for a better knowledge, not only of Rajab's own *sākhī*s and the literature of the Dādūpanth, but also of Kabīr and the Sant literature in general. Manuscripts of the *Sarvāṅgī* are found in many collections in Rajasthan, differing slightly in the order of titles and the amount of material.

Language of the Rajab-vāṇī (Varma edition)

The language of the *Rajab-vāṇī* can be called "non-descript", for two reasons. First, the (one) manuscript used for the latest edition of the *Vāṇī* (V. Varma) is not dated and till further evidence is found, the degree of relationship of this text with the original tongue of Rajab cannot be established with certainty, for the text may have been subject to many successive alterations. Secondly, like many of the popular poet-mystics of the period, Rajab, too, underwent a variety of religious and literary influences and addressed a variety of people. For example, there are clear instances of his having repeated himself, at one time in Sanskrit vocabulary, and at another in Sufi terminology.[26]

Yoga and Sufi Terminology in the Rajab-vāṇī

Like the *nirguṇa* tradition in general, Rajab's writings, too, present a remarkable syncretism of ideas, with contributions from the Vedāntic Hindu tradition, (Buddhist) tantra, the Siddha and Nātha

25. In the Introduction to his *रज्जब की सरबंगी*, pp. 148ff. B.K. Singhal describes the six manuscripts of the *Sarvāṅgī* which he consulted (काम में ली गई हैं), but in the text-edition (pp. 201-687) no critical apparatus or reference to any manuscript is given.

26. Varma, *संत कवि रज्जब*, pp. 222-23, defines Rajab's language as "basically Rājasthānī (dialectically Ḍhūḍhārī) with a good deal of influence of Braj, Avadhī, Kharī Bolī Hindī, Punjābi, Gujarātī, Marāṭhī, Persian and Sanskrit".

literature, the Yoga philosophy and practices and Sufism. The two latter trends are briefly discussed here.

Yoga

Steeped in the Hindu tradition of the Upaniṣads, the *nirguṇa* authors too have their roots in the Buddhist Vajrayāna school, i.e. the branch of Mahāyāna Buddhism which turned to the sexo-yogic practices of Tantra Yoga. The link with that tradition was provided by the Gorakhnāth sect. Rajab was not only well acquainted with the Nātha literature — in his *Sarvāṅgī* we find ten quotations from Gorakhnāth — he surely came also into contact with the yogic practices of the Nātha devotees, popular among the ordinary people. However, following his master Dādū, Rajab did not rely much on the severe body exercises of the *haṭha-yogī*s, who aim at awakening the serpent-power (*kuṇḍalinī-śakti*) and make it climb through the six/seven centres (*cakra*s) up to the centre of supreme experience in the top part of the skull (*brahmarandhra-cakra*). Keeping the same goal in mind, i.e. the experience of God in the interior of man, Rajab rather advocated the practice of mental yoga, the interior discipline of purification. This practice can be termed *laya-yoga*, the discipline of absorption, of union with the Eternal One. Considering the emphasis put on devotion (*bhakti* and *upāsanā*) and love (*prema* and *iśka*) we may also call it *bhakti* yoga.

The basic insight is that God dwells in the heart of man and that He cannot be found in the places of devotion of the *saguṇa bhakta*s. We read in the chapter on "The middle path and one's own place on it"[27]:

The 490 millions (of winds) roam about day and night, the sun

27. Chapter 57, *Madhya māraga nija thāna niranai kā aṅga*. *Madhi māraga* has with Kabīr and Dādū the Buddhist meaning of "middle path". Cf. C. Vaudeville (*Kabīr-Granthāvalī*, Pondicherry, 1957), who translates the title of chapter 31 as "*chapitre du milieu*". Orr: 1947, p. 81, translates the title of the 16th chapter of the *Dādū-vāṇī* as "Chapter of Impartiality". Madhyamāraga has with Rajab generally the specific meaning of "interior path", the path of *laya-yoga*. The English translation of Rajab's couplets in this article is my own.

and the moon are unceasingly moving; yet, both these travellers do not know the Imperishable Lord. —57/10

Travel over the seven isles and over the nine parts (i.e. over the whole world), yet your hand will not rise even one inch. (Rajab says) enter the dwelling of the heart in order to find perfection. —57/13

Within your heart you must go across the whole earth, in your heart visit the unlimited bathing-places. Along the path of the heart does the devotee meet the Indweller (*antarajāmī*). —57/19

O ignorant people, you search Him outside, but He is within you, pervading your whole body; (Rajab says) Rām and I are closely together, believe the wise men (Santa Sujāna). —57/6

To which Mecca did Muhammad go, and in what place did Mahādeva reside? Follow that path rather where the travellers are wise people. —57/29

The hypocrisy and inefficacy of exterior practices and the superiority of the interior discipline are emphasized throughout the *Vāṇī*, especially in the chapter entitled "On Hypocrisy" (ch. 132, *svāṅga kā aṅga*).

The *haṭha-yogī* who believes in the efficacy of his bodily postures and exercises believes that his own energy, when properly directed, leads to liberation. For him no exterior agent is necessary. The *laya-yogī* contemplates the Indwelling Lord and relies on God's grace. The term *rahīm kari* (rendered as "with His grace", or "showing mercy") is frequently used by Rajab and properly fits only in this system of *bhakti-yoga*. In the chapter on "Supplication" (*bīntī kā aṅga*) Rajab says:

Showing mercy from on high, Harijī gives me His hand. Protect my union with Your name, Lord, You who keep me out of hell. —45/2

Brahmā is like a bird and man is His egg; if God does not take care, how can the body of man even start to live? —45/30

The total reliance of the *bhakti-yogī* on God finds its most humble expression in the acceptance of one's sinfulness. The *haṭha-yogī* aims at transcending his weakness and contingency; the *bhakti-yogī* asks for God's help:

> I never stopped sinning, I am always in sin; Lord, why are you forgetful of me, why do you not save me?
>
> —45/56, also 45/114

Haṭha-yoga terminology is used by Rajab to describe the higher levels of experience. Amidst the misery of the dark night (described in the chapter on "Desolation", *viraha kā aṅga*) Rajab hopefully yearns for the sweetness of former experiences. The terms are fully yogic, e.g.:

> Rise up to your own heaven, in the centre of the forehead (the *ājñācakra*); reverse the movement towards *śūnya* (*brahmarandhra*), the safe dwelling-place of the travellers. —10/30

When describing the inner experiences of the encounter with the Divine, Rajab uses the words *sunni* (*śūnya*) which literally means "void". The term was often used in the Yoga and Siddha literature, to denote the state of supreme bliss experienced at the moment when the energy-serpent (*kuṇḍalinī*) has traversed the six centres and has reached the lotus of a thousand petals (*sahasra-dal*), said to be located at the top of the skull. At that moment the unheard sound (*anāhat sabad*)[28] is heard. Rajab, like Kabīr and Dādū, uses the term *śūnya* to indicate the state of supreme bliss (*unmani*). In the chapter on the "Fire of Brahma" (*brahma agini kā aṅga*) we read:

> The body and the wood of the *karama* (tree) burn, but the fire of Brahmā is in the forehead (i.e. in the *ājñācakra*); the life of holiness starts with this fire, equal to *śūnya*. — 12/3

He also uses the term *śūnya* in the general meaning of "the sky".

When describing the supreme Deity, he compares His infiniteness with the vastness of the sky:

28. Cf. e.g. *nāda dhuni* in chapter 3/112 of the *Rajab-vāṇī*.

> The One Lord and the sky (*śūnya*) alike have no beginning, middle or end. All seekers have searched in vain, but Rajab is in Him.
> —61/3

Sufism

Although the Sufis formed only a marginal group in northern India, they nevertheless exerted a distinct influence on the religious life of the period. Dādū and perhaps even Rajab were of immediate Muslim descent and at one time were surely much in contact with the Quran. Yet, many Sufi elements in their spirituality they share with their Sant predecessors. The *Rajab-vāṇī*, too, shows many affinities with the Sufi theology. Leaving aside the question of their contact with contemporary Sufis, I only want to point out in the *vāṇī* some apparent affinities with Sufism.

1. Although the guru is important in the Bhāgavat tradition too, he attains a nearly superhuman status in the Dādū tradition and in the *Rajab-vāṇī*, to the extent that even starting a religious quest is impossible without a guru:

   > The divine perfection is like a jewel; a diamond cannot be pierced; but if the guru makes a hole, the disciple can fit in a thread (the thread of devotion) (3/18). Rajab received the grace of his vocation and of the vision of God through the intermediary of his guru (3/15 and ff.) and all his good actions are the result of Dādū's help (e.g. 3/6).

   The distinction between the human guru Dādū and the divine *satguru* is not always clear, as appears from, e.g. this couplet of the third chapter:

   > The guru is the tailor, His word is the needle, His love-rope is the thread; (Rajab says) only the *satguru* can stitch the devotee and Rām together.
   > — 3/49[29]

---

29. A particularly clear exposition of the meaning of the word guru as an expression of the divine initiative and of *satguru* as the initiative itself, is given in McLeod: 1968, pp. 196-99.

2. The relation between God and the devotee is one of intense love and is often described as being the relationship between husband and wife, lover and beloved. The most penetrating description of the devotee (woman)'s love for God (lover) is found in the chapter on "Desolation":

   > The wife, when separated from her husband, roams about day and night. The servant Rajab goes on burning (in the absence of God), his endless pain is always alive. — 10/5
   >
   > Separated from my beloved, I am a dumb child, an animal. My desires are left unfulfilled and I cannot find the beginning of the road (towards salvation). — 10/9
   >
   > The separation from my beloved hurts like a snakebite; only the vision of God is a suitable medicine. Without seeing Him I remain sad, I find no peace in body or soul. — 10/14
   >
   > Listen, O Beloved friend, Rajab has forgotten everything, like the woman who in the absence of her husband no longer cares for her beauty. — 10/17

   Applying a human experience unto the relation with God, Rajab says that love for God must be exclusive and tolerates no division:

   > If I have one; I will have all, but if I want to have all, I'll have none. This is the way of the world and Rajab has with great discernment understood. — 66/12

3. The mirror (*darpana, darpaṇa*) is a common Sufi simile, often used by Rajab. In this mirror of human faculties, cleansed of the obscurities of sin and negligence, the image of the Divine is received and retained. In this inner mirror the purified man reflects and hence resembles the Divine. For Rajab, the guru is often the mirror reflecting divine wisdom:

   > The mirror of the guru is very shiny, from it the servant Rajab acquires great knowledge. — 3/48

> The knowledge of my guru is penetrating, the disciple reads in it and learns, as when looking in a mirror we clearly see a reflection. — 3/123

The image is also used to denote the presence of the divine in the heart:

> The world is visible in the mirror of the heart.
> — 66/10

God Himself is sometimes the mirror:

> Rām is a mirror, immaculate and pure.
> — 50/15
>
> In the mirror (I see) the ocean which is the Lord.
> — 50/18

2

The Anabhay-Prabodh of the Dādūpanthī Garībdās

[1973/1977][1]

THE *Anabhay-Prabodh* was written in 1608 (VS 1665 *māse phāgun* in manuscript no. 2, fo. 78a) to meet the requirements of the disciples and followers of Dādū (1544-1603) for whom the meaning of the *nirguṇa bhakti* literature may apparently have become as puzzling as for the modern reader. The meaning is difficult for mainly two reasons. First, the Sants were popular reformers and at times critics of both the Hindu and Muslim religious customs. Influenced by both religions and addressing a wide range of people, they borrowed vocabulary not only from Sanskrit, the Prākr̥t languages, *deśī* "Hindī" and the Rājasthānī dialects but also from Persian which was the current administrative language in northern India. Secondly, like most mystic authors, they used words in a second and third meaning in order to explain their inner experience and to describe the component elements of mind and body in the process towards this experience. Because of the abundant use of yogic terminology and of complicated metaphors, the reader of the *nirguṇa bhakti* literature is often at a loss as to the exact meaning of a particular verse or word.

In this "Key for Understanding Mystical Terminology" Garībdās gives in 141 couplets a series of synonyms for the most

1. In: *Orientalia Lovaniensia Periodica*, 5, 1974: 163-85, and *Orientalia Lovaniensia Periodica*, 8, 1977: 309-30.

frequently occurring terms in Sant literature. It should be noted that in the list below the same term has at times been used to denote different concepts. Also, it would seem that words are often grouped merely for the effect of alliteration, as with म for मन ("mind", line 28) or माया (line 34), च for चित (line 31), क for कुबुधि (line 38), स for संसा (line 39) and for सुरति (line 57). It is also evident from the synonyms used for a particular keyword what the degree of respect for the denoted concept was in the mind of the *bhakti* poets; see, e.g. the synonyms for माया in line 34 and on the other hand the terms used for सतगुर in line 74. Certain synonyms are rather unusual, like कलस, or कुंभ (pot) for प्राण ("spirit", line 53). Synonyms of मन (mind) appear to be masculine whereas those of मनसा (mind) are feminine.

Since my translation of this list is especially meant to provide a tool to the readers and translators of a *nirguṇa* text, I have given the terms, as far as possible, also in an alphabetical glossary, and not only (as far as possible) in a verse-to-verse translation. At the same time, the list may be useful for a general study on symbolic terminology in literature.

The first part (1-81) gives a general exposition on the origin of the world and on the constitution of the created world and of the human body and mind.

The list "Names for God" (82ff.) shows a remarkable mixture of Hindu and Muslim terminology. This work was fairly important in the early Dādū Sampradāy and it most probably also influenced the *Gyān-samudra* of Sundardās.[2] In *The Nirguṇa School of Hindī Poetry*[3] P.D. Badathval gives a "Mystery Code", in which he enumerates a limited number of synonyms and symbols used in *nirguṇa* literature, and he states: "Garībdās's *Anabhay-Prabodh granth* has been of great help in compiling this list".

2. This "Ocean of Knowledge", written in 1643 gives in much more detail definitions of similar terms and topics. See, Sharma: 1936, pp. 1-83.

3. Benares, 1936, pp. 270-72.

The Author

The Dādūpanthī Garībdās should not be confused with Garībdās (1717-98), founder of the Garībpanth, whose *Vāṇī* was published by the Belvedere Press, Allahabad.[4] As is the case for many Dādūpanthī *bhakta*s the sources about Garībdās are partly historical and partly legendary. Without trying to clearly distinguish between the two, I list here the earliest sources.

The *Dādūjanmalīlā* by Dādū's disciple Jangopāl is, according to Orr[5] "believed to have been written shortly after Dādū's death" (in CE 1603; see below, pp. 173ff. in which see p. 137 for the references to Garībdās).

In the Narayandas, edition of the Rāghavdās *Bhaktamāl*[6] the notes on Garībdās are found on pp. 677-80 and on pp. 183-85 in the edition of A. Nahta, Jodhpur, 1965. The संवत् सत्रह सै सत्रहोतरा (*Bhaktamāl*, no. 651) was translated by P.H. Sharma[7] as Saṁvat 1700 + 77 (or CE 1720; see below, pp. 156-57). However, both editors[8] of the *Bhaktamāl* of Rāghavdās translate सत्रहोतरा not as 77 but as 17, i.e. Saṁvat 1717 or CE 1660.

The *Santa Guṇa Sāgar* by Mādhavdās (referred to in the Rāghavdās *Bhaktamāl*, pp. 735-36) is a vast work of 2,000 couplets supposed to have been completed in 1604. This work has not yet been published and I rely on the quotations given by Sukh Dayāl Dādū in "आचार्यवर श्री स्वामी गरीबदासजी महाराज का आदर्श जीवन चरित्र" in the periodical *श्रीदादूसेवक*, 5 (1947), nos. 4 and 5. Although the manuscripts of the *Santa Guṇa Sāgar* are said to give Saṁvat 1661 or CE 1604 as date of compilation, its composition was probably later, as is also suggested by P.H. Sharma.[9]

4. Chaturvedi: 1964, pp. 728ff.
5. Orr: 1947, pp. 26ff.
6. Narayandas: 1969.
7. Sharma: 1936, Introd., p. 2.
8. Narayandas: 1969, p. 899, and Nahta: 1965, p. *ś*.
9. Sharma: 1936, p. 93.

We also find some information about Garībdās in the work of Rajab, a disciple of Dādū and contemporary of Garībdās.[10]

"Son" of Dādū?

The ninth chapter of the *Dādūjanmalīlā* (ch. 9; see below, pp. 173ff.) relates that as to Kabīr was born Kamāl, so Dādū, too, had children.

To his wife, eager to have children, Dādū gave two cloves and two peppercorns and as a result Garībdās and his brother Maskīndās were born. Incidentally, both *garib* and *masakīn* mean "poor, humble".[11] This happened in Sāmbhar (north of Jaipur), probably around 1575. In chapter 9:2-6 Jangopāl describes the birth of Dādū's children:

> In Sāmbhar when Dādū was thirty-two, during the rainy season, the Lord of the world gave him children. Dādū was with us as a father, the first son born to him was Garībdās. As the child grew up corresponding to his age, he acquired full wisdom, like Nārad playing the flute, like *gandharvas* singing loudly, like Tumbar clapping his hands for rhythm, with a nectar-like voice and sweet speech: enumerate all the talents in the world, Garībdās was endowed with them. An ascetic from birth, totally detached as a youth, wise Garībdās knew no passion. Jangopāl sings his praise and tells you about Dādū's other children. The second son is Maskīn. . . .

In chapter 15:1 (1ff.) is given an interpolated section in which the miraculous passing away of Dādū is told. Garībdās plays an prominent role in this passage and this leads naturally to chapter 16:16:

> The Sants anointed Garībdās as the successor, he was given the seat and place of the guru. Garībdās began to be considered as equal to Svāmījī, with the support of the Sants.

---

10. Narayandas, श्रीरज्जबवाणी, 1967, pp. 1180ff.: *Śrī svāmī garībadās ke bhẽṭ ke savaiye*.

11. See Mangaldas, दादूवाणी, 1951, chapter 23.27.

In the context of Garībdās the *Bhaktamāl* (ed. Narayandas, pp. 677-79) mentions Dādū *suvan* and Dādū *nanda*, i.e. son of Dādū. According to modern Dādūpanthī sources Garībdās was only Dādū's spiritual son, in the way even today *sadhus* may adopt children to educate them. Sukh Dayāl Dādū (*श्रीदादूजन्मलीला परची*, Jaipur, 1947) gives the following account:

> When Dādū resided in Sāmbhar a childless brahmin couple (Dāmodardās and his wife Umā) came to him; they were given miraculous seeds, got two sons and gave them to Dādū for adoption.

This effort to make Garībdās the son of a brāhmaṇ follows the pattern applied to Dādū's and even Rajab's origin. In the nineteenth-century biography *Bhagavat Līlā Advaita Siddhānta* by Daulatarām, Rajab, too, is said to have been a foundling educated in a brāhmaṇ family. With Dādū this literary strategy is all the more important because of the traditional argument that he started his ascetic life in his childhood and was never married. The fact that the short *Bhaktamāl* of Jaggā[12] (one of Dādū's disciples) mentions Garībdās and Maskīn only as *sevaks* or disciples or that the *Bhaktamāl* of Caina (another disciple, ibidem, p. 283) does not mention the parental relationship with Dādū is not a clear proof for the absence of such a relationship.[13] All sources agree on the point that after Dādū's death Garībdās, at the age of 28, was chosen as successor on the seat of the main monastery in Narainā, south of Jaipur.

Garībdās died in 1614 or in 1636. The first date is suggested by Sukh Dayāl Dādū (see Bibliography, आचार्यवर श्री. . .), the second by Swami Mangaldas (*गरीबदासजी की वाणी*, 1947, p. छ). The date 1636 looks more acceptable if we take into account the story[14] of emperor Jahangir's presence in Narainā and the miracle performed by Garībdās on his lute: at the emperor's request he played the *megh rāg* (melody of the clouds) and caused an abundant

12. Nahta: 1965, pp. 274-79.
13. Ibid., pp. 280-86.
14. Narayandas: 1969, pp. 678ff.

rain during a period of drought. Emperor Jahangir was in Ajmer in CE 1615.[15] The *jayantī* of Garībdās is celebrated each year about 25 May in Narainā, where his sandals and lute are still kept.

The Text

The text of the *Anabhay-Prabodh* was published by Svami Mangaldas in *गरीबदासजी की वाणी*, (Jaipur, 1947, pp. 1-28) along with the *Vāṇī* of Garībdās, which consists of *sākhī*s (fo. 29-40), *caubolā*s (fo. 41-47), *kavitta*s (fo. 48) and *pad*s (fo. 49-75). The booklet is out of print and hard to find. Svami Mangaldas gives the reading of words which "he found was most common in the manuscripts consulted" (Introd., p. ङ) but he does not mention which manuscripts he consulted nor does he include a critical apparatus. In the Introduction Mangaldas wrongly thinks that the work entitled *Adhyātmabodh*, in *Hastalikhit Hindī Pustakon kā Saṁkṣipt Vivaraṇ*, vol. I, Benares, 1964, p. 17, should be of a different Garībdās. The manuscript which I copied for the present edition has at the beginning (fo. 74b): *granth adhyātam anabhay prabodh*, and at the end (fo. 78a): *iti śrī adhyātam bodh sampūrṇa samāpta.*

I found the following manuscripts during my search in Rajasthan:

Dādū Mahāvidyālaya, Jaipur: no. 2, fo. 62ff., dated 1676;

Vidyā Bhūṣaṇ Saṁgraha, Jaipur:

No. 34, fo. 435-44 (dated 1658),

No. 12, fo. 265-68 (CE 1684).

Without trying to establish an authoritative text, I give here a transcript of manuscript no. 34, with the relevant variant readings in manuscript no. 2 in footnote. In some cases the meaning of certain words could not be known for sure. Instead of attempting a misleading translation, these words are left untranslated, marked with the siglum "x". In manuscript no. 2 we find often ष for the spelling ख in manuscript no. 34. The translation given below

15. See V. Smith, *The Oxford History of India*, 3rd edn., repr., 1967, p. 368.

should be a much improved version, as in the 1970s *The Oxford Hindī-English Dictionary* of R.S. McGregor (1993) and my *The Dictionary of Bhakti* (2009) did not exist.

१ वोॐ प्रणऊं गुर के पाइ　　मति बुधि ग्यांन देहु संमझाइ ।
जासूं बरणौं प्यंड ब्रह्मंड　　सातौं साइर अरु नव खंड ॥

Oṁ. I bow [my head] at the feet of my guru, who gives total insight. Who is proclaimed by all beings in the whole universe, over the seven oceans and over the nine parts.

2 आदि अनादैं जोति अपार　　ताथैं प्रगट्यौं वो ॐकार ।
वो ॐकार थैं पांचौं तत्त　　राजस सातिग तामस मत्त ॥

At the beginning there was eternal and unlimited light, from which originated Oṁkār. From Oṁkār originated the five elementary substances (*tattva*), and the idea of [the constituents of nature: *guṇ*] *rajas*, *sattva* and *tamas*.

3 धरती पांणी अगनि मिलाव　　पवन अकास ऐ पंचूं नांव ।

Earth, water, fire together with/wind, ether: these are the five names [of the elementary substances].

3b राजस ब्रह्मा बि न कै सातिग तामसि महादेव की क्रांति ॥
4 राजस बरिषा सातिग सीत　　तामस ग्रीष्म तीन्यूं रीत ।
राजस जल सातिग मत पवन　　तामस अगंनी तीन्यूं भवन ॥
5a ब्रह्म नाभि बि न उरि बास　　महादेव मस्तकि कविलास ।

3b-5a: the three constituents of nature (*guṇas*):

	[deity]	[season]	[house]	[dwelling]
rajas	Brahmā	rainy	water	navel
sattva	Viṣṇu	cold	wind	heart
tamas	Mahādev	hot	fire	top of the skull[16]

5b देही मांहीं तीन्यूं देव　　गुर बिन कैसै पावै भेव ॥

5b These three divinities are present in the body. How can I find the mystery without the help of the guru?

16. See कबिलास, Callewaert: 2009, p. 299.

Below I give a brief survey of the five elementary substances (*tattva*), their twenty-five characteristics (*prakṛti*, verses 8-10), and their colours, tastes, nature, house, gate, food, behaviour, and body (verses 11-18). The relevant elements of these verses may be represented as follows (11-13):

tattva	**colour**	**taste**	**nature**
Earth	yellow	sweet	forgiveness
Water	red	salty	coolness
Fire	black	pungent	burning [?]
Wind	green	pure	moving around
Ether	blue	fragrant	organizing

Verses 14-18

The house, gate, food, behaviour and body of the twenty-five characteristics (*prakṛti*); "body" (देह) does not seem to be clearly mentioned in the verses.

tattva	**house**	**gate**	**food**	**behaviour**
Earth	heart	mouth	grain	greed
Water	forehead	senses	[?]	passion
Fire	yellow place	eyes	eyes	delusion
Wind	navel	nose	fragrance	anger
Ether	top of the skull	ears	stories	vanity

6 अष्ट धात का प्यंड जु बांध्या पवंन थंभ दे तामैं सांध्या ।
प्राण पातिसाह मन प्रधांन पांच पचीसौं मांनै आंन ॥

The body was created with eight substances (*dhātu*),[17] wind[18] gives it support and effects a union.

17. 6a: for अष्ट धात Mangaldas: 1947 glosses: fluid (*ras*), blood (*rakta*), flesh (*māṁsa*), fat (*med*), bone (*asthi*), marrow (*majjā*), semen (*śukra*), energy (*oj*). The last substance is usually not mentioned in the works on Indian medicine. See further, "seven" substances in verse 22. See सप्त धात in Callewaert: 2009, p. 1962.

18. 6a: *pavan*, lit. "purifier": wind, air, vital, breath, life.

The vital breath (*prāṇ*) is the Lord, the mind (*man*) is the most important, others speak of five and twenty-five.

7 पांच पचीसौं सब कौ भाषै तिन के नांव कवन बिधि राखै ।
एक तत्त की पांच प्रकीरति सतगुर बिंन कैसै पावै गति ॥

They maintain that everything is made of five and twenty-five but how can we give a name to these?
Five characteristics of one elementary substance: how can I understand this process without the guru's help?

प्रकीरत्यां के नाम Names for the characteristics

8 प्रथमि पृथ्वी प्रकीरति देस अस्थ मास तुचा नाडी केस ।
आप[19] प्रकीरति लाल नीति प्रसेद सुकल सनेव च जीति ॥

First, places of the Earth-characteristics: bones, flesh, skin, veins and hair. Water-characteristics: redness, perspiration, whiteness,[20] love [?], victory [?].

9 तेज प्रकीर्ति खुध्या प्यास निद्रा आलस[21] क्रोध अभ्यास ।
वाइ प्रकीर्ति गावै धावै ज्ञान कथा अगोचर पावै ।

Fire-characteristics: hunger, thirst, sleepiness, laziness, anger.
Wind-characteristics: singing and running, (true) knowledge and (right) speech about the Invisible.

10 आकास प्रकीर्ति माया मोह लज्या करै राग अर द्रोह ।
...पचीस प्रकीर्ति पांचूं तत्त भिन भिन ब्यौहारा यहु मत ॥

Ether-characteristics (*ākāś*): illusion, attachment; it causes shame, passion and enmity. These are the five characteristics of the

19. 8b: आब or "water" in ms. 2. I translate लाल नीति as "redness". It is noteworthy that लाल is also given as the colour of water in verse 11.
20. 8b: the reading सुकल सनेव is preferred to सुकल सनेवच जिति in ms. 2 and सुकल सने वल [for which Mangaldas: 1947 glosses: वाणी] जीति in the edition. In fact, the whole line is not certain. I understand सनेव as a form of सनेह (<स्नेह), or "love".
21. 9a: The reading आलस (Skt. आलस्य) is preferred to आलकस in ms. 2 and आलक in Mangaldas: 1947.

elementary substances, each with a different behaviour.[22]

पांच तत्त के वर्ण नाम

Names for the colours of the five elementary substances

11 प्रिथमी पीत आप रंगि राता तेज स्यांम वाइ हरि कहाता ।
...नीला आकास ये पंचूं वरण जे चीन्है सो मेटै मरण ॥

Earth: yellow; Water: red; Fire: black; Wind: green; Ether (*ākāś*): blue.

You can destroy death, if you recognize these five colours.

पांच तत्त के स्वाद नाम

Names for the tastes of the five elementary substances

12 प्रिथमी मधुर खार है आप तीखा तेज कहीऐ ते ताप ।
...अमल वाइ कषाइ आकास पंच तत्त के स्वाद निवास ॥

Earth: sweet; Water: salty[23]; Fire: spiced.

Wind: sour [<अम्ल]; Ether (*ākāś*): pungent [< S. कषाय]: these are the names for the tastes of the five elementary substances

पांच तत्त के सुभाव नाम

Names for the nature of the five elementary substances

13 बैठी खिमा सीतल गुन सरं बहनीं तपति नांव जंन धरं ।
...फिरता पवन गगन है ठाटा पंच सुभाव खोजि तनं काटा ॥

13[24] Earth: forgiveness; Water: coolness; Fire: burning,[?].

Wind: moving around; Ether (*gagan*): organizing [?]. Cutting [or releasing?] the body to find the nature of the five elementary substances.

---

22. 10b: or "different description"?; बोरा in Mangaldas: 1947 and ब्यौरा in ms. 2.
23. 12a: खार < क्षार; छार in edition and ms. 2.
24. 13: The meaning is not fully clear; only an attempt to translate is made here. बैठी (<?) is translated as "earth".

धरती का घर द्वार अहार व्यौहार देह कै विषै

Names for the house, gate, food, behaviour, body of Earth

14 कुभनी घोष कलेजा अस्थित मुखद्वार सौ कह्यौ सोधि चित ।
...भखि अंन जल करै अहार लालच लोभ सदा व्यौहार ॥

House: heart[25]; Gate: mouth; [?][26].

Food: grain; Behaviour: greed; Body: [?]

पाणी का घर द्वार अहार व्यौहार देह कै विषै

Names for the house, gate, food, behaviour, body of Water

15[27] तोया धाम लिलाट बषाणैं इंद्री द्वार बिंषै रस माणैं ।
...भष्य जोषिता जे नर करैं काम व्यौहार कलेवर हरै ॥

House: forehead; Gate: senses[28].

Food[29]; Behaviour: passion[30]; Body: [?]

अगनी का घर द्वार अहार व्यौहार देह कै विषै

Names for the house, gate, food, behaviour, body of Fire

16 पावक का घर पीता ठांव चखि[31] द्वार कही येते नांव ।
...नेत्र अहार ज दे रूप मोह व्यौहार सु प्रतखि कूप ॥

House: gall-bladder[32]; Gate: eye.

---

25. 14a: lit. "the sound of the earth resides in the heart". It is noteworthy that these "houses" do not correspond to the "mansions" in verses 4b-5a.
26. Lit. "the gate is the mouth", also called सोधि चित [?].
27. Verse 15 is omitted in ms. 1; the correction in the numbering in ms. 2 is made after verse 22; verse 23 is "missing" in the numbering and the numbering continues with verse 24, on a new folio.
28. Lit.: "the senses are the gate and the sense-objects are the fluid".
29. 15b: lit. "the food of water is जोषिता [S. योषिता], giving new life to man".
30. This passion is said to "remove the body".
31. 16a: चखि is चक्षु in ms. 2.
32. Mangaldas: 1947 (p. 4) explains पीता ठाव as पित्त स्थान, or "the place of the bile".

Food: eye that gives form [?]; Behaviour: delusion[33]; Body: causing anger [?]

पवन का घर द्वार अहार व्यौहार देह कै विषै

Names for the house, gate, food, behaviour, body of Wind

17 पवन भवन नाभि अस्थान द्वार नासिका सों यूं जांन ।
...अहार इहै जे लीजे वास क्रोध व्यौहार थैं होइ निवास ॥

House: navel; Gate: nose.

Food: fragrance [?]; Behaviour: anger; Body: [?]

आकास का घर द्वार अहार व्यौहार देह कै विषै

Names for the house, gate, food, behaviour, body of Ether

18 अंब[34] का घर मस्तक होइ करंण द्वार कही जैं सोइ ।
...सुणैं कथा सोई जु अहार डंभ[35] करै पखंड ब्यौहार ॥

House: forehead; Gate: ear.

Food: hearing stories; Behaviour: vanity; Body: [?]

19 तीनि सै साठि रेज[36] गती जोङी बहतरि कूप लगाइ खोडी ।
...नौ नाङी नौ द्वार बनाए तीनि गुप्त यूं बारह गाए ॥

In the body there are 360 pieces [of bone], 72 limbs;

nine veins; nine openings and three hidden (openings) make a total of twelve.

20 तेरहै द्वारि मुक्ति की आस भै भ्रंम भागै प्रेम पियास ।
...बाजै अनहद गरजै प्राण देह विचारै पद निर्वाण ॥

The thirteenth door gives hope for salvation; through it fear, illusion, love and thirst are chased.

33. 16b: this delusion "is said to promote anger" [?].

34. 18a: अंबर or "the sky" in ms. 2.

35. 18b: ड्यंभ in ms. 2.

36. 19a: रेजगी in ms. 2 and edition. I translate रेज as "small piece" (Pers. *riza*); *gati* as "condition". In a footnote (p. 5) Mangaldas: 1947 refers to the 5th chapter, "On the Body", in the *Suśruta* of the Vedas, which reportedly mentions these 360 bones in the body and to the Āyurvedic literature which mentions 300 bones in the body.

When the unheard sound resounds the vital breath thunders; the body is the basis of salvation.

21 अहूठ हाथ का पांड विस्तार अहूठ कोडि रोमावली भार ।
...काया का कछू नांही छेह मिलै सतगुर जाइ संदेह ॥

This body[37] of three and a half hands carries 35 million hairs. This body knows no limit and if you meet the *sadguru* all doubts disappear.

22 सप्त धात की काया कहिए पांचूं इंद्री मन जीव गहिए ।
...मन चंदा जीव सूरिज रूप सप्त धात का अरथ अनूप ॥

The body is composed of seven substances (*dhātu*; see above, v. 6); the five senses, the mind and the spirit (*jīva*).[38]
The mind is the moon and the spirit is the sun: the seven substances have a wonderful meaning.

23 नैंना रूप र जिभ्या स्वाद घ्राण[१] वासना श्रवां नाद ।
...इंद्री भोग विषै का मूल पांचूं इंद्री यहु अस्थूल ॥

The eyes perceive forms and the tongue tastes, the nose perceives scents and the ears hear sounds.
The senses are [thus] the basis of sensual pleasure; they seize what is gross.[39]

24 मन आकार कवन विधि सूझै जीव कवन गति प्रकट बूझै ।
...मन आकार ज सूषिम डोलै जीव पवन ता मांहि बोलै ॥

How can one understand the size of the mind and the movement of the spirit?

---

37. 21a: पांड is given in Lalas, Sitaram, राजाथांनी सबद कोस (III.1, p. 2432) as a variant form of पिंड or "body". Both ms. 2 and Mangaldas: 1947 have the reading प्यंड.

38. In contemporary religious poetry, *jīv* is frequently used with the meaning of *ātman*, or "spirit".

39. अस्थूल is to be read and understood as स्थूल; see Callewaert: 2009, p. 140: "gross".

The mind is swinging the subtle,[40] the spirit is the wind talking in it.

Verses 25-81: No systematic translation is further given of those verses which are meant to give only synonyms of a particular keyword. Those synonyms are listed alphabetically in the glossary below, with reference to the respective keyword and the verse in which they occur.

19-25 names for काया (*kāyā*, the body)

27 names for वो ॐकार (Oṁkār)

28 names for मन (*man*, the mind)

31 names for चित (*cit*, the understanding)

32-33 names for मनसा (*manasā*, thought, with various meanings: desire, understanding)

34 names for माया (maya, Skt. *māyā*, illusion)

35 names for बिकार (*bikār*, change)

36 names for इंद्री (*indrī*, senses)

37 names for व्यंद (*vyanda* or *binda*, semen)

38 names for कुबुधि (*kubudhi*, evil mind)

39 names for संसा (*saṁsā*, doubt)

40 names for काम अग्नि (*kām agni*, fire of passion)

41-43 names for उभै गुण (*ubhay guṇ*, the two qualities)

44-45 names for कर्म (*karma*)

46-48 संसार (*saṁsār*, the world compared to a tree)

49-50 सरीर सरोवर/व्रिष (*śarīr*, the body)

51-53 names for प्राण (*prāṇ*, vital breath; life-energy)

54 names for ज्ञान (*gyān*, knowledge)

55 names for गोष्ठि (*goṣṭhi*, conversation)

56 names for वाणी (*vāṇī*, the word)

---

40. 24b: सूक्ष्म, "subtle", as opposed to स्थूल, "gross".

57 names for सुर्ति (*surati*, hearing/remembering)

58 names for सुबुधि (*subudhi*, good understanding)

59 names for सुमिरण (*sumiraṇ*, remembering/recitation)

60 names for भगति बंदिगी (*bhakti* and *bandagī*, religious devotion, devoted service)

61 names for ब्रह्म अग्नि (*brahma-agni*, Brahma-fire[41])

62 names for विरह (*virah*, separation)

63 names for विरही (*virahī*, the separated)

64 names for ध्यान (*dhyān*, meditation/contemplation)

65-66 घट मैं तेतीस कोङि देवता के नाम

names for the 330 million gods in the body

67-68 घट मैं ब्रह्मा इन्दु महेस के नाम

names for Brahmā, Indra and Maheś in the body

69 comparing आतम सरवर, the *ātmā* (soul) to a lake

70 the life-breath प्राण तरवर (*prāṇ*) as a lake

71-72 ब्रह्म सागर/व्रिष Brahma as a lake and as a tree

73 names for गुर सबद (guru *sabad*, the word of the guru)

74-81 names for गुरदेव (*gurudev*)

82-116 names for परमेस्वर (*parameśvar*)

117-128 तुरकी, Turkī (or Muslim) names

129 names for न्रिंजन अस्थांन (the place of *nirañjan*)

काया के नाम Names for the body

25 काया सरीर प्यंड वपु देह घट आकार नांव बन एह ।
...पृथ्वीसमुद्र वावी[42] कूप भोमि षाड गोकल जु अनूप (?) ॥

---

41. See Svami Narayandas, *श्रीरज्जबवाणी*, p. 102, chapter 12, v. 6.

42. 25b: ms. 2 gives बांबी. The meaning of वावी or of बांबी is not clear. One can possibly understand बांबी as "hill of white ants" or as "hole of a snake" (see *Hindī śabaa śāgar*, VII, p. 3434); the meaning given in *Raj. sabad kos* (III, p. 2967) is not helpful. The corresponding word in Barathval: 1936 (p. 272, *śarīr*) is बंक कूप; कूप (lit. "well") has possibly to be understood in a compound with वावी.

26 व्यंद्रावन व्रिष वेलि[43] वबूल नींब[44]पूतिला कलि अस्थूल।
...जान औजूद देहरा हार महल मसीति ब्यावर परिवार ॥

वो ॐकार के नाम Names for Oṁkār

27 वो ॐकार पवन अर सास जीव सबद सुर सूर उजास ।
...ससा संख सेस कहि[45] नाद स्यंघ स्याल सीन अर साद ॥

मन के नाम Names for the mind

28 मन मीन म्रिग मंडक[46] मंजार मूसा म्रकट मोतीहार ।
...मोर गरद गज[47] पसु पतंग सुनहा सूवा कउवा रंग ॥

29 महादेव अवधूत देव रावल ल्यौरू डवा[48] भेव ।
...बगुला बाज काइथ मन जोगी खूंटा बंधू भंवरा भोगी[49] ॥

30 फटक धौं[50] कलाल मन मही मुलां मुसला करहा कही ।
...रयंद[51] सैतान जिनि राख्या जीति कबहूं न टूटै प्रीति ॥

चित के नाम Names for the understanding[52]

31 चित चात्रिग चीता चकोर चकवा चक्र चिडा[53] अरु चोर ।
...चूल्हा चाकी चरखा सोइ एते नाम चित के होइ ॥

---

43. See below, Glossary, वेलि.
44. 26a: for वबूल नींब we read बबूलनी in Barathval: 1936, p. 272, *śarīr*.
45. 27b: like ms. 2, Barathval: 1936 (p. 270, *Oṁ*) gives the reading सेसदम [?] for सेस कहि. In ms. 2 सिंघ for स्यंघ, and बाद for साद.
46. 28a: in Barathval: 1936 (p. 272, मन): मेंधक for मंडक.
47. 28b: in Barathval: 1936 (p. 272, मन): हाथी for गज.
48. 29: the meaning of ल्यौरू डवा (लौरू डऊवा in ms. 2 and ed.; डऊवा in Barathval: 1936) is not clear. After verse 29a, Mangaldas: 1947 inserts the heading रावल लौरूड लौरूड उभाव (not found in the mss.) as an introduction to verses 29b and 30ab. Perhaps we may consider the words in these verses as synonyms of मन.
49. 29b: in Barathval: 1936 (p. 272, मन): भोमि for भोगी.
50. 30a: धौल in ms. 2.
51. 30b: रिंद in ms. 2.
52. 31a: the term चित (Skt. चित्त) is used to denote the faculty of reasoning or the intellect: understanding.
53. 30b: रिंद in ms. 2.
53. 31a: चिडिया in Barathval: 1936, p. 271: चित.

मनसा के नाम[54] Names for thought

32 मनसा गावत्री सुरही वछी[55] नारी जमुना तरंग मृग मछी ।
...मषी[56] मूंगी देवी सक्ति डीबी जोगणी मांनी जगति ॥

33 मनसा मालनी कलाली गोरी[57] पारवती त्रिया दामिनी मोरी ।[1]
...मंजारी बगुली चांवडी[58] चंडी चांदी चील्ह चोरटी मंडी ॥

माया के नाम Names for *māyā* (illusion)

34 माया मैंणी मोहनी मंजारी मगहर मकड़ी मास पसारी ।
...सापिणी पापिणी कोढणी डंकणी कांमिनी भांमिनी गनिका संखिणी[59] ॥

विकार के नाम Names for changes (or sins)[60]

35 खलि विषै स्वाद विकार जंजाल व्याल रोग रंज दुसमन काल ।
...जुरु[61] व्याधि असाधि मनोरथ दुंदर दोजग छोडि सबै सथ ॥

इंद्री के नाम Names for the senses

36 इंद्री अस्व बछर[62] नांव पांडौ पांचूं लरिका ठांव ।
...ऐई बैरी ऐई मीत सकल लोक मैं इंद्री अजीत ॥

The Names for the senses are "horse" and "calf" [?]; they are like the five Pāṇḍav brothers. For some an enemy, for others a friend; the senses are invincible throughout the world.

---

54. The terms in this verse are in Barathval: 1936, p. 270, listed as synonyms of इच्छा.
55. 32a: मछीय बच्छी in Barathval: 1936, p. 270; मछी in ms. 2. For मृग मछी, we read मृगछी (मृगाक्षी, "having lovely deer-eyes") in Barathval: 1936, p. 270.
56. 32b: माषी in ms. 2.
57. 33a: गौरी in ms. 2.
58. 33b: चामुंडा in Barathval: 1936, p. 270.
59. 34b: the second half of the line is संखणी कांमिनी भांमिनी गनिका जसणी in ms. 2.
60. See Callewaert: 2009, p. 1873
61. 35b: जुरहा (<ज्वर) in ms. 2.
62. 36a: बछरवा in ms. 2.

व्यंद के नाम Names for semen

37 सुकल जलंध्र कंद्रप मैन मदन कांम गहि गुर के बैन ।
...व्यंद अनंग ग्यांन सौं दहै सकल लोक मैं कीर्त्ति रहै[63] ॥

कुबुधि के नाम Names for the evil mind

38 कुबुधि कोल केतुकी कुमति विलाई दुबध्या द्रोपती[64] दुर्मति ।
...कुदाली कागली कुही कहीजैकसाइणी सेती कांठौ दीजै ॥

संसा के नाम Names for doubt

39 संसा संक्या श्रप स्यंघ[65] स्याल सुसा और भै भुवंग ।
...सुनहा दुविध्या रज विकार प्रतिब्यंब देखि तन करहि छार[66] ॥

काम-अग्नि के नाम Names for the fire of passion

40 काम अग्नि काया का नाम क्रोध अग्नि मन जाइ निरास ।
...मोह अग्नि प्राणी दुख पावै लोभ अग्नि सूं मूल गंवावै ॥

The fire of passions pertains to the body; the fire of anger makes the mind desperate. The fire of delusion causes sorrow for a being, and through the fire of lust the root is lost.

उभै गुण के नाम Names for the two [opposite] qualities

41 द्वै द्वै गुण का बंध्या मूर[67] धर आकास चंद अर सूर ।
...राति दिवस पुरिष अरु त्रिया संपति विपति सबनि कूं दीया ॥

Both (opposite) qualities are tied in the root, like the earth and the heavens, the moon and the sun. Like the night and the day, like man and woman, like wealth and poverty given to all.

42 सुभ असुभ हरिष अरु सोक खपा पर तैं राग[68] दोस ।
...सीतल तपति र आवागवन नीच ऊंच अरु जांमण मरण ॥

---

63. Probable meaning: "(this fluid) is burnt through knowledge, it is well known throughout the world".
64. 38a: The words द्रोपति and following are listed separately in Barathval: 1936, p. 271, under the keyword दुबिधा.
65. 39a: सिंह in ms. 2.
66. 39b: possible meaning: "its reflection turns the body into ashes".
67. 41a: बांध्या मूल in ms. 2.
68. 42a: राग र in ms. 2.

Auspicious and inauspicious, joy and sadness, [?].

Cold and heat, coming and going, high and low, birth and death.

गुणहुं[69] के नाम Names for the qualities

43[70] गुण म्रजाद उकरि[71] डर घाटी परबत कंटिक सेन्या ठाठी ।
...जामचर सूदर मेर अहंकार गुडिया तारा गुण ब्यौहार ॥

कर्म के नाम Names for *karma*

44 कर्म कर्म सब कोइ कहै गुर बिन प्रचा[72] कैसै लहै ।
...पांचूं इंद्री मांगै पोष दीजै भगितौ लागै दोष ॥

Everybody speaks about *karma* but without the guru, how can one have a real knowledge of it. The five senses require food but when food is given, sin is the result.

45 हतै जीव तौ लागै कर्म सकल संतोषैएही ध्रम ।
...छोडि जगतपति जे कुछ करै सोई क्रम जन नाम धरै ॥

If you murder a living being, *karma* sticks to you; only in continuous contentment is there real *dharma*. When people ignore God, all their actions are called *karma*.

संसार के नाम Names for the world

46 संसार समुद्र भौवन वारी विस्व जगत[73] दूतर भारी ।
...दुसह असह मांड जंजाल म्रिग जल चिलका[74] कहिए काल ॥

संसार-सुंदर के नाम Names for the beautiful world

47 संसार भौवन विषै विकार त्रिविधि भंग चिलक विस्तार ।
...जे लागे ते खीणै कहियैं झीवर काल जाल मैं गहियैं[75] ॥

---

69. गुणसंबूह in ms. 2.

70. The meaning of v. 43 is not clear.

71. 43a: ऊकरी in ms. 2.

72. 44a: परचा in ms. 2.

73. 46a: this world is further said to be "hard to pass" (दूतर), "heavy" (भारी) and "unbearable" (दुसह and असह).

74. 46b: चिलका, lit. "bright, shiny", can probably be understood as an adjective qualifying mirage.

75. 47b: दहिये in ms. 2.

Comparing the world (of rebirth) to an ocean, [?].

If you get involved, you are bound to die. Death like a fisherman will catch you in his net.

संसार-व्रिष (करि बरण्या[76]) The tree of the world

48 जगत बिटप स्वारथ की छाया ओऽंकार ईला सब माया ।
...रज तम सत साखा जुगपत फल दोई पाप पुनि मैं रत ॥

In the comparison of the world (of rebirth) to a tree, selfishness is the shade, when *oṁkār* and the earth are in the power of *māyā* [?]. *Rajas*, *tamas* and *sattva* are the branches; good and evil are the double fruit, mixed (one in the other).

सरीर-सरोवर करि बरण्यौ Describing the body-lake

49 वपु विधा कर जीवन वारि त्रिस्ना विभ्रम लुबधि नित नारि ।
...मन अरबक माखंड[77] है माया सलीन सरोवर कहिये काया ॥

[The meaning of the metaphor in this line is not clear].

सरीर व्रिष करि बरण्यौ Describing the body-tree

50 देही द्रुम मोह की छाया कुल परिवार गहबरी लाया ।
...साखा गुंण प्रकीर्ति पान फूल कांमना फल अभिमांन ॥

In the comparison of the body to a tree, delusion is the shade, bringing misfortune to all. The *guṇa*s are the branches and the characteristicss[78] are the leaves; desire is the flower and pride is the fruit.

प्रांण[79] के नाम Names for the vital breath/life-energy

51 प्रांण पातिसाह अरजन अंस औधू जोगी प्रीखत हंस ।
...महरू गूजर परजापति राजा साह काजी खग सती ॥

76. Missing in ms. 34

77. 49b: माकड in ms. 2.

78. See above, vv. 8-10.

79. In contemporary religious poetry, the term प्राण or "vital breath" is at times used with the meaning of आत्मा, "spirit"; see v. 6 and v. 52. The terms in this verse are in Barathval: 1936 given as synonyms of आत्मा (p. 270) and of अंतहकरण (p. 271).

52 आत्म इंद ऊटि कुरि कुंज विरहनि वैरागनि वियोगिनी बंझ ।
...सुंदरि दुलहनि रूह अरवाह बेलि अंजनी नांव अथाह ॥

53[80] कंवल[81] कुंभ कलस दिल गगन कौंला कोमल अंतरि मगन ।
...अंतहकरण आंगण ताषा कुवा कवल पदम यूं भाषा ॥

ज्ञांन के नाम Names for knowledge

54 ज्ञांन दीप पंगुल मत सार गाडर गाइ गयंद विचार ।
...सूरिज चंद बोध प्रकास ज्ञांन चांदणा तत उजास ॥

गोष्ठि के नाम Names for conversation

55 कथा उचार चाचरी चरचा निज गोष्ठि स्यूं कीजै प्रचा ।
...गुरबति नांव पारस पाई सब्द मांहि सतगुर समझाई ॥

वांणी के नाम Names for word

56 वांणी गंगा भागीरथी सारद बछी कोकिल कथी ।
...घंटा सुरसरी जाहनवी[82] तारुणी अरूपरी बेणाचवी ॥

सुर्ति के नाम Names for hearing/remembering[83]

57 सुरसुति सुषमनां सुंदरि सुर्ति सींगी सुई सखी संमझि मति ।
...सासू सीप सूर्ति जङ कहिए कुदाली नांव कहे तैं लहिए[84] ॥

सुबुधि के नाम Names for good understanding

58 आतमां मांहैं उपजै सुमति सुबुधि बहु रहै इक तति ।
...बेटी धीय सुभ परिवार आतम के अंग हैं निज सार ॥

सुमिरण के नाम Names for remembering/recitation

59 सुमिरण भजन रटणि अरु जाप रैरेकार[85] धुनि प्रगटै आप ।
...डोरी सुत्र ल्यौ तांतूं रहै धूरि गरज नांव जन कहै ॥

---

80. Some of the terms in verse 53 are given in Barathval: 1936 (p. 270) as synonyms of अंतहकरण.
81. 53a: पदम मैं in ms. 2.
82. 56b: जाहरनई in ms. 2.
83. The term सुरति was used with various, often vague, meanings in the contemporary *nirguṇa* literature. See Callewaert: 2009, p. 2088.
84. We read कुदाली श्रुक चेत नां लहिये in ms. 2; Barathval: 1936 (p. 272. सुरति) gives कुदाली, श्रुक, चेत.
85. 59a: रंकार in ms. 2.

भगति बंदिगी के नाम Names for devotion

60 पूजा अरचा सेवा बंदन चांटी चाकरी अर दासातन ।
...बंदगी इबाबत खिजमत कीजै एते नांम भगति के लीजै ॥

ब्रह्म-अग्नि के नाम Names for the Brahma-fire

61 ज्ञान अग्नि काया प्रजारै विरह अग्नि मन मनसा बारै ।
...ब्रह्म अग्नि प्रांण मैं प्रगटै तिन सूं पाप क्रम अघ कटै ॥

The fire of knowledge burns the body, the fire of separation burns the mind (*man, manasā*). The fire of Brahma appears in the vital breath (*prāṇ*), burning *karma*, sin and faults.

विरह के नाम Names for separation

62 बिछोह वैराग विरह तनि प्यास तपति औचाटत लघु अभ्यास[86] ।
...तालाबेली उदास बिवोग फिकर फिराक अंदेसा सोग ॥

विरही के नाम Names for the separated lover

63 विरही वैरागी वियोगी प्यासा अनुरागी उदासी आसिक आसा ।
...सोषता सुहदा दरदबंद कहिए तालिब नांव तलब मैं रहिए ॥

ध्यांन के नाम Names for meditation/contemplation

64 ध्यान चितवन ताली त्राटिक निद्रा समाधि जडै नव फाटिक ।
...यहु मन ले उनमनी लगाव दसवैं द्वार परम पद पावै ॥

64b. [In this contemplation] the mind becomes *unman* (i.e. is destroyed) and through the tenth door the highest bliss is experienced.

घट मैं तेतीस कोडि देवता के नाम

Names for the 330 million gods in the body

65 कोडि तेतीसौं मिलै जु आई इंद्रादिक ब्रह्मादिक चाई ।
...स्यौपुर मांहै भया अनंद भेट होइ भागै बहु दंद ॥

The thirty-three gods,[87] Indra and the others and Brahmā and

86. 62a2: अवचाट तलफ अभ्यास in ms. 2; अवचाट (Hindī अवचाट or "distracted"). Possible meaning: "(separation) burns the person who lacks concentration and who has little experience".

87. 65: the term कोडि (< कोटि, lit. "ten million" or a very large number) is not →

the others are experienced [in desire?]. In Śivapur bliss is felt; with this encounter all strife disappears.

66 पचीस प्रकीर्ति इंद्री पांच तीन्यूं गुंण जब पाया सांच ।
...कोडि तेतीसौं एइ देव पाइ अलख पुरिस की सेव ॥

When you have understood the truth about the twenty-five characteristics,[88] the five senses and the three *guṇa*s, [i.e.] the thirty-three gods, then you have found the service of God (*alakha puris*).

घट मैं ब्रह्मा इन्दु महेस के नाम

Names for Brahmā, Indra and Maheś

67 घट मांहै इंद्रादिक कोइ ब्रह्मादिक क्यूं परचा होइ ।
...स्यौंपुर कैसैं चीन्ह्या जाइ तीन्यौं ठौर कहौ समझाइ ॥

Brahmā, Indra and Maheś in the body; how can you recognize Indra-and-the-others and Brahmā-and-the-others in the body and how can Śivapur be recognized? Explain these three places.

68 इंद्रादिक मन सहजै होइ ब्रह्मादिक वांणी रटि सोइ ।
...स्यौ तौ प्राण पुरी मत सार तीनि ठौर का इहै विचार ॥

Indra and the others come in the mind, Brahmā and the others are pronounced in the words and the essence of Śiva is realized in the vital breath (*prāṇ*).

आतम-सरवर बाहिरि वरण्यौ

Comparing the soul to a lake

→ clear, in juxtaposition with "thirty-three". Dādū mentions, in *Dādū-vāṇī* 24.8: देवा सकल तेतीसूं कोडि. *Taitīs devatā* is also found in the writings of Dādū's disciple Rajab. Commenting on v. 66.2 of the *Rajab-vāṇī* Narayandas glosses for 33 gods: "Eleven Rudra, 12 Aditya, 8 Vasu, 2 Asvinī". Incidentally, *indra* is also a synonym of the "sun", which is the first of the 12 Ādityas and is also synonymous of Viṣṇu, as appears below in verses 67 and 68. The meaning of the "thirty-three" gods is perhaps more clear in the light of verse 66, where Garībdās speaks of the 25 characteristics, the five senses, and the three *guṇa*s, which make a total of 33.

88. 66: see above, vv. 8ff.

69 आत्म तत्त पति नांव रन सार प्रेम कलोल अनंत अपार ।
...पवन हंस सुरति[89] है मछी आत्म सरवर की गति अच्छी ॥

[the metaphor in v. 69 is not fully clear]: love is the endless game [of the waves?], breath is the swan and love is the fish.

प्राण-तरवर The vital breath (*prāṇ*) as a tree

70 प्राण व्रिष संतोष सत छाया ब्रह्मा बनी जड सुति[90] दिखाया ।
...साखा सबद प्रीति पत होइ आर्ति पुहुप दरस फल दोइ ॥

The spirit is a tree and contentment is its shade; Brahmā is the forest and roots are love. The branches are the words and love is the leaves; worship is the flowers and vision is the double fruit.[91]

ब्रह्म-सागर Brahma as a lake

71 ब्रह्म अपार जीवना नूर तरंग पालि बिन है भरपूर ।
...तामैं हंस प्रांण मन मीन साधू सकल भये लैलीन ॥

Brahma is endless, the being are light [?]; waves without limit [?]. In it the swans are the beings, the mind the fish; in it the saints are always immersed.

ब्रह्म-व्रिष Brahma as a tree

72 ब्रह्म व्रिष पूरण है छाया धर आधार नही सौ राया ।
...साखा पत्र पेड नही करम संत बमेकी पावै मरम ॥

The Brahma-tree is full of shade, [?]. There are no branches, leaves, trees [?J, or *karma*: wise saints understand this mystery.

गुर-सबद के नाम Names for the word of the guru

73 सबद सिचांणां पलीता कूंची बांण मसक लागति गहि ऊंची ।
...अनभै न्रिभै अनहद वाणी तांति की गुरी लेहु पीछांणी ॥

गुरदेव के नाम सोभा Names for the *gurudev*

89. 69b: सुरति in ms. 2.

90. 70a: सुरति in ms 2.

91. 70b: for the double fruit, see above v. 48.

74 सतगुर गरवा वैराग र खांणि गुर उसताद सुत्रधार पिछाणि ।
...मुरसिद पीर सीकलीगर[92] सार गंभीर सबुधि साह सुनार ॥

75 सतगुर चंदण चिंतामणि नांव कामधेन कलपब्रिछ भाव ।
...रवि ससि कंवल पारस अर हीरा कहिये वैद ज मेटै पीरा ॥

76[93] अनलपंखि पारजातिक भ्रिग मेघ नदी सूर अरु स्यंघ ।
...हंस भंवर धर पवन आकास कुसमल धोवैं करैं उजास ॥

77 सतगुर सोभा अस्तुति कीजै ता समि और पटतर नही दीजै ।
...चंदन काठ चिंतामणि कंकर काष्ठ नाव कामधनि पसूवर ॥

78 कलपव्रिछ रवि तपति समाइ चंद्र कलंक कंवल मुरझाइ ।
...पारस हीरा पत्थर होइ बैद मरै गुर समि नही कोइ ॥

79[94] अनलपंखि पारजाति दार भ्रिग जंत घन पंगा खार ।
...सूर स्यंघ जीवनि कूं दह हंस भंवर पंखेरू कहै ॥

80 जुगति जङ पवन बहु डोलै सूनि आकास खगपति क्यूं तोलै ।
...बहु गुण देखे सतगुर मांहि सब सोधे पटंतरि कूं नांहि ॥

On the lifeless earth the wind moves around; why do we compare [the guru with a bird moving in an empty sky? I saw very many qualities in the guru and nothing equals them.

81 श्रवन नैन नासिका रसना नख सिख अंग बैंन मुख डसना ।
...फेरै घाट अनूप संवार गुर दादू सब कारिज सारै ॥

His eyes, ears, nose, tongue; his whole body, limbs, words, teeth. My guru Dādū transforms my sinful works and makes them outstanding.

परमेस्वर के नाम Names for *parameśvar*[95]

82 रमिता रांम रंकार रसाल राषणहार राइ रछिपाल ।
...रचणहार रसरूपी रतन राषौ रिदै बहुत करि जतन ॥

---

92. 74b: for सीकलीगर [?] we read किसलीगर [?] in ms. 2.
93. 76: see below, v. 79.
94. 79: see above, v. 76.
95. All nouns used here as a name or epithet of God are written with capital in the translation.

He is all-pervasive, *rām*, *ra*-sound,[96] melodious; Protector, King, Maintainer.

Creator, nectar-like, Jewel; with all His might He protects the heart.

83 मोहन मुरारि माधवा महाराजि मंगलकारी मूल जिहाज ।
...मणि मोती मनोहर महिमंडण मूरति मधुर महा दुषखंडण ॥

Mohan, Murārī, Mādhav,[97] Emperor; beneficient, Root and Boat. Jewel, Diamond, Heart-stealing, Decorator of the earth [?]; attractive Mūrtī,[98] mighty Destroyer of sorrow.

84 अपरंपार अगोचर अपर अजप[99] अचिंत अकथ अरु अकह ।
...अबिनासी अबरंण अनंत अभेव अपार अगाध अरंग अछेव ॥

He is endless, invisible and cannot be grasped in recitation, reflection, description or definition.

He cannot be destroyed, He is colourless, limitless and without division; He is unsurpassed, unfathomable, without colour and endless.

85 अलोप अतीत अभेद अथाह अछेद असंष अघट अगाह ।
...अषिर अबिहड अधर अनाहद अबिचल अमर अषै आनंदपद ॥

He is invisible, passed beyond, undivided, bottomless; unbroken, uncounted, unchangeable, immeasurable.

End [?], uninterrupted, He cannot be grasped, unstruck; He is motionless and immortal, indestructible, Bliss.

86 अभै अनूप अभंग अडोल अलेष अलेप अषिल अमोल ।
...अजोनीं आस्थेर अजरांवर अजित अगिणत अबिगत अतोल अमित ॥

---

96. As first letter of the word *rām*, the *ra*-sound has a sacred meaning. In manuscripts of the Dādū-panthī literature, the letter *ra* is often written at the end of a work, as follows: *rām dādū rām dādū ... rarararara . . .*

97. Names of Viṣṇu.

98. The *mūrtī* or clay-representation of the divinity in the temple is, after a blessing, the visible presence of God before the devotees. He is accordingly dressed, decorated and fed.

99. 84a: अजय in ms. 2.

Fearless, wonderful, without division, immobile; He cannot be described nor painted, He is omnipresent and precious.

He is not dependent on the *yonis*,[100] immobile, beyond birth and death, invincible; He cannot be counted, known, weighed or measured.

87 आपैं आप अप्रमित अकल अघजारण अघमोचन अटल ।
...अंतरजांमी आरति हरंण अनभूत अरचित अकरणकरण ॥

He is self-sufficient, endless and timeless,[101] He burns away sins and liberates from sinfulness, He cannot be moved; He is indwelling, removing sorrow, without past, not made, He is the causeless Cause.

88 अघबिदार अघहरंण अनूप आतमराम आनंद सरूप ।
...अप्रवांण अघदहण अजाचिक वोषदि अजरा अघदलन अबंछिक ॥

He destroys and removes sin, He is wonderful, Rām in the soul,[102] the Essence of bliss; He is endless, burning away sins, not begging, He acts like medicine, He is ageless, destroying sin, without desires.

89 अधम अधारंण उपावणहार अंम्रित अपलट अव्यापक सार ॥
...अगम अलंग अडिग निज अंग अषंडित अचल नहीं तिहिं भंग ॥

He saves the downtrodden, He gives birth, He is Nectar, never changing, unlimited Essence. He cannot be reached, He is insurmountable,[103] not moving limbs (like man); He is not divided, He does not move and there is no division in Him.

90 आदि पुरिस उजल अटूट असरंणसरण उतिम अषूट ।
...अनाथबंध आश्रम सोइ जाणराइ जगजोति जोइ ॥

100. 86b: the word *yoni* (the womb) is used to denote the 8.4 million bodies of plants, animals and human beings in which a "self" can be born and reborn, according to the laws of *karma*. The human body is the last stage in this cycle and the most difficult to reach and pass.

101. 87a: अकल probably < कलारहित, i.e. beyond the *kalā*s, or divisions of time.

102. 88a: see आत्मा–राम, Callewaert: 2009, p. 167.

103. 89b: अलंग could perhaps be read as अलंघ (< Skt. अलंघनीय, "insurmountable, unattainable".

He is the primaeval Man, immaculate, undivided; not having yet giving shelter, He is supreme, unbreakable. He is Shelter for helpless people, king of the wise and Light of the world.

91 निरलेप त्रिबिग्रह त्रिबांण त्रिबंध त्रिलोभी त्रिगुंण त्रिसंध ।
...निरंजन निरालंभ निरकार नरहरि निवास नाथ त्रिधार ॥

He is authentic,[104] without decay,[105] He is Salvation (*nirvāṇ*), without ties; He has no greed, He is *nirguṇa*, uninterrupted.

He is pure (*nirañjan*),[106] self-supporting, without form, Lord of men; Lord of the dwelling,[107] without support.

92 त्रिमोही त्रिमल निहक्रंम निहक्रोध त्रिविष निहभ्रंम ।
...त्रिसंसै निजपद त्रिधांम निकुल निस्वादी है निहकांम ॥

He knows no illusory love (*moh*), He is free of stains (or sin), above (the laws of) *karma*; without anger, free of poison and illusion. Beyond doubts, His own support; He has no dwelling place, human descendance, taste or desires.

93 नारायंण निज सरूप निज सार त्रिबिकार निस्तारंणहार ।
...त्रिसंक निसहरा त्रिसंदेह निहप्रपंची सौं कीजै नेह ॥

(Called) Nārāyaṇ (Helper of men), He is His own form and essence; beyond decay, Saviour. Without hesitation, destroying darkness, free of snares: love Him.

94 नि चल निस्तरंग निरहार निरामय निगुरा त्रिधार ।
...तेज तत त्रिभुवन पति तारण तारिक तापत पति हरि हंरण ॥

He is immobile, quiet like a waveless lake (*nistaraṅga*), invincible; above sickness, without a guru's initiation and support. He is the Energy-element, Lord of the universe, helping across (the ocean of rebirths), Lord of the fire, Hari, Remover (of sins).

104. 91a: lit. "not painted", like an image in clay.

105. 91a: for त्रिबिग्रह, नरविग्रह in ms. 2.

106. 91b: the term निरंजन as a name for God is frequently used by Kabīr and the Dādūpanthīs and literally means: "without stain"; *añjan* (lit. "collyrium, stain") symbolizes the *guṇas*; see Callewaert: 2009, p. 1072

107. 91b: नवास in ms. 2.

95 त्रिधन कौ धन निरासने की आसात्रिधारनि आधार बेसासा ।
...निगंधरूप महमहण सुजांण महापुरिष महीपाल बिनाण ॥

He gives wealth to the poor and hope of good fortune to the despairing, He is Support for the helpless believer.

He is without smell or form, the biggest of all, wise; outstanding Person (*mahāpuruṣ*), Sovereign of the earth, Knower.

96 साषीभूत सुषदाई सुषदाइक सुषकारी सुषकरंण सुषनायक ।
...सुषरासी सुषरूपी सचर सुषनिधांन सुषमंडण सधर ॥

He gives testimony (about man's *karma*) and provides happiness.[108]

97 संम्रथ सुंदर सीतल सारंग सुधा सधीर श्रबगति श्रबंग ।
...सकलकरा श्रीपति स्यौ सार सुंनि संनेही सिरजनहार ॥

He is almighty, beautiful, refreshing Moon, like nectar, patient, all-pervading and omnipresent; *sakalakarā*,[109] Lord of wealth, the Essence of Śiva, *śūnya*, loving, Creator.

98 सुषसागर अरु संत सधीर सुभकरण श्रवैं सुष सीर ।
...साचा सजीवनिं संपूरंण साह सुत्रधार सुंमिरौ सुर ताह ॥

He is an Ocean of happiness, patient, holy Man (*santa*), providing good fortune, shining forth rays of happiness; He is truthful, eternal, accomplished Lord, Stage-director: remember that Lord of gods.

99 सरस सिरोमणि सोहै स्वांमी सकल समंगल है घंण नांमीं ।
...सकल धांम संकोच निवारण सोभा सिंध सब साज संवांरण ॥

He is full of nectar, *śiromaṇi*,[110] beautiful Lord, always with abundance of bliss, with many names; He dwells everywhere,

---

108. 96: several synonyms are here translated only once.
109. 97b: as a conjecture, I read सकलकला and translate as "provided with all the sixteen *kalās*", although this seems to contradict the अकल of verse 87.
110. 99a: *Śiromaṇi* or *cūḍāmaṇi* (lit. "a specific jewel of the head"), is used metaphorically for "an outstanding person".

removing doubts, Ocean of beauty, uniting all splendour in Himself.

100 सकल बियोगी सुयंसिंभ   सव गुंण रहता नांही डिंभ ।
...सदई सदा संतनि की संपति सुधन संनेही साधू जंपति ॥

He is present everywhere,[111] (x),[112] free of all specifications (*sava guṇa rahit*) and without vanity; He is always the wealth of the holy men, rich, loving for the seeker calling on Him.

101 श्रबरूप सजन संगाती   सहजरूप सूषिम थिति थाति ।
...सारग्राही सबीर्ज[113] थीर   अनाथनि कौ नाथ उधांरण धीर ॥

In all His forms He is the Companion of man; His natural form is a guarantee for happy days.

He grasps the essence, He is full of energy, yet motionless; He is the Lord of the helpless, the patient Saviour.

102 प्रमातम पूरण प्रकास   परंम पुरिस परब्रह्म उजास ।
...परंमगुरू पवित्र प्रतिपाल   परमानंद प्रांनपति लाल ॥

He is the supreme Soul (*paramātmā*), full of Splendour; greatest Person, highest Brahma, Brightness. He is the highest Guru, holy Governor, supreme Bliss, Lord of all beings, beloved.

103 पतितपांवन प्रगट परसोतम   परमेस्वर परंमहंस प्रभु वोपम ।
...प्रम ईस प्रमारथ पालिक   प्रांणनाथ प्रसिध संभालक ॥

Purifying the sinners, appearing as first of men (*puruṣottama*); greatest Lord (*parameśvar*), most outstanding ascetic (*paramhaṁsa*), worthy Lord. Supreme Lord, He observes the ultimate purpose; Lord of beings, famous Preserver.

---

111. 100a: the reading सकल बियोगी can perhaps be rendered as "entirely separated, unattached".

112. 100a: सुयंसिंभ is probably a corrupt reading; as a conjecture, I read it as a compound of सुभम < Skt. सुजन, "relative" and ˙सिंभ < Skt. सिम [?], "all, best, the self", i.e. "having the self as (the only) relative". ?

113. 101b: सवीरज in ms. 2.

104 परंमपुज[114] परभेव पुनीत परापरी परषोतम मीत ।
...पारसरूपी प्राण का प्रांण प्रमसिंध पुंज पद प्रांण ॥

Most venerable, He is the holy; Supreme Being, full of opposites, First of men (*puruṣottam*), Friend. Vital breath of vital breaths like a Philosopher's Stone (turning iron into gold), He is the biggest Ocean and Treasure-store of salvation and life.

105 प्रीतम ब्रलंभ[115] प्रांणपियार हितकारी अरु प्रंम प्रगार ।
...परंम उदार परंम उदीत प्रम प्रभास सु कीजै मीत ॥

He is the beloved of beings; Benefactor and biggest Shrine (storing the good deeds of people). He is a very generous Friend, exerting His good influence.

106 जगत प्रणांमीं[116] जगत प्रकास जोति सरूपी जगत उजास ।
...जगतपति जगदीस जगतगुर जगजीवन जगसोभा ईसवर ॥

He transforms the world, He is light of the world.

He is Lord of the world (*jagatpati, jagadīś*), guru, Life and Splendour of the world, our Lord.

107 जीवनमूरी जगत निवास जग उदीत जग करण बिगास ।
...जगमणि जगतारण जगनाथ जंत्रक जांण जीवनि सब साथ ॥

Root (or medicine) of life, Dwelling-place of the world;[117] Origin,[118] Cause and Developer of the world. Jewel of the world, Saviour and Lord, Sculptor of beings and of life.

108 बिस्वंभर बिस्वनाथ विनांणी विस्वरूपी व्यापक ब्रह्म जांणीं ।
...बंनमाली बषिहरण बिधाता बिधनां बेहद बेकीमति दाता ॥

Lord over the whole universe, Knower; Brahma pervading the whole universe. Owner of the forest, Remover of poison, Creator, unlimited and precious Giver.

---

114. 104a: परमपूज्य in ms. 2.
115. 105a: बल्लभ in ms. 2. Several words are here translated with "beloved".
116. 106a: परणामी in ms. 2.
117. 107a: जगदनिवास, i.e. "in whom the world resides".
118. 107a: उदित in ms. 2.

109 बिस्वासरूप बिमल बिद्याधर बडा धंणी बमेकी बहुकर ।
...बासदेव बा नांरूपी बैराठ बिचारी बस्त अनूपी ॥

Source of faith, pure Store of all knowledge; great and wealthy, full of understanding, having many hands. Fire (*vāsudev*), like desire (*vāsanā*); Virāṭ;[119] reflect on this wonderful fact.

110 दयानिधि देवाधिदेव दयासिंधे कहूं नहीं छेव ।
...दीनबंध दीरन नांव दांमोदर है सब ठांव ॥

Ocean of mercy, God of all the gods; Sea of pity, hurting nobody. Friend of the small (*dīn*), with an immense name, Dāmodar, present in all places.

111 दयाल देव दई दुषहरण दुषखंडण दरीया दुषदहंण ।
...चिंताहरंण चित्रीव चितेरा चिंतामणि छत्रपति चित नेरा ॥

He is a merciful God, Remover of sorrow; River tearing apart and destroying sorrow. He takes away worries, peculiar Painter, Cintāmaṇi,[120] King, present in the mind.

112 गुंण सागर गंभीर गहगरा गोपाल गंणेस्वर गगनधरा ।
...गुर गोब्यंद गुपत गहि ग्यांन गुरवा गोरष गढीया ध्यांन ॥

Ocean of virtues, impenetrable, (x),[121] Gopāl (Protector of cows), Lord of people (*gaṇeśvar*) in heaven and on earth; the Guru Govinda masters all hidden knowledge, great Gorakha,[122] fixed in meditation.

113 भगत बछल भांवतौ भारी भंजन भीड बहुत सुषकारी ।
...त्रिभुवनदेव त्रीलोकनाथ त्रकंम तार सकल कै साथ ॥

Lover of devotees, very lovable, Destroyer of calamities, He goes

---

119. 109b: बैराठ ? < विराट or the personified form of Brahmā in whom the whole world resides.

120. 111b: *cintāmaṇi* is the legendary jewel granting all wishes, the Wishing-stone.

121. 112a: गहगरा can perhaps be read as गहगहा or "full of joy".

122. 112b: Gorakha-nātha, as "protector of cows", or perhaps referring to the (legendary) poet-mystic Gorakhanātha.

on providing happiness; He is the God of the three worlds, Lord of the three worlds, liberating from the triple *karma*, Helper of all.

114 भै भंजन भौ तारंण भगवंत भू परवन भू धर नहीं अंत ।
...भावग्राही भैहरण भगवांन धरणीधर भरतार सुजांण ॥

Freeing from fear, the Bhagavant[123] takes across the world, Enchanter of kings, Upholder of the earth, without end; giving heed to the feelings of men, the Lord (*bhagavān*) removes fear, He is the wise Lord of the earth.

115 कालहरंण अरु कलहनिवारंण करता पुरिस कलि मांहिं उबारंण ।
...कल्यांणकारी चतुर चितचोर छबिरूपी झिलिमिलि चहुं वोर ॥

He removes death, does away with calamities and saves man in the dark era; Benefactor, wise, Enchanter of hearts, everywhere shines His beauty.

116 केसौ करुणामै क्रिपाल कारीगर करतार कुलाल ।
...कोमल कंवल किरंणि ततसार करंणहार के नांव अपार ॥

Keśav is full of mercy and pity, He is Craftsman, Creator, Potter; soft Lotus, Sunray, Essence of things: these are the unsurpassed names for the Creator.

तुरकी नांम Muslim names

117 अलिफ आप पाक महबूब साफ लतीफ षुलासा षूब ।
...मिहरवांन मालिक करीम राजिक रब सांई रहींम ॥

God is Beginning[124] and Father, He is holy, beloved, pure, pleasing, the Final End;[125] He is a merciful Lord, generous,[126] feeding us, the Lord,[127] the Compassionate.[128]

---

123. 114a: भगवंत or भगवान, originally meaning "the venerable, the Lord", is commonly used as a name for God.

124. 117a: as the first letter of the Hebrew and Arabic alphabet, *aliph* stands for God "who is at the beginning".

125. 117a: <u>*kh*</u>*ulāṣa* in Arabic.

126. 117b: *karīm* in Arabic.

127. 117b: *rabb* in Arabic and साइ < Hindī स्वामी.

128. 117b: *rahīm* in Arabic.

118 माजर पिजर मासूक षांन कांइम करता तूं दींवांन ।
...दस्तगीर दोस्त सतार हाजिर नाजिर जहांदार ॥

Mother, Father,[129] beloved, Refuge, firm,[130] Creator and Organizer; Helper, Friend, (x), ever present, watching carefully, Protector of the world.

119 मीरां मीयां सुलितांन गंनी सलौंनां सुबहांन ।
...सुरजन सांईं दिलदार अजब अजाइब आलेयार ॥

Knight, Lord, Governor, wealthy, beautiful and rich;
Surajan,[131] Lord, Friend, Wonder of wonders,[132] great Friend.

120 जा फिरि जाहिर जहूर साचा साहिब हक नूर ।
...अला इलाही पिरी ऐक बहु गुंणवंता पीव नेक ॥

Giver of life,[133] the Apparent,[134] true Lord, Reality[135] and Light; Alā, Ilāhī, beloved one, full of virtues, Lover of all.

121 क़ादिर लासरीक मौजूद मवलक मौला है माबूद ।
...षालिक षुदाइ इलिला दांनांबींनां बेपरवाह सयांनां ॥

Almighty,[136] without companions,[137] present, Maulavī (priest) and Revered;[138]

---

129. 118a: I translate here मादर and पदर as found in Mangaldas: 1947, p. 24.
130. 118a: the form कांइम can perhaps be related to *al.kayyūm*, "the self-subsisting" in Arabic.
131. 119b: सुरजन as a name for God is possibly derived from सुजन, "a gentle, good person".
132. 119b: अजाइब, as a plural form of अजब, is here repetitive.
133. 120a: I translate here the rendering जा आफिरि in Mangaldas: 1947, p. 25.
134. 120a: the composite जाहिर may refer to *ẓāhir* in Arabic.
135. 120a: see हक is related to *ḥaqq* in Arabic.
136. 121a: see *qādir* in Arabic.
137. 121a: the meaning of लासरीक is not certain. As a hypothesis it can perhaps be related to *lā-·šărīk* or *lā·šărīk*, "without companions".
138. 121a: माबूद is related to *ma'būd*, "the Revered", in Arabic.

Creator,[139] Khudā,[140] *il Ilā*, wise, clearsighted,[141] free of worries and full of understanding.

122 पाक प्रवर्दिगार फारीक बेबहा जाति तारीक ।
...बारीक हजूर लाप्रद अलाह रहमांन षता बकसिंद ॥

Holy, Protector,[142] boundless, totally detached, [x];[143]

infinitely small, Lord, unveiled, Allah, Benefactor,[144] forgiving faults and sins.

123 नांव कहौं बहु भांति अनेक हिंदू तुरक कां करता ऐक ।
...अरथ बिचारि राषीये भाव तौ पावै अंम्रित का साव ॥

People call Him with many names, yet the Creator of Hindus and Muslims (*turakī*) is the same; reflect on the deep meanings, protect your (religious) experience and you will taste the nectar.

124 त्रिनांमींक निरंजन सोइ ताकै पटंतरि नांव न कोई ।
...सेवग सेवा मांहैं रहै जैसौ देषै तैसौ कहै ॥

Nirañjan is without name and He cannot be compared with any name; the disciple should remain in (His) service and (only) speak according to what he experiences.

125 तात मात नहीं बंधू जाती रूप रेष नहीं प्यंडन भांती ।
...नेत्र रसन कर नांहीं श्रवन अरध उरध नहीं मस्तक चरंन ॥

He has no father or mother, friend or caste, He has no form or beautiful body; He has no eyes, tongue, hands or ears, front or back, head or feet.

---

139. 121b: *ḫāliq* in Arabic.
140. 121b: *khudā* is a Persian name for God; षुदाइ (ms. 2) means "divinity".
141. 121b: बींनां is perhaps related to the Persian participle adjective *binā*. Cf. J.T. Platts, *A Dictionary of Urdū, Classical Hindī and English*, Oxford University Press (1884), 1968, p. 211.
142. 122a: प्रवर्दिगार, Persian *parvardigār*; फारीक and बेबहा are synonymous.
143. The translation is not certain; perhaps *jāti* (Arabic) or "own", and तारीक <Arabic *tārik*: "one who gives up".
144. 122b: see *raḥmān* in Arabic.

126 पेट पीठि तुचा नहीं अस्त नाडी जीव रेत नहीं रकत ।
...नाद बिंद काया नहीं छायाधात घात ग्रेह नहीं माया ॥

He has no stomach, back, skin or bones; no veins, sperm or blood like living beings. The shadow of a body or *nād binda*[145] is not on Him, maya (x) has no effect on Him.

127 बीज अंकूर ब्रिछ नहीं मूल साषा पत्र पलव नहिं फूल ।
...बेली तांतू फल नहीं बास न्रिंगुंण रांम श्रबंग निवास ॥

He is (like) a tree without seed, germ, roots, branches, leaves, shoots or blossoms; there are no creepers on Him, no fruits or fragrance, He is absolute (*nirguṇa*), Ram, His dwelling is everywhere.

128 अषंडित तेज निवास समंगल सब ठां रसन श्रवण चक्षु न्रिमल ।
...चरंण हस्त सीस मुष बांणींसकल संबूह श्रबंग बिनांणीं ॥

He is undivided Energy, Dwelling full of bliss, everywhere are His pure tongue, ears and eyes; His feet and hands, head, face and voice, everywhere He is, all-knowing and wise.

न्रिंजन अस्थांन के नाम Names for the place of Nirañjan

129 प्रथम अस्थांन गगन कविलास सुन्य सकति आसंण आकास ।
...बल पोरिष छाजा केदार तषत अरस अरु नांव अपार ॥

The highest place (of His presence or of man's union with Him)

---

145. 126b: *Nād bindu* is a yogic term (see *Nād bindu upaniṣad* in M. Eliade, *Le Yoga*, pp. 137f.) used in a specific sense by the *nirguṇa bhaktas*. Literally meaning "sound", *nad* stands here for the mystic sound heard by the *yogī* only after long discipline, at the height of his experience; *bindu*, literally "fluid, sperm", also "point", stands for the essence of man, and metaphorically means the core of Being, the vital power which the *yogī*, through discipline, has to keep inside his body and under his control. Dādū used the term to denote the discipline as well as the goal of the discipline. In the *Dādū Vāṇī*, v. 26,3 we read: "That *yogī* lives, who fills his body with the *nad bindu*; he will not die but he will drink the nectar of Rām". In the context of verse 126 of the text here we may perhaps suppose that *nād bindu* belongs to the realm of the seeking human being and cannot be applied to God.

appears in the *gagan;*[146] it is *śūnya*, energy (*śakti*), residing in the sky. It is the strength and the guardian of the roof, the field, the throne and the palace [i.e. of the whole body?], innumerable (are His) names.[147]

130 तुमकौं कैसी वोपमा दीजै जे कुछ कहौं संबेदी कीजै ।
...तेरी गति तूंहि भल जांनैं हंम अयांन का तुंमहिं बषांनैं ॥

What can we compare You with? Any comparison is an offence to You. You alone know Your own nature: we are so ignorant, what can we say about You?

131 जप तप ब्रत कोटि जगि करै तीरथ सकल पलटि तंन हरै ।
...तुला ध्रम दांन बहु दीजै तउ न नांव सरभरि कीजै ॥

If a man would recite Your name, do penance, take vows and offer a million sacrifices, if a man would run to all holy places, fast away his body; give in charity his own weight in gold, even then he will not be able to find an adequate name for You.

132 पंचा अगनि अ टांग जोग साधैं पवन करैं रस भोग ।
...लुंचित कथा उपाव सबहुं राषै नांव पटंतरि साधन न भाषै ॥

If a man does the penance of the fivefold fire, practises the eightfold yoga, does breathing exercises and enjoys the nectar of experience; if he chastises his body[148] and does severe penance, yet he will not be able to compare You adequately with any name.

133 वेद पुरान सिंम्रित सब सोधैं लाला तिलक पहरि परमोधै ।
...अंतरि कपट नहीं मनि साचास्वांग बणावै करणी काचा ॥

The seeking of man is recorded in the Vedas, Purāṇas and Smṛtis,

---

146. 129a: *gagan* (sky) means the top part of the skull (*brahmarandhra*) in yogic terminology; it is said to be the place of the highest experience. For कविलास, see Callewaert: 2009, p. 299: कबिलास.

147. The translation of verse 126 is not fully certain, if not misleading.

148. 132b: I translate here the rendering given by Mangaldas: 1947, p. 27: लुंचित काय उपवास बहु.

people move the beads of their rosaries, anoint their head and meditate all night; yet, only in the truthful mind is there no division and corruption, hypocrisy makes all action ineffective.

134 काची मुला पढ़ैं कुरांन रोजा बंग निवाज बषाण ।
...काबै हज मके कूं जावै इसक दरद बिंन जांति न पांवैं ॥

*Qāzī*s and *maulavī*s read the Quran, fast and say their prayers; people go on pilgrimage to the Ka'ba in Mecca, yet without the pain of (true) love, they do not attain the birth (unto the real life).

135 ईदि बकरीद बिसमला करैं हलाल कहैं अरु दोजक भरैं ।
...कहूं रीकरि बांटैं षांण मंदे अमल भिस्ति क्यूं जांण ॥

If one celebrates Īd and Bakrīd and eats only the religiously permitted meat,[149] even then one may go to hell;

even if he prepares frankincense[150] and distributes food (in charity), how could an evil man go to heaven like a pure man?

136 नेकी करैं पाक दिल राषैं जीव संतोषै झूठ न भाषै ।
...हक बंदगी षिजमति सार ते आसिक पावैं दीदार ॥

The true disciple (*āśik*) is good and keeps a pure heart, he is contented and does not speak falsely; he finds joy in service and he experiences the (mystical) vision.

137 अध्यात्मबोध बिचारै कोई कोईसुधि बुधि ग्यांन बमेकी होई ।
...नई रसन श्रवन चषि आवै प्रांण हत पद हरि धन पावै ॥

If a man reflects on this Introduction to the inner Life, he will enjoy good knowledge, understanding and discernment;

he will get a new tongue, new ears and eyes, he will enjoy the richness of Hari in his whole body.[151]

---

149. 135a: *halāl*, or "lawful as food"; *halāl karanā*: "to slaughter an animal in accordance with Islamic law".

150. If we read कहूं रीकरि as कंदूरी करि we may perhaps translate as "if one prepares frankincense".

151. In the remaining four couplets the author states that he composed this book through the grace of his guru Dādū and that immense benefits will result from its reading.

Glossary

Verses 25-81: no systematic translation is given of those verses which are meant to give only synonyms of a particular keyword. Those synonyms are listed alphabetically in the glossary below, with reference to the respective keyword and the verse in which they occur.

अंजनी (mother of Hanumān)	:	vital breath/life-energy (*prāṇ*) - 52
अंतहकरण (अंत:करण: heart, soul, conscience)	:	vital breath/life-energy (*prāṇ*) - 53
अंदेसा (अंदेशा)	:	विरह - 62
अनंग (a N. of Kāmadeva)	:	व्यंद (semen) - 37
अंनभै(-वाणी)	:	गुर-सबद - 73
अनलपंखि (अनलपक्ष, Fire-bird[152])	:	गुरदेव – 76, 79
अनहद(-वाणी)	:	गुर-सबद - 73
अनुरागी	:	विरही - 63
अरचा (अर्चना)	:	भगति/बंदगी - 60
अरजन (अर्जुन, Arjuna)	:	प्राण (vital breath/life-energy) - 51
अरवाह (Ar. *arvāḥ*)	:	प्राण (vital breath/life-energy) - 52
अरूपरी (?)	:	वाणी (word) - 56
अवधूत (an ascetic)	:	मन - 28
असाधि (असाधु, evil)	:	विकार – 35
अस्थूल (=स्थूल, visible; with कलि?)	:	काया - 26
अस्व (अश्व, horses)	:	इंद्रिय - 36
आकार (form)	:	काया - 25
आकास (आकाश, the sky, heavens)	:	गुरदेव – 76

152. See Callewaert: 2009, p. 68.

आंगण (आँगन, courtyard[153]) : प्राण (vital breath/life-energy) - 53

आत्म : प्राण (vital breath/life-energy) - 52

आसिक (आशिक़, Ar.) : विरही - 63

इंद (the moon, or Indra?) : प्राण (vital breath/life-energy) - 52

इबाबत (इबादत, Ar.) : भगति/बंदगी 60

उचार : गोष्ठि (conversation) - 55

उजास (light) : ॐकार - 27

उदास : विरह - 62

उदासी : विरही - 63

उसताद (उस्ताद, P.) : गुरदेव - 74

ऊट (ऊँट, a camel?) : प्राण (vital breath/life-energy) - 52

औजूद (existence, body) : काया - 26

औधू (अवधूत, an ascetic) : प्राण (vital breath/life-energy) - 51

कउवा (H. कौवा, a crow) : मन - 28

कथा : गोष्ठि (conversation) - 55

कंद्रप (कंदर्प, a N. of Kāmadeva) : व्यंद (semen) - 37

करहा (a camel, or a rabbit?[154]) : मन - 30

कलस (कलसा, an earthen pot; see below, कुंभ) : प्राण (vital breath/life-energy) - 53

कलाल (a liquor-seller) : मन - 30

कलाली (f., a liquor-seller) : मनसा - 33

कलि (the *baheḍā* tree or its fruit [into which the demon Kali — see Nal/Damayantī — is said to have come) : काया - 26

कलपबृछ (कल्पवृक्ष, a tree that grants all desires) : गुरदेव - 75, 78

---

153. See Callewaert: 2009, p. 149.

154. See Callewaert: 2009, pp. 315-16; camel, cont. "consciousness", "after which the soul wanders like a widow after her camel" (Kabīr).

कंवल/कवल (a lotus[155]) : प्राण (vital breath/life-energy) -53; गुरदेव - 75

कसाइणी (क़साइन, a butcher's wife) : कुबुधि (evil mind) - 38

काइथ (कायस्थ) : मन - 28

काग[ली?] (काक, a crow?) : कुबुधि (evil mind) - 38

काजी (क़ाज़ी, a muslim judge or magistrate?) : प्राण (vital breath/life-energy) - 51

काम (a N. of Kāmadeva) : व्यंद (semen) - 37

कामधेन (कामधेनु, Cow of plenty) : गुरदेव – 75, 77

कांमिनी (कामिनी, a beautiful, or amorous woman) : *māyā* - 34

काल (death) : विकार - 35; world (of rebirth) -46 (47)

कुंज (a bower?) : प्राण (vital breath/life-energy) - 52

कुदाली (a grub-hoe?) : कुबुधि (evil mind) - 38; सुर्ति - 57

कुंभ (a pot; see above, कलस) : प्राण (vital breath/life-energy) - 53

कुमति : कुबुधि (evil mind) - 38

कुरि (?) : प्राण (vital breath/life-energy) - 52

कुही (कुहर, S. कुधि, an owl?) : कुबुधि (evil mind) - 38

कूंची (कुजी, a key?) : गुर-सबद - 73

कुवा (कुँआ, a well) : प्राण (vital breath/life-energy) - 53

केतुकी (केतकी, the screwpine or *ketakī* flower[156]) : कुबुधि (evil mind) - 38

कोकिल (-कथी, song of the cuckoo?) : वाणी (word) - 56

कोढणी (f., a leper) : *māyā* - 34

---

155. See Callewaert: 2009, p. 339.

156. The black bees are said not to sit on this flower because the intoxication of its fragrance reportedly kills them.

कोल (a boar)	:	कुबुधि (evil mind) - 38
कौंला (कमल, a [lotus-shaped] shallow cup)	:	प्राण (vital breath/life-energy) - 53
खग (a bird)	:	प्राण (vital breath/life-energy) - 51
खलि (खल?, wicked)	:	विकार - 35
खिजमत (ख़िदमत, Ar.)	:	भगति/बंदगी - 60
खूंटा (खँटा, a stake?)	:	मन - 29
गंगा (the Ganges)	:	वाणी (word) - 56
गज (an elephant)	:	मन - 28
गनिका (a prostitute)	:	*māyā* - 34
गयंद (गजेंद्र, an elephant)	:	ज्ञान (knowledge) - 54
गरज (the noise of thunder)	:	सुमिरण - 59
गरद (an eagle)	:	मन - 28
गाइ (a cow)	:	ज्ञान (knowledge) - 54
गाडर (H. भेड़, a sheep)	:	ज्ञान (knowledge) - 54
गावत्री (the *gāyatrī mantra*)	:	मनसा - 32
गूजर (a Rājpūt Gūjar, or cowherd?)	:	प्राण (vital breath/life-energy) - 51
गोकल (गोकुल?, herd of cattle)	:	काया – 25
गोरी (गौरी in ms. 2; गौरि or Pārvatī?)	:	मनसा - 33
ज्ञान–अग्नि	:	see v. 61
घट : काया – 25		
घंटा (a bell)	:	वाणी (word) - 56
चकवा (the *cakavā*)	:	चित्त - 31
चकोर (the *cakor*)	:	चित्त - 31
चक्र (चक्रवाक, the *cakavā*)	:	चित्त - 31
चांवडी (चामुंडा in Barathval: 1936)	:	मनसा - 33

चंद (the moon)	: ज्ञान (knowledge) - 54
चंदण (चंदन, sandalwood)	: गुरदेव – 75, 76
चरखा (चरख़ा, a [spinning-] wheel[157])	: चित्त - 31
चरचा (चर्चा)	: गोष्ठि (conversation) - 55
चाकरी (P.)	: भगति/बंदगी 60
चाकी (चक्की, a millstone)	: चित्त - 31
चाचरी (a song[158])	: गोष्ठि (conversation) - 55
चांटी (Raj.)	: भगति/बंदगी - 60
चात्रिग (the *cātak* bird)	: चित्त - 31
चांदणा (चाँद, the moon)	: ज्ञान (knowledge) - 54
चांदी (silver)	: मनसा - 33
चांवडी (a whisk)	: मनसा - 33
चिडा (चिड़ा, a sparrow)	: चित्त - 31
चितवन	: ध्यान - 64
चिंतामणि ("jewel of thought", granting all desires)	: गुरदेव - 75, 77
चीता (a leopard)	: चित्त - 31
चील्ह (चील, a kite)	: मनसा - 33
चूल्हा (a fire-place)	: चित्त - 31
चोर (a thief)	: चित्त - 31
चोरटी (a fem. thief, or hypocrite; see Callewaert: 2009, p. 645)	: मनसा - 33
जगत	: संसार (world of rebirth) - 46
जंजाल (snare[s] of the world)	: विकार - 35; संसार (world of rebirth) - 46

157. For the "contextual" meanings, see Callewaert: 2009, pp. 602-03.

158. See Callewaert: 2009, p. 611.

जङ (root?) : सुर्ति - 57

जमुना (the Yamunā River) : मनसा - 32

जलंध्र (जलंधर, the demon Jalandhara?) : व्यंद (semen) - 37

जाप: सुमिरण - 59

जाहनवी (जाह्नवी, the Ganges) : वाणी (word) - 56

जीव (spirit) : ॐकार - 27

जुरु (जुर, ज्वर, fever?) : विकार - 35

जोगणी (योगिनी, a female ascetic) : मनसा - 32

जोगी (a *yogī*) : मन - 29; प्राण (vital breath/life energy) - 51

डंकणी (डाकिनी, a demoness) : *māyā* - 34

डीबि (?) : मनसा - 32

डोरी (a string?) : सुमिरण - 59

तनि–प्यास (thirst in the body) : विरह - 62

तरंग (a wave) : मनसा - 32

तांतू (ताँत, a string of musical instrument) : सुमिरण - 59

तारुणी (तारण, liberating) : वाणी (word) - 56

तालाबेली (restlessness[159]) : विरह - 62

तालिब (Ar. *ṭālib*) : विरही - 63

ताली (also तारी, trance) : ध्यान - 64

त्राटिक (त्राटक, त्राटिका: a specif. yogic exercise) : ध्यान - 64

त्रिया (a woman) : मनसा - 33

दरदबंद (adject., badly hurt) : विरही - 63

दामिनी (lightning) : मनसा - 33

दासातन : भगति/बंदगी 60

159. See Callewaert: 2009, p. 858.

दिल (-गगन, heaven of the heart?) : प्राण (vital breath/life-energy) - 53

दीप (दीया, a light) : ज्ञान (knowledge) - 54

दुंदर (द्वंद्व, conflict) : विकार - 35

दुबध्या (दुबधा, doubt) : कुबुधि (evil mind) - 38

दुविध्या (दुबधा) : संसा (doubt) - 39

दुर्मति. : कुबुधि (evil mind) - 38

दुलहनि (दुलहन, a bride) : प्राण (vital breath/life-energy) - 52

दुसमन (दुश्मन, enemy) : विकार - 35

देव (a god) : मन - 29

देवी (a goddess) : मनसा - 32

देह : काया – 25

देहुरा (temple) : काया - 26

दोजग (दोज़ख़, [leaving?] hell) : विकार - 35

द्रोपती (द्रौपदी) : कुबुधि (evil mind) - 38

धर (the earth) : गुरदेव – 76

धीय (daughter) : सुबुधि (good understanding) - 58

धुनि (ध्वनि, sound[160]) : सुमिरण - 59

धौं (धौल?, a bullock[161]) : मन - 30

नदी (a river) : गुरदेव – 76

नाद (sound) : ॐकार - 27

नारी (a woman) : मनसा - 32

निद्रा : ध्यान - 64

त्रिभै(-वाणी) : गुर-सबद - 73

पंगुल : ज्ञान (knowledge) - 54

पतंग (a kite) : मन - 28

पदम (पद्म, a lotus) : प्राण (vital breath/life-energy) - 53

160. See Callewaert: 2009, p. 1009.

161 See ibid., p. 1017.

परजापति (प्रजापति, emperor) : प्राण (vital breath/life-energy) - 51

परिवार (family) : काया - 26

पलीता (P.; the wick of a candle?[162]) : गुर-सबद - 73

पवन (the wind) : ॐकार - 27; गुरदेव – 76

पसु (पशु, an animal) : मन - 28

पांडव : see 36 (इंद्रिय)

पातिसाह (पातशाह, emperor) : प्राण (vital breath/life-energy) - 51

पापिणी (पापिनी, f., a sinful or wicked woman) : *māyā* - 34

पारजातिक (पारिजात, the coral tree[163]) : गुरदेव – 76, 79

पारवती (Pārvati) : मनसा - 33

पारस (philosophers' stone) : गुरदेव - 75, 78

पीर : गुरदेव - 74

पूजा : भगति/बंदगी 60

पूतिला (a puppet) : काया - 26

प्यंड : काया - 25

प्यासा : विरही - 63

पृथ्वी (the earth) : काया - 25

प्रीखत (?[164]) : प्राण (vital breath/life-energy) - 51

फटक (crystal) : मन - 30

फिकर (फ़िकर, A.) : विरह - 62

फिराक (फ़िराक़, A.) : विरह - 62

बगुला (a heron) : मन - 29

---

162. See Callewaert: 2009, p. 1179.

163. The *pārijāt* tree, in Indra's heavenly garden, is said to produce any scent according to the wishes of people and to carry many precious stones on its branches.

164. Barathval: 1936 (p. 271, जीव) gives प्रषित for प्रीखत.

बगुली (a female crane)	:	मनसा - 33
बछर	:	see 36 (इंद्रिय)
बछी (?)	:	वाणी (word) - 56
बंझ (बाँझ, a barren woman)	:	प्राण (vital breath/life-energy) - 52
बंदगी (P.)	:	भगति/बंदगी 60
बंदन (वंदन)	:	भगति/बंदगी 60
बंधू (a relative)	:	मन - 29
बाज (Braj, a horse, or बाज़, a hawk?)	:	मन - 29
बाण (an arrow?)	:	गुर-सबद - 73
बिछोह (विछोह)	:	विरह - 62
बिवोग (वियोग)	:	विरह - 62
भागीरथी (the Ganges)	:	वाणी (word) - 56
बेटी (daughter)	:	सुबुधि (good understanding) - 58
बेणाचवी (?)	:	वाणी (word) - 56
बेलि (बेल, a creeper[165]; see also below, बेलि)	:	प्राण (vital breath/life-energy) - 52
बैद (वैद्य, an Āyurvedic doctor)	:	गुरदेव – 78
बैराग (वैराग)	:	विरह - 62
बोध(-प्रकाश: light of understanding?)	:	ज्ञान (knowledge) - 54
ब्यावर[166] (<व्यावर)	:	काया - 26
ब्रह्म-अग्नि	:	see v. 61
भजन	:	सुमिरण - 59
भंवरा (भँवर?)	:	मन - 29
भंवर (भ्रमर, a black bee[167])	:	गुरदेव - 76

165. See Callewaert: 2009, p. 1504.

166. "Bringing forth". In the *हिन्दी शब्द सागर*, 1972, vol. 9, p. 4652 Dādū is quoted wrongly: दादू कापा ब्यावर . . . instead of दादू काया ब्यावर.

167. See Callewaert: 2009, p. 1532.

भागीरथी (the Ganges) : वाणी (word) - 56

भांमिनी (भामा, a passionate or angry woman) : *māyā* - 34

भुवंग (a snake) : संसा (doubt) - 39

भोमि[168] (भूमि, the earth) : काया - 25

भवन : संसार 46, 47

भ्रिंग (a large black bee) : गुरदेव - 76, 79

मकड़ी (a spider) : *māyā* - 34

मषी (मक्खी, a fly) : मनसा - 32

मगहर (?,मगर, a crocodile, or : *māyā* - 34
मगहर, Magahar; see :
Callewaert 2009, p. 1606)

मछी (मच्छी, a fish?; see below, मृग) : मनसा - 32

मंजार (a cat) : मन - 28

मंजारी (मार्जारी, a female cat) : मनसा – 33; *māyā* - 34

मंडक (H. मेंढक, a frog) : मन - 28

मंडी (a market) : मनसा - 33

मदन (a N. of Kāmadeva) : व्यंद (semen) - 37

मनोरथ (heart-felt wish) : विकार - 35

मसक (?) : गुर–सबद - 73

मसीति (मसजिद, mosque) : काया - 26

महरू (master?[169]) : प्राण (vital breath/life-energy) - 51

महल (palace) : काया - 26

महादेव (Śiva) : मन - 29

मांड (universe) : संसार -46

मांनी (मानी, a proud, resentful [woman]) : मनसा - 32

168. मोम in Barathval: 1936.

169. See Callewaert: 2009, pp. 1648 and 1647.

मालनी (a. fem. gardener[170])	: मनसा - 33
मास-पसारी (?,मांस-आहारी, meat-eating)	: *māyā* - 34
मीन (a fish)	: मन - 28
मुरसिद (मुरशिद, A.)	: गुरदेव - 74
मुला (मुल्ला, a Muslim priest?)	: मन - 30
मुसला (मुसल्ला, a prayer mat?)	: मन - 30
मूंगी (an ant[171])	: मनसा - 32
मूसा (a mouse)	: मन - 28
मृग (a deer) or "having lovely deer-eyes?; see note with v. 32.)	: मनसा - 32
मेघ (a cloud)	: गुरदेव - 76
मैंणी (f.; मैंण, or मेन, मेदन, is a N. of Kāmadeva)	: *māyā* - 34
मैन (मेन, मेदन, a N. of Kāmadeva)	: व्यंद (semen) - 37
मोतीहार (a garland of pearls)	: मन - 28
मोर (a pea-cock)	: मन - 28
मोहनी (a charming woman)	: *māyā* - 34
मौरी (a wedding-crown)	: मनसा - 33
म्रकट (H. मर्कट, a monkey)	: मन - 28
मृग (a deer)	: मन - 28
मृग-जल (deer-water: a mirage)	: संसार - 46
रटनि (रटन)	: सुमिरण - 59
रंज (sorrow)	: विकार - 35
रवि (the sun)	: गुरदेव - 75

170. मालनी is also used as an epithet of Pārvatī, whose name is mentioned in the same verse as a synonym for मनसा.

171. See Callewaert: 2009, p. 1704.

राजा (king) : vital breath- (प्राण) - 51

रावल (a king) : मन - 29

रूह (Ar. *rūḥ*) : प्राण (vital breath/life-energy) - 52

रैरैकार (रंकार)[172] : सुमिरण - 59

रोग (disease) : विकार - 35

र्‍यंद (रिंद, a dissolute person[173]) : मन - 30

ल्यौ[174] : सुमिरण - 59

वछी (?; see note with v. 32) : मनसा - 32

वपु : काया - 25

वबूल (बबूल, the acacia tree[175]) : काया - 26

वियोगिनी (a separated person) : प्राण (vital breath/life-energy) - 52

विरहनि : विरही - 63

विरह-अग्नि : see 61

विरहनि (a separated person) : प्राण (vital breath/life-energy) - 52

विलाई (बिलाई, a cat) : evil mind - 38

विषै (विषय [-स्वाद?] sensual enjoyment?) : विकार - 35

विश्व : संसार - 46

वेलि (बेल, a creeper[176]); see also above, बेलि) : काया - 26

वैद (वैद्य, an Āyurvedic doctor) : गुरदेव – 75

---

172. See Callewaert: 2009, p. 1739.

173. Ibid., p. 1810: "this mind is a र्‍यंद", Dādū.

174. Ibid., p. 1857.

175. Ibid., p. 1344.

176. Ibid., p. 1505: "In Dādū the creeper is symbolic for the soul, or for उनमन, that is the stage where the union of the soul with the Supreme Being is experienced". Dādū and Kabīr have a separate chapter in their *sākhī* collection, resp. 36 and 16, with the title बेली को अंग. See also Callewaert: 1978, p. 416.

वेरागनि (one who is free from worldly desires)	:	प्राण (vital breath/life-energy) - 52
वैरागी	:	विरही - 63
व्यंद (बिंदु)	:	semen - 37
व्यंद्रावन [वृंदा-forest]	:	काया - 25
व्याधि (disease)	:	विकार - 35
व्याल (wicked; also a snake)	:	विकार - 35
वृष (a tree)	:	काया - 26, 50; संसार - 48; Brahma - 72
श्रप (सर्प, a snake)	:	संसा (doubt) - 39
षाड (a pit in which a weaver sits)	:	काया - 25
सक्ति (शक्ति, Durgā?)	:	मनसा - 32
संक्या (शंका)	:	संसा (doubt) - 39
संसा (संशय)	:	संसा (doubt) - 39
सती (शक्ति, power)	:	प्राण (vital breath/life-energy) - 51
सबद (word)	:	ॐकार - 27
समाधि	:	ध्यान - 64
समुद्र (the ocean)	:	काया - 25; संसार - 46
सरीर	:	काया - 25
(मलीन)-सरोवर	:	सरीर - 49
संख (conch)	:	ॐकार - 27
संखिणी (शंखिनी, a shameless woman)	:	*māyā* - 34
सखी (a female companion)	:	सुर्ति - 57
ससा (a hare, or rabbit)	:	ॐकार - 27
ससि (शशि, the moon)	:	गुरदेव - 75
साद (Skt. शब्द, sound)	:	ॐकार - 27
सापिणी (साँपिन, a female snake)	:	*māyā* - 34

सारद (शारदा, the Sarasvatī River) : वाणी (word) - 56

सास (breath) : ॐकार - 27

सासू (सास, mother-in-law) : सुर्ति - 57

साह (शाह, emperor) : प्राण (vital breath/life-energy) - 51

सतगुर : गुरदेव - 74

सीकलीगर[177] : गुरदेव - 74

सींगी (a horn, used as trumpet) : सुर्ति - 57

सीन (chest?) : ॐकार - 27

सीप (सींप, shell, mother-of-pearl[178]) : सुर्ति - 57

सई (a needle) : सुर्ति - 57

सुकल (शुक्ल, white?) : व्यंद (semen) - 37

सुत्रधार (thread-holder : stage-manager, or puppeteer) : गुरदेव - 74

सुत्र (a string?) : सुमिरण - 59

सुंदरि (a beautiful woman) : प्राण (vital breath/life-energy) - 52; सुर्ति: - 57

सुनहा (a dog) : मन - 28; संसा (doubt) - 39

सुनार (goldsmith) : गुरदेव - 74

सुमति : सुबुधि (good understanding) - 58

सुर (sound) : ॐकार - 27

सुरसरी (S. सुरसरित्, the Ganges[179]) : वाणी (word) - 56

सुरसुती (सरस्वती, the Sarasvatī River) : सुर्ति - 57

177. See *हिंदी शब्द सागर*, p. 6009, Ar.+P.: "sharpening, brightening" (?).

178. See Callewaert: 2009, p. 2054.

179. Ibid., p. 2091.

सुरही (सुरभि, a cow)	: मनसा - 32
सुषुमना (सुषुम्ना[180])	: सुर्ति - 57
सुहदा (A. शोहदा, a rogue?)	: विरही - 63
सुसा (शश, a rabbit)	: संसा (doubt) - 39
सूर (सूर्य, the sun)	: ॐकार - 27; गुरदेव - 76, 79
सुरिज	: ज्ञान (knowledge) - 54
सूवा (H. सुवा, a parrot)	: मन - 28
सेवा	: भगति/बंदगी 60
सेस (शेष, Śeṣa?)	: ॐकार - 27
सैतान (शैतान, a devil)	: मन - 29
सोग (शोक, P. *sog*)	: विरह - 62
सोषता (तन–सोषता, "draining the body"[181])	: विरही - 63
स्यंघ (a lion)	: ॐकार - 27; संसा (doubt) - 39; गुरदेव - 76
स्याल (a fox)	: ॐकार - 27; संसा (doubt) - 39
हंस (goose, *poet.* swan[182])	: प्राण – vital breath/life-energy 51; गुरदेव - 76, 79
हीरा (diamond)	: गुरदेव - 75

180. See Callewaert: 2009, p. 2092: सुरसुती.

181. Ibid., p. 2128: सोषता.

182. Ibid., p. 2145.

3

Dādū and the Dādūpanth
The Sources

[1987][1]

DURING the past few decades [1987] some lengthy studies have been devoted to Dādū Dayāl and the Dādūpanth.[2] However, most biographical literature about Dādū is, to a great extent, the result of a mere copying from a few and the same earlier writers. Also, a mass of details about Dādū is given without a clear distinction between the early documents and the later (hagiographical) information from tradition. In most cases the composition of an original work was followed by a number of sectarian writers who indulged in laudatory embellishments to the point of the most fanciful miracle-mongering. For most sectarian biographers, Jangopāl's account (*Dādūjanmalīlā*, *c.* 1620; see below, pp. 173ff.) has served as the basic source.

For the history of the Dādūpanth written by English authors,

---

1. In: K. Schomer & W.H. McLeod, eds., *The Sants: Studies in a Devotional Tradition of India*, Berkeley, Religious Studies Series, 1987, pp. 181-89.
2. Vasudev Sharma, *संत कवि दादू और उनका पंथ*, New Delhi, Shodhaprabandha Prakashan, 1969; K.P. Simha, *दादूपंथ एवं उसके साहित्य का समीक्षात्मक अध्ययन*, Banaras, Kashi Vidyāpīṭha, 1971. W.G. Orr, *A Sixteenth-Century Indian Mystic*, London: Lutterworth Press, 1947. For a complete survey of the sources (till 1977), see Callewaert: 1978, pp. 21-56; 55 references. For a recent article on Dādū, and for a recent bibliography, see Monika Horstmann, Dādū Dayāl, in: Brill's *Encyclopedia of Hinduism*, vol. IV. pp. 209ff.

the basic source is an article written by H.H. Wilson in 1828.[3] In its basic data it has been copied again and again with only minor additions and changes. W.G. Orr applied a critical test to some oral traditions about Dādū and gave a summary and analysis of Dādū's teaching, with a translation of many representative verses. His study of Dādū's life is divided into two parts. In the first part, *The Life of Dādū in Tradition* (pp. 26-44), the narrative "is based almost entirely on a little work entitled *The Life Story of Dādū*" (p. 26; is the *Dādūjanmalīlā*). Although Orr agrees that "this poem has undergone considerable revision at the hand of later editors" (p. 26), he fails to distinguish the earlier accounts from those of later editions (see further, pp. 173ff.). In the second part (chapter 4) Orr critically examines the historicity of four points which have given rise to some debate: (1) Dādū's birthplace, (2) his caste and profession, (3) his religious teacher, and (4) his interview with Akbar. The abundance of additional information which Orr includes seems to be presented with a critical mind, but would have been much more valuable if the sources had been mentioned regularly. It seems as if he has gathered most of his information from oral informants who in turn relied mainly on sectarian sources and oral traditions.

When trying to find the kernel of truth from which later Dādū traditions grew, it is necessary to consider the two following factors: (a) the time-lag between the life of Dādū and the date of compilation of his biography, and (b) the tendency of both oral and written traditions to conform to certain archetypes for the behaviour of Sants, telling us how they should or may have acted. To give only one example, illustrating the last factor: even if it would not be historically correct that Dādū was invited by the Mughal emperor Akbar and went to see him in Fatehpur Sikri, it was fitting that such an incident be recorded, since not a few other Sants were said to have been invited by Akbar. Thus, an examination of the sources must consider not only their date of composition but their sectarian assumptions as well.

3. 'A Sketch of the Religious Sects of the Hindus', in: *Asiatic Researches*, vol. XVI (1828). See Callewaert: 1978, p. 32.

Sectarian Sources

The earliest source for the biography of Dādū (1544-1603) is the *Dādūjanmalīlā* written by his disciple Jangopāl, probably soon after Dādū's death (see further, pp. 173ff.).

The second (early?) source for Dādū's life is the *Sant Guṇa Sāgar* by Mādhavdās, who may have been one of Dādū's disciples. Information about this work (supposedly two thousand verses, not edited) was given to me for the first time in 1973, by Sukh Dayal Dadu of Delhi, who attributed it to Mādhavdās. According to him, the work was composed in 1604, i.e. one year after Dādū's death. If this is correct, then most of the fanciful details in the later *Dādūjanmalīlā* would have their origin in the *Sant Guṇa Sāgar*. However, P.H. Sharma of Jaipur has already expressed his doubts about the authenticity of this date.[4] The doubt was confirmed by the octogenarian Dādūpanthī *sādhu* Svami Narayandas of Ajmer, who writes that many manuscripts of the *Sant Guṇa Sāgar* have now been found, but that none is dated before 1910.[5] He refers briefly to the details about Dādū's life in the *Sant Guṇa Sāgar* which differ from Jangopāl's account and presumes that the work was written at the beginning of the twentieth century.

Orr also refers to the *Sant Guṇa Sāgar* when he writes:

> A second *Janmalīlā* [after Jangopāl's] on much the same lines is ascribed to another of Dādū's disciples, Madhu Das. This, too, is probably a re-edited version of a genuinely early work. In its present form it can hardly be placed earlier than 1800.[6]

Considering the uncertain date of composition I classify the information found in this biography as a recent, sectarian tradition.

A third early source is the *Bhaktamāl* by Jaggā, a first generation disciple of Dādū. In verses 33-69 a description is given of Dādū and

---

4. Sharma: 1936, I, pp. 3, 93, 129.
5. Narayandas: 1975, pp. 5-6.
6. Orr: 1947, p. 209.

his disciples. The work was edited by A. Nahta in his edition of the Rāghavdās *Bhaktamāl* (see further, p. 148).[7] Unlike both the early and the later versions of Jangopāl's *Dādūjanmalīlā*, verse 34 in this *Bhaktamāl* already makes mention of Dādū's foster-father "by the name of Lodi". This seems to indicate that the change in the account about Dādū's origin (see further, pp. 173ff.) was brought about at an early stage in the tradition.

Rajab's *Sarvāṅgī* (see further, pp. 143ff.) a fourth major source, contains an important variant reading concerning Dādū's alleged *dhuniyā* origin. In the fourteenth verse of the *Grantha sādha mahimā* chapter (following chapter 22, *Bhajana pratāpa*) the texts of all the manuscripts used in my edition (except for F and J) agree in writing *dhuniyā grahe utapanno dādū mahāmuni*.[8] This verse is often quoted in the controversies about Dādū's origin and can be translated in two ways, on account of the double meaning of *dhuniyā*, viz. "*dhūnī*-woman" and "river": "Dādū was born in the womb of a *dhūnī*-woman", or "Dādū was found in a river". Two later manuscripts (F and J, dated 1790) give a different reading: *dariyā madhye utapanno mahāmuni*, in which *dariyā* can only be translated as "river".

The *Bhaktamāl* of Rāghavdās (CE 1720), with a *ṭīkā* or commentary by Chaturdās (CE 1800), is a gigantic work dealing with about 1,200 *bhakta*s. (The Nābhādās *Bhaktamāl* mentions only about 600 *bhakta*s). For the lengthy description by Orr, and the discussion about the date of composition (CE 1660 or 1713?), see below p. 155 The details about Dādū's origin, caste, etc. are in agreement with the enlarged version of Jangopāl's *Janmalīlā*.

In the *Sarvāṅgī* of the *Dādūpanthī Rajab*, I have listed a total of 55 works dealing with biographical data about Dādū.[9] They range from *c.* CE 1620 to 1912. As stated above, most of these works repeat what Jangopāl wrote but they also add a few further details. Only one

7. Nahta: 1965, pp. 275-79.

8. Callewaert: 1978, p. 81.

9. Ibid., pp. 21-56.

example will be given to illustrate this. In Jangopāl's work, it is merely said that Dādū was born in Ahmedabad in CE 1544. Nowadays, a big annual festival is held at Narainā (Rajasthan) on the birthday anniversary of Dādū, which is said to be the eighth day of the bright half of Phālgun, i.e. about the end of February. The accurate date (*phālguṇa śukalāṣṭamī*) appears for the first time in Ātmabihārī's *Śrī Dādūcaritra* (about CE 1830).

Non-sectarian Sources

Besides the sectarian works which have been discussed above, there are several sources which have their origin outside the Dādūpanth. They are among the earliest sources available and the information they give about matters such as Dādū's profession as a cotton-carder is all the more important, since these sources seem to be free of sectarian bias. What is probably the first reference to Dādū outside the Dādūpanthī literature is found in a verse of Eknāth and is quoted in the Marāṭhī work *सकलसंतगाथा.* In his poem on the Nānak-panthīs, Eknāth says: नानक घर दादू पिंजारी नाम जपन,[10] which may be rendered as: "The *piñjārī* Dādū is like Nanak in the meditation on the Name".

The second non-sectarian reference to Dādū is found in *abhaṅga* 4299 of Tukārām's *Gāthā*.[11] The dates of Tukārām are generally taken as CE 1598-1650. Since Dādū died in 1603, the year 1635 seems to be a reasonably approximate date for this piece of information. It begins with the statement "Pride of caste has never made any man holy, says Tukā. The untouchables have crossed the ocean of life by God-devotion, and the Purāṇas sing their praise." Then follows a list of those who were saved in spite of their low caste or different religious faith. The list includes Gorā the potter, Rohidās (Raidās) the cobbler, Kabīr the *momin* (weaver), Latīf the Muslim, Senā the barber, Kānhopātrā the daughter of a concubine, Dādū the cotton-carder, Chokhāmelā and Bāṅkā the untouchables, Janī the maidservant and Mairālā, the low caste woman. The *abhaṅga* is said to be authentic.

10. T.H. Avate, ed., *सकलसंतगाथा,* Poona, 1924, no. 3964.
11. Tukārām, *श्रीतुकारामाञ्छागाथा,* 2 vols., Bombay: Government Central Press, 1950, 1:594.

In it, Dādū is specifically mentioned by Tukārām as a *piñjārī*, or "one engaged in the profession of carding (or rather loosening or breaking up of) cotton".

Another early reference is found in a Persian work called the *Dabistān-i-mazāhib*, written in the mid-seventeenth century. If the work was written about 1665, as maintained by Blochmann, it is a relatively close witness:

> Another sect is that of the Dādū Panthians. Dādū was one of the cotton-carders in the village Narainā, in the district of Marwar. In the time of the Padshah Akbar (who inhabits heaven) Dādū devoted himself to the state of a Durvesh, and assembled many disciples about him. He prohibited his followers to worship idols, to eat the flesh of any animal or to hurt any living being; but he did not order them to abandon woman and wife or to withdraw from all business of the world; but he left it free to anyone to give up or to cultivate the connection and the intercourse with men.[12]

The quotation not only confirms the statement in Tukārām about Dādū being a cotton-carder but also throws light on the already existing sect, known to outsiders for its rules governing external behaviour.

Western Sources

The first known account about the Dādūpanth written by a Western author is in H.H. Wilson's "A Sketch of the Religious Sects of the Hindus".[13] The note by the editor introducing Wilson's account in the *Journal of the Asiatic Society of Bengal*, 6 (1837) says that Wilson's "notice of the sect was chiefly obtained from Lieut. Col. Smith and

---

12. D. Shea and A. Troyer, eds., *Dabistān-i-mazāhib*, 3 vols., Paris, 1843, 2:233.
13. H.H. Wilson, "A Sketch of the Religious Sects of the Hindus," in: *Asiatic Researches*, 16 (1828), pp. 79ff., quoted as a Preface to the contribution made by G.R. Siddons, "Extract and Translation of one of the Granthas, or sacred Books, of the Dādūpanthī Sect," in: *Journal of the Asiatic Society of Bengal*, 6 (1837), pp. 481-87 and pp. 751-56. These excerpts are the first known English translation of any Dādūpanthī literature. Wilson's article was later reprinted in H.H. Wilson, *Religious Sects of the Hindus* (London, 1861; reprinted, Calcutta: Sushil Gupta, 1958), pp. 57-58.

partly from verbal information at Banaras, where the elder branch of the same dissenters, the Kabīrpanthians, have a principal establishment". This account by Wilson is very important since the information given in it (at Banaras) will be found in most subsequent articles on Dādū in English, for nearly a century, with only a few minor additional details. In *The Sarvāṅgī of the Dādūpanthī Rajab* (pp. 34-56) I refer to twenty-four such works or articles published after Wilson's article, which give descriptions of the origin of the Dādūpanth, the contemporary situation and the growth of the military branch of the Dādūpanth (the Nāgas). Wilson calls the Dādūpanth "one of the direct ramifications of the Rāmānandī stock; its founder is said to have been a pupil of one of the Kabīrpanthī teachers, and to be the fifth in descent from Ramanand, viz. 1. Kabīr; 2. Kamāl; 3. Jamāl; 4. Bimal; 5. Buddhan; 6. Dādū".[14]

Finally, a synopsis of biographical data relating to Dādū and commonly accepted in the *panth* now, is given in the *Śrī Dādū Mahāvidyālaya Rajat Jayantī Grantha*, a memorial volume on the 25th anniversary of the foundation of the school, in Jaipur (1919-44), published in 1952. I summarize the description given in the (Hindī) Introduction:

> On the eighth day af *phalgun sudi* Saṁvat 1600 (CE 1543) Dādū was found in a basket on the Sābarmatī River, near Ahmedabad, by the Nāgar brāhmin Lodīrām. At the age of eleven, near the Kānkarīyā tank, an old *mahātmā* appeared to him and instructed him. A few days later, Dādū left his home and went to Peṭalād, where he met Mānakdās and Gyāndās; then he travelled over Ābū and Sirohī to Kalyānpur where he stayed for six years. Then he travelled over Ajmer, Bhīlvārā and Chittor to Karaulī and then to Sāmbhar; he was about 19 years old then.
>
> In 1562, the composition of the *Vāṇī* was begun and at the age of 25 Dādū started to preach. He encountered opposition from the local Qāzīs and Hindu priests; people were forbidden to see him. In 1569, Baṛe Sundardās of Bikaner became his disciple; many other

14. Quoted in Siddons, "*Extract and Translation . . .*", p. 480.

> disciples soon followed Dādū. He stayed in Sāmbhar from 1562 till 1574. His father's brother, Ānandī Rām Nāgar, came to see him there.
>
> In 1575 he went to Amer, where Bhagavantdās, the father of King Mān Singh was the ruler. Several disciples joined him there. Mohandās Daftarī started writing down his sayings. King Bhagavantdās persuaded Dādū to accept Akbar's invitation to go to Fatehpur Sikri, about CE 1587.
>
> Afterwards, he travelled again around Rajasthan and in 1590 he left Āmer, for Āndhī (two years), Kalyān (one year) and other places in Rajasthan. In 1598 he went to Narainā where he sat down underneath the *khejarā* tree. He died there on the 8th of *jeṭh badī* and was exposed to the wild beasts, near Bharainā, on a place now called Dādū Khol".

The two most recent [in 1988] biographical works of Dādū and the early history of the *panth*, have been produced by the prolific writer Svami Narayandas: *Śrīdādūcaritāmr̥t*, Ajmer, 1975, 2 vols., 580 and 558 pp., and *Śrīdādūpanthaparicay*, Pushkar, 1979, 3 vols., 952, 1032 and 951 pp.

Conclusions

On the basis of my research on the sources for the biography of Dādū and the history of the Dādūpanth, I have reached the following conclusions:

The earliest biography of Dādū (Jangopāl's *Dādūjanmalīlā*) has been changed and enlarged at a very early stage after its composition. Most interpolated details are encomiastic and more miraculous. This fact emphasizes the need to work on reliable manuscripts. Later biographies only add more details, which clearly grew out of the oral tradition. These additional elements seem to conform to an Indian archetype for the behaviour of Sants, which involves the performance of miracles in order to impress their audiences, even the Emperor Akbar.

In the early hagiography of Dādū, we notice a tendency towards Brahmanization. Although Dādū himself stressed that caste in fact was not important, later disciples in the sect tried to hide his (possible) Muslim origin and Muslim preceptor (?) and invented an explanation for his connection with the *dhuniyās* (cotton carders).

The basis for English writings (and recent Hindī writings) on the subject of Dādū and the Dādūpanth is Wilson's article of 1828. Relying mainly on informants in Banaras, Wilson started the tradition of calling Dādū "a disciple in the lineage of Rāmānand and Kabīr."

4

Nāmdev's Poems in Rajasthan and Punjab

[1989][1]

THERE is as yet no convincing explanation why the very popular songs of Sants in north-west India started to be written down only around CE 1600 and not before. Nāmdev, Kabīr and others were certainly popular during the sixteenth century, as will appear from the analysis of musical repertoires below. But why are the earliest manuscripts dated around CE 1600[2] and after, and only in Rajasthan? Would they be lost, while we have many Jain manuscripts in Rajasthan and Gujarat, or Sanskrit manuscripts of, e.g. the *Gītagovinda*? Was there for the singers handling these repertoires no need to write the songs in a "proper" way? Or did the technology to produce home-made paper in plenty become easy only after the impetus given to miniature painting at Akbar's court? Like a sudden blizzard in the desert or the first monsoon in fertile Punjab, an abundance of manuscripts with the songs of the Sants appears around CE 1600. And then hundreds, if not thousands of manuscripts started to be written in the seventeenth century in Rajasthan. The Dādūpanth has undoubtedly been a nucleus of high literary activity, rivalling the production in Punjab around 1604.[3]

---

1. In: *Annali ISMEO*, Napoli, 49 (1989), fasc. 3, 301-08.
2. The earliest manuscript giving the "Hindī" poems of Nāmdev (11) and of Kabīr (15) is found in the City Palace, Jaipur (Fatehpur Manuscript, CE 1582).
3. See W.M. Callewaert, "Search for Manuscripts of the Dādūpanthī →

Travelling Singers

Let us imagine we are travelling from Banaras to Rajasthan, around CE 1520, on sandy tracks or on bumpy roads after the rainy season. We spend the nights on the floor in temples and watch the audiences drawn by travelling singers singing their songs of *bhakti*. These singers — like the Purāṇic bards — received extended hospitality depending on the quality and depth of their performance. We are on the way to Rajasthan after a visit to Banaras, where a few years before Raidās had died and where the grandfather of one of the singers had heard a person called Kabīr. And this grandfather's great-grandfather — in this family of travelling musicians — may have been to Maharashtra where he had heard a poet called Nāmdev.

The singers sang the songs which were most in demand, such as those of Nāmdev and Kabīr, which they had learned from their fathers. They also kept enlarging their repertoire when, during their travels, they heard a new song by a famous *bhakta*. Inspired by a particular environment, they added new songs to the repertoire. Memory was their only way of recording, but as the repertoires grew bigger, some musicians started to keep little (or big) notebooks as an aid to their memory. The earliest manuscripts seem to have had these notebooks as their basis. The manuscripts of the seventeenth century that have been preserved are copies of these early manuscripts now lost. Scholars of the twenty-first century have to rely on seventeenth-century manuscripts which are copies of the scribbled notes of singers in order to reconstruct and edit what the singers were singing. I do not say: "to reconstruct what Nāmdev or Kabīr had sung".

Why Do We Bother?

Why do we bother to prepare critical editions of poems sung in the fifteenth-sixteenth centuries, and committed to writing only

→ Literature", in: *Orientalia Lovaniensia Periodica*, 4, 1973, 155-67; and Ibidem, in: *cit.*, 8, 1977, 305-08; also "Nirguṇ Literature on Microfilm in Leuven", Belgium, in: *IAVRI Bulletin*, London, IX (December 1981), pp. 24-48.

after a long period of oral transmission? Students of comparative religion need critical editions. Often the analysis of the development of thought and of the interaction between Hindī poets of particular periods is based on a text which post-dates the poets by centuries. Unless we work on "critical" editions we end up studying the influence of, e.g. a seventeenth-century Gorakhnāth text on the fifteenth-century Kabīr, or of a seventeenth-century Kabīr text on sixteenth-century Dādū. Comparisons of this kind may give an attractive result but not necessarily a correct one. Further, linguists and philologists, too, are often misled by a wrong chronology of editions which are based on manuscripts of a later period. It does no harm periodically to shake up academic or sectarian complacency, and to remind us that the *bhajan*s we hear and read have been mediated by unknown singers and known scribes. Very few of them passed on the songs of a poet-mystic without changing them. Musicians adjusted the metre to suit the rhythm, they adapted the language for the convenience of the audience as they went from village to village, from one region to another.

Studying the songs of a *bhakta* like, e.g. Nāmdev is quite different from the study of Shakespeare. It is the ambition of a textual critic studying Shakespeare to bring out the text "written" by the author, looking at the various versions available in manuscripts. The textual critic soon realizes that this is impossible in the case of Nāmdev or Kabīr. It is not easy to reach beyond the oral tradition to the *bhakta*s themselves. This oral tradition, unlike that of the Vedas, did not shun variety and creativity. Consequently, the oeuvre of, e.g. Nāmdev has come to us in a multiciplicity of forms, changing over both space and time. We should rather look for analogy in the Purāṇas, rather than in Shakespeare.

In north-west India we find three distinct examples of anthologies of songs classified according to *rāg*. Two of these are from Rajasthan (one Dādūpanthī, one Nāth) and one is from Punjab (the *Gurugranth*).

THE ĀDIGRANTH

In 1604, Guru Arjan Dev compiled the *Gurugranth*, an anthology of 5,000 songs and 500 distichs (roughly 2 Megabyte) with 61 songs of Nāmdev, 225 songs of Kabīr and so on.[4] His gigantic work was most probably based on an earlier written document.[5]

SARVĀṄGĪS

In 1627, the Dādūpanthī Gopāldās compiled his *Sarvāṅgī* of 730 pages, quoting extensively from more than 180 poets, both Sant and Vaiṣṇav.[6] This anthology is representative for what a growing sect like the Dādūpanth thought was important *bhakti* literature, at the beginning of the seventeenth century in north-west India. A similar, though smaller *Sarvāṅgī*, was compiled by Dādū's disciple Rajab, around CE 1620.[7] Like Gopāldās, Rajab quotes extensively from the five important Sants whose works appear in separate collections called *Pañcavāṇī*: Dādū, Nāmdev, Kabīr, Raidās and Hardās. Scores of manuscripts with the *Pañcavāṇī* collection have been written.

Both compilers, Gopāldās and Rajab, arrange thematically *sākhī*s, *savaiyā*, *ślok*s, *kavitta*s and *pad*s of different poets; such a feature is not found in the manuscripts which give only the *Vāṇī* of a particular poet, where usually a *sākhī-bhāg* and a *pad-bhāg* is given. It is interesting to note that very few poems of, e.g. Nāmdev appear in the same one thematic chapter in the *Sarvāṅgī* of Gopāldās and the *Sarvāṅgī* compiled by Rajab. In view of the argument of this article, it should further be noted that the *pad*s of different poets are consistently grouped according to their common *rāg* or tone.

4. See Pritam Singh, "Bhai Banno's Copy of the Sikh Scripture", in: M. Thiel-Horstman, *Bhakti in Current Research, 1979-1982*, Berlin, 1983, p. 338, n. 3.
5. See W.H. McLeod, *The Evolution of the Sikh Community*, Delhi: Oxford University Press, 1975; The Clarendon Press, 1976, pp. 60-61.
6. See W.M. Callewaert, "A 17th *c.* Anthology of Hindī Poetry", in: *Orientalia Lovaniensia Periodica*, 5, 1974, 163-85. See also below, pp. 139ff.
7. See Callewaert: 1978, p. 446.

PAÑCAVĀṆĪ[8]

Travelling singers classified the songs of their performance according to the *rāg* and scribes kept that *rāg* label when copying manuscripts. One of the earliest, *rāg*-oriented collections made in the Dādūpanth is the *Pañcavāṇī* or "Songs of the Five". These five highly respected *bhaktas* in the early Dādūpanth are: Dādū (1544-1603), Kabīr (*c.* 1450-1518?), Nāmdev (*c.* 1270-1350), Raidās (*c.* 1450-1520) and Hardās (floruit *c.* 1600?). This repertoire, classified in clusters under a particular *rāg*, comprised more than 1,000 songs. Later, several compilers wrote the huge collection on paper and it became known as the *Pañcavāṇī*. Scores of manuscripts with *different versions* of the *Pañcavāṇī* are even today found in the manuscript collections in Rajasthan, Punjab and Banaras. A comparison is not an easy task, because each *Pañcavāṇī* manuscript is about 1.6 Megabyte of text, rougly the equivalent of 333,000 words. It is not only the enormous size of the collection, at first definitely only available in the memory of singers, that makes the *Pañcavāṇī* an amazing feature. What baffles us even more is the fact that different singers, possibly in different places, had memorized five repertoires that were very different in size and in the order of songs, and clearly had variant "readings". As a result we do not have only one *Pañcavāṇī* recension but several, each one relying on a different oral tradition.

Looking at the consistent order (Dādū, Nāmdev, Kabīr, Raidās and Hardās) in all the *Pañcavāṇī* manuscripts, scholars thought that the numerous *Pañcavāṇī* manuscripts all go back to a single, scribal archetype, compiled by one of the learned disciples of Dādū, perhaps even under the guru's direct inspiration. They thought that this archetype served as the basis for all later copies, most of the seventeenth century. Such an idyllic thought, cherished by textual critics upto the present, must be given up. The *Pañcavāṇī* manuscripts now at hand cannot go back to one archetype or to

---

8. For the detailed contents, see below, *An Early Hindī Databank in the Computer.*

any single compiler. There must have been several *Pañcavāṇī* compilers, each working separately either from existing manuscripts or in direct contact with the oral tradition. A critical analysis of these manuscripts takes the researcher much further into the period of oral transmission than was possible for S.S. Das (1928) or Parasnath Tivari (1962) for their edition of Kabīr. Because of a plainly direct link with different musical traditions, we find in the *Pañcavāṇī* manuscripts variants which were introduced during the musical transmission, along with those produced by scribes.[9]

Musical Variants

I argue that we have to look for traces of the singing tradition in the manuscripts at hand if we hope to get close to what the original corpus of a Sant may have been. Because of a plainly direct link with different musical traditions, we find in our manuscripts variants which were introduced during the musical transmission, along with those produced by scribes. Keeping both the oral and the scribal variants in mind and clearly distinguishing between these two streams is a gigantic task for the unaided human memory which has to collect its data over a span of several years of study. A hypothesis about this phenomenon could be formulated only with the help of computer programmes[10] developed to count and compare variants, making a distinction between the variants that are oral and those that are scribal.

The Rāg Tag

A consideration about musical variants in the text is not the only clue pointing to an independent development of, e.g. Nāmdev's

9. This hypothesis was first formulated and tested in our edition of the *pad*s of Nāmdev. See Callewaert & Lath: 1989. We applied the same method for the edition of the *pad*s of Raidās, see Callewaert & Friedlander: 1992.

10. For a description of these programmes, see W.M. Callewaert, "The Leuven Text Composition System in Indian Alphabets", in: *ALLC Bulletin*, vol. 12, 1 (1984), 5-8; and "Indian Manuscripts without Autograph? : A Computer Analysis", in: *The Indo-Iranian Journal*, 30 (1987), 65-71.

pads during the oral period. The available manuscript tradition does allow us to enter beyond the threshold of the oral tradition, or the moment when *pads* started to be written down, some time before CE 1600 (while the oral tradition continued as well). Indian musicians used to sing clusters of songs according to particular modes, called *rāg*. It appears that first the singers sang a particular *pad* in a particular *rāg*; then they grouped together the *pads* which were to be sung in the same *rāg*. Scribes kept the *rāg* tag of each *pad*. Consequently, a *rāg* is like an identity-card for the earliest period of oral transmission. It was only later, when compilers took over, that *pads* were classified in *aṅgas*, according to the main theme. The same *pad*, apparently, could be sung to different *rāgs*. As a result we find *pads* classified under different *rāgs* in different manuscripts. This variation in classification is obviously not due to a scribe's intervention but stems from the oral period itself, when the *pads* were in the hands of singers. Subsequently, the songs were transmitted under different *rāgs* and appeared as such also in the manuscripts later on. Thus, looking at the *rāg* structure we are able to make a preliminary classification of the musical recensions. The statistical computer count corroborates this classification, adding nuances.

Repertoires That are not Pañcavāṇī

Not all our Rājasthānī manuscripts are of the *Pañcavāṇī* type. Manuscript *u* (dated CE 1684) is Dādūpanthī but not *Pañcavāṇī* and ms. *c* (dated CE 1660) may by defined as "Nāth-Siddha". Manuscript *c* is a huge compilation of the songs and utterances of the *siddhas*, which includes along with Nāmdev other *nirguṇa* poets like Kabīr and Raidās, who seem to have been popular in seventeenth-century Nāth circles. Like the *Pañcavāṇī* collections, these Nāth collections are of a musical kind, classifying *pads* according to their *rāg*. Although post-dating the Dādūpanthī collections, they are independent repertoires, relying on an independent source. Again, although they are sometimes quite different, the songs of Nāmdev in these Nāth collections often have much in common with the versions we find in the Dādūpanthī collections.

Differences in Rāg

When we compare the *rāg* structure in the *Gurugranth* with that in the Rājasthānī repertoires, we find considerable differences. The Punjabi singers handled a text which was musically and morphologically different from what their colleagues in Rajasthan had.[11] I am tempted to propose that the *pad*s which have the same *rāg* in the *Gurugranth* and in the Rājasthānī mss. are likely to have belonged to a very early common source.

One important point can be made at this stage: we can no longer call the *Gurugranth* the oldest available version of, for example, Nāmdev's or Kabīr's *pad*s. What we find in the seventeenth-century Rājasthānī mss. is a variant musical version which may well be as old as the musical version from which the Punjabi singers drew their inspiration, if not older. At what muddy or sandy crossroads did singing families go their own way, and at what point in history? We do not know but the division certainly set in quite early.

When we look at the 11 *pad*s of Nāmdev which are classified under the same *rāg* in the *Gurugranth* and in the Rājasthānī mss., we notice that these *pad*s are also found in all the Rājasthānī recensions (with only one exception), and we see that these *pad*s have exactly the same *rāg* in all these recensions. On the other hand, when we look at those *pad*s which do not have the same *rāg* in all the Rājasthānī mss., they are also the *pad*s which are not given in all the mss., often occurring only in a few mss. And, all *pad*s which have a different *rāg* in the *Gurugranth* appear under the same *rāg* in all the Rājasthānī mss. This suggests the hypothesis

11. For his critical edition of the *pad-bhāg* of Kabīr, P.N. Tivari finally selected 200 *pads*. Of these 121 are found in the *Gurugranth* also, and of these 121 only 55 are classified under the same *rāg* as in the Rājasthānī tradition. Out of the 35 common *pad*s under *rāg gauḍī* in the Rājasthānī tradition, 31 are under the same *rāg gauḍī* in the *Gurugranth*. Further, *āsāvarī*: 8 out 23; *rāmkalī*: 3 out of 6; *kedārau*: 1; *bhairū*: 8 out of 11; *vasanta*: 4 out of 5. For the other *rāg*s, nothing is common. On the other hand, most *pads* of Kabīr I looked at in three Rājasthānī mss. (one *Pañcavāṇī* manuscript, ms. *u* and ms. *c*) are there classified under the same *rāg*.

that the singers walking on the Rājasthānī roads around, let us say, CE 1520 drew their repertoires from a common source. But this source is different from the source which gave us the *Gurugranth* repertoires.[12]

Language

Traditionally language has been considered a reliable clue to arrive at the authentic version of a text. Many textual critics have used it to define the genuineness of an expression, a line or a whole *pad*. They have also used it as the basis for making ammendations in a text. However, in the case of *bhakti* texts the linguistic test is often contradicted by the musical (*rāg*) pattern in which, e.g. the *pad*s of Nāmdev were arranged. *Pad*s of Nāmdev which are found under the same *rāg* in all the consulted manuscripts, and presumably belong to an old layer in the oral tradition, are linguistically quite a mixed bag: we have songs in almost pure Gujarātī, others in a kind of Marāṭhī-Rājasthānī and still others in Braj.

Must the textual critic stick to the assumption that the *bhakta* sang in his own dialect only? As is the case even today, musical repertoires were not language-oriented. To take one example, Dādū, whose works survive without much change because they were almost immediately written down, has left us *pad*s in more than one language. In the musical tradition, too, it was common to compose in more than one language. Certain kinds of songs are traditionally associated with certain dialects and musicians composed in those dialects, whatever their "own" language was. It is also likely that certain *rāg*s or certain ways of singing were associated with a particular dialect. "Language" is not a reliable clue for our text edition.

---

12. With regard to Raidās, when we add up all the *pad*s which we find in the *Gurugranth*, in the Rājasthānī mss. and in the Belvedere edition, we get a total of 117 *pads*. Out of the 40 *pad*s found the *Gurugranth*, only 14 are also found in the Rājasthānī mss. and of these 14, only 6 are given under the same *rāg*.

Is There a Pattern at All?

When we construct a tentative stemma on the basis of the similarity in the order in which the songs were arranged under the heading of a *rāg*, then our effort is continually contradicted by the dissimilarity of the oral and scribal variants. The result is a totally blurred and confused pattern, if any pattern appears at all. If, after having the computer count the variants and count the variants that are identical in particular manuscripts, we draw the proper conclusions, we despair of ever finding a classical stemma and an archetype.[13]

The computer count establishes that, in the case of Nāmdev's *pads*, there is no consistent relation between two manuscripts of the same "recension". We notice also that, when looking at variants from different angles, no consistent relation even between manuscripts is seen throughout. This suggests a very nebulous interaction between singing traditions. If we seek to establish an "original text" on the basis of stemmatic clues, we deceive ourselves for the simple reason that there hardly ever existed a "critical text". Or, if Nāmdev one day sang his *pads*, very soon they became the property of singers who handled them according to their own inspiration, musical genius and particular dialect. We may assume that it was mostly the capable singers, those who were more poetic and creative, who prevailed and we notice the consequences of this in the stemmatic chaos before us.

What then have we looked for? We have looked for a text which is found in many musical traditions. We have tried to isolate an old Rājasthānī core, without suggesting that the songs of this core are in any way closer to the poet.

If there is no stemma and no justified "critical" text, then what do we have? We have the conviction that, possibly for centuries, a Nāmdev enthusiasm had gripped people in Rajasthan and Punjab,

13. For a study on the same line, see John G. Griffith, "Non-stemmatic Classification of Manuscripts by Computer Methods", in: Jean Irigoin and Gian Piero Zarri, eds., *La Pratique des ordinateurs dans la critique des textes*, Paris, CNRS, 1979, pp. 73-86.

and that this enthusiasm was linked somehow to Nāmdev's songs of the fourteenth century. Full of enthusiasm for Nāmdev's songs, poets and musicians sang and recited his verses, adding songs or lines of their own or changing the lines according to their own taste and genius. This "Sant-enthusiasm" theory may well apply to many more *nirguṇa* and *saguṇa* mediaeval poets than has hitherto been believed. Still, even if we cannot get to Nāmdev himself, the result of our search is worthwhile. We discover poetry that is often very beautiful and a mystical literature which has influenced the religious life of thousands, from the beginning of the fifteenth century until the present day.[14]

Nāmdev in Punjab?

In Ghuman (Punjab) we find Nāmdev's *samādhi*, while another *samādhi* is found in Pandharpur, Maharashtra. The traditional "Punjabi" view suggests that Nāmdev sang *abhaṅga*s in Maharashtra and that he spent his latter days in Punjab. There is more than one problem in this view. With due respect for oral traditions, it should be noted that the first document referring to Nāmdev's presence in Punjab is W. Crooke, *The Tribes and Castes of the Western Provinces*, 1896, and M.A. Macauliffe, *The Sikh Religion*, 1909. So far I have not found any reference to Nāmdev's presence in Rajasthan.[15] The Maharashtrian oral tradition reflected in Mahipati (1762) mentions Nāmdev's journey to Banaras. Isn't it even today a respectable reference to be able to say you have been to Banaras and that you have studied there? Mahipati makes no mention of Rajasthan or Punjab.

---

14. A selected 125 "Hindī" songs of Nāmdev are rendered into English, in Callewaert & Lath: 1989.

15. In interviews in Jaipur, in 1986, tailors and *chimpī*s claimed to be of the *vaṁśa* of Nāmdev. Should this be rendered as "in family-lineage linked to Nāmdev"? They also stated that originally they were not from Rajasthan but from Gujarat. There are two distinct groups, apparently not inter-marrying, in Chār Pol Bāzār, Thakur Bagru kā Rāstā, near the Raghunath Mandir, Jaipur. There are also clans in south India which claim a connection with Nāmdev.

It is hard to explain how a Punjābī influence could have caused so many and so varied musical repertoires of Nāmdev's *pads* to be popular in Rajasthan around 1500. We remember that 61 *pads* of Nāmdev are given in the *Gurugranth*. Of these only 25 are found in the Rājasthānī mss., and only 10 are found under the same *rāg*. This suggests a weak rather than a strong connection between Punjab and Rajasthan. If we suppose, as I have done, that the presence of Nāmdev's *pads* in Punjab and in Rajasthan is explained by a transmission through wandering musicians, and not by Nāmdev's physical presence, we still have problems. How can we understand the relation between the quite different Rājasthānī and Punjābī repertoires? It is hard to argue that the abundant material in Rajasthan is a later offspring of an original corpus in Punjab, presumably of pre-Nānak times. There are too few *pads* in common, considering the abundant material found in Rajasthan. One may perhaps try to explain the phenomenon by supposing Nāmdev travelled through Rajasthan, spending time in temples and villages so that his songs and message became popular. He then went to Punjab and from the repertoire which developed there independently of Rajasthan 61 *pads* found their way into what later would be known as the Sikh tradition. No other repertoire seems now to be found there.

But is the physical presence of Nāmdev at all necessary to explain the popularity of his *pads*? Kabīr and Raidās are not known to have been to Punjab or Rajasthan; yet, we find a large number of their *pads* (and *sākhīs*) in both regions. In the *Gurugranth,* we find 225 *pads* of Kabīr, 61 of Nāmdev and 40 of Raidās, while in the Rājasthānī *Pañcavāṇī* manuscripts we find *c.* 400 of Kabīr, 258 of Nāmdev and *c.* 80 of Raidās. What evidence do we have to believe that Nāmdev was in Punjab, while Kabīr and Raidās supposedly were not? Perhaps we should not forget that Kabīr lived around 1500 and Nāmdev around CE 1300. Two centuries at that time may have been sufficient to allow devotees (in the eighteenth century?) to "know" that the great Sant Nāmdev had actually been in their region. Of course, there is no point in "proving" that Nāmdev did *not* go to Punjab. The point is that enough importance has not been given to travelling singers and their repertoires. They spread the *nirguṇa* message; the traces of their handling of *pad*s is seen in the manuscripts. We reached this conclusion early in our study when we realized that looking for a scribal archetype or the hypothesis of a mammoth scribal contamination could not bring clarity in the abundant seventeenth-century manuscript material.

We may have to conclude that singers were responsible for both the spreading of the message and for the stemmatic chaos.

5

Can the Bhagavad-Gītā Be Translated?

[1990][1]

IN the present article[2] I survey the different factors essentially required for a good translation. The first is the critical text.

The Critical Text

The science of textual criticism is a relatively new phenomenon in Indian studies, especially among traditional scholars. Yet, as long as the accuracy of the original text is not established, translations can only be provisional. Of course, there will always be a tension between the devout reader and the critical scholar, and it is not clear which value — the historical or the devotional one — is more important. However, both values have their relevance, and ignoring either will do injustice to the sacred text. In the traditional view about the redaction of the *Gītā*, the original author is said to have been the great sage Vyāsa Kṛṣṇa Dvaipāyana, the author of the *Mahābhārata* and if there are any obscurities in the text, they must be attributed to the speed at the time of dictation by Vyāsa:

> While Vyāsa composed the *Mahābhārata*, Gaṇeśa was his scribe. The condition between the author and the scribe was that the former would not stop dictating the verses till the completion of

---

1. In: C.D. Verma, ed., *The Gītā in World Literature*, Delhi, 1990. pp. 89-100.
2. *Gītā* is here used as an abbreviation of *Bhagavad-Gītā*. A very detailed analysis of this problem, with an exhaustive list and a comparative study of the existing translations, has been prepared and published in Callewaert & Hemraj: 1983.

> the book, and the scribe would not write without understanding the meaning of the verses. Vyāsa at times dictated extremely difficult verses known as *vyāsa-kūṭas*. During the time Gaṇeśa took to understand the meaning of these verses, Vyāsa composed new stanzas. . . .[3]

Later on, it was even said to be nearly impossible for a copyist to tamper with the original text. The story goes that Vyāsa dictated the verse बलवान् इन्द्रियग्रामो विद्वांसम्-अपि कर्षति or "the strong pull of the senses will distract even the scholars". A copyist called Jaimini, confident of his power of self-control, is said to have changed only one syllable, as follows: बलवान् इन्द्रियग्रामो विद्वांसम् न-अपि कर्षति or "the strong pull of the senses will *not* distract even the scholars". Some time later, Jaimini was sitting in his hut. It was evening, and a big storm broke out. A beautiful woman soaked in the rain asked for shelter. There was a fire lit in the hearth, and while she sat there to dry her clothest Jaimini felt attracted to her. She tried to stop him, then gave in on condition that he should carry her three times around the fire. Jaimini lifted her, but she began to hit his head, saying विद्वांसम् नापि कर्षति! He was amazed to hear the very words he had changed in his guru's text. He stopped and, indeed, there stood Vyāsa himself, looking at him with a meaningful smile. Jaimini repented, hurried back and changed the verse to its original form.

Further, scientific theories about the redaction of the *Gītā* make the question of translation very complex, because one has to consider the consequences of a very long period of oral transmission. Oral traditions in India connected with Vedic studies are certainly very ancient, and even when written texts did exist, their transmission through writing seems to have been of secondary importance to the oral transmission. Although some art of writing was known in India from the time of the Indus Valley Civilization, and traces of inscriptions are found in documents belonging to the fourth century BCE, the existence of extensive written texts is

3. S.C. Banerji, *A Companion to Sanskrit Literature*, Delhi, 1971, p. 115.

not much in evidence. It should be conceded that as a result of the orthodox and religious attitude in ancient India, the religious texts were preserved with great accuracy, as the pupil had to learn the text, word by word, from the mouth of the teacher and "put it in his throat" (*kaṇṭhastha*).

Only centuries after its composition, the *Gītā* was written down in its final form, with the result that we deal with an oral tradition to which traditional textual criticism does not strictly apply. The question became very complex, however, when scholars realized that after the text was eventually written down, the oral transmission continued as well. The implications of the oral transmission of epics in world literature have not yet been studied thoroughly enough to guarantee the exactness of all hypotheses regarding structure, interpolations, formulaic expressions, thematic compositions, etc. Dealing with a text transmission through manuscripts, a translator should be acquainted with the basic principles of the science of textual criticism and with the results of their application.

The textual critic seeks to ascertain, from the different copies at hand, which form of the text should be regarded as most nearly conforming to the original. In some cases the evidence will be found to be so evenly divided that it is extremely difficult to decide between two variant readings. In other instances, however, the critic can arrive at a decision based on more or less compelling reasons for preferring one reading and rejecting another. A translator should consider the decisions and preferences of the critic and study also the variants and rejected readings, as they may throw light on the meaning of a particular word at a particular time.

One example may be verse 2.38c of the *Gītā*: युद्धाय युज्यस्व or "prepare yourself then for battle", rendered as "do battle for battle's sake" by K.M. Ganguli, with the remark:

> Most texts read युद्धाय युज्यस्व. A manuscript belonging to a friend of mine has a correction in red ink, युद्धाय युधस्व. It accords so well

> with the spirit of the lesson sought to be inculcated here that I make no scruple to adopt it.[4]

Incidentally, the reading युधस्व adopted by Ganguli is given in Belvalkar's critical edition ([1945], 1968, p. [10]) as a non-adopted variant reading in the oldest manuscript consulted (Ñ1).

Manuscripts of The Gītā

Among the more than one million manuscripts in Indian languages one can easily count 5,000 Sanskrit mss. of the *Gītā* text. The Sarasvati Bhavan Library of Banaras alone has a list of about a 314 *Gītā* mss. The handwritten text of the *Gītā* is preserved in all shapes and sizes. The British Museum, London, for instance has a *Gītā* manuscript (catalogue of Sanskrit mss., 1902, no. 84) of 41 folios, in Nāgarī characters, on leaves of hexagonal shape, each side measuring about 1 cm. A. Weber describes a *Gītā* ms. in Berlin in very small handwriting: the complete text is written on a long and narrow scroll, enframed in gold, and rolled up in a tiny little pipe of reddish colour. The library of St Petersburg, Russia, possesses an even smaller manuscript, kept in a bronze container which does not exceed the size of an ordinary needle-holder. The letters have to be deciphered with a magnifying glass. Another curiosity is the voluminous *Gītā* ms. of 3,304 folios at the Raghunatha Temple of His Highness the Maharaja of Jammu & Kashmir. It was completed in 1860 under Maharaja Ranavira Simha. The text is written in the Kashmiri script and each *ślok* has a set of 18 Sanskrit commentaries ending with the Maharaja's *Raṇavīra Samudbodhinī* commentary and a Hindī *bhāṣānuvāda*.

The *Gītā* text is often accompanied by translations and commentaries, while sometimes only selected verses have been copied. Besides the mss. of the complete *Gītā* there are about 212 mss. with *Gītā ṭīkā*s and abstracts in the Library of the Sanskrit University, Banaras (although it is not certain that all mss.

---

4. *The Mahābhārata*, vol. V, Bhīṣma-parva, 3rd improved edn., New Delhi, 1953, p. 56, n. 1.

mentioned in the Catalogues are at this moment still available!). Another treasure-trove with *Gītā* mss. is the Sarasvati Mahal Library of Thanjavur. It has 116 *Gītā* mss. in its collection and the oldest dated ms. available there is of 1653. It is rather rare to find manuscripts dated before the fifteenth century. The oldest dated ms. (no. 1597) used by S.K. Belvalkar for the critical edition of the *Gītā* is a Nepali ms. The oldest mss. seem to be related to Śaṅkarācārya's commentary: one Devnāgarī ms. of the *Gītā* with the *Śāṅkarabhāṣya* is dated VS 1468, or CE 1411.

Printed Editions of The Gītā

The story of the printed editions starts in 1808-09 when, at the suggestion of Colebrooke, the Baburama Press, Calcutta, printed the Editio Princeps of the *Gītā* (23.5 x 12.5 cm lithographed, 60 folios, VS 1730). A.-W. von Schlegel counted 60 wrong readings in this edition, which he could easily correct without having recourse to conjectural emendations. Only the last verse (18.78), he felt, was to be rejected as spurious. Von Schlegel himself published the first critical edition of *Gītā*, together with a Latin translation, in 1823: "the first book ever printed on the continent of Europe in the Sanskrit language and in the original Devanāgarī character".[5] Von Schlegel collated the Editio Princeps on the basis of 4 mss. preserved in the Royal Library, Paris, and one "codex micrographicus" in small script with five illustrations (preserved in the Royal Library of Berlin). He considered every word and syllable very carefully. Obvious corrections he did not hesitate to make to the text itself but the less certain ones he reserved for the footnotes, with the intention of marking the unsolvable passages as suspect.

C. Larssen, a disciple of von Schlegel and author of the 4-volume *Indische Altertumskunde* (Bonn, 1843), revised his master's edition in 1843. Further, J. Garrett made use of it for his polyglot *Gītā* edition in parallel columns in Sanskrit (in Kannada characters),

5. A.-W. von Schlegel, "Letter to the Honorable Court of Directors of the Honorable East India Company", in: *Réflexions sur l'Etude des langues asiatiques*, London, 1828, p. 182.

English (C. Wilkins' version) and Kannada (Garrett's), (Bangalore, 1849; Foreword of 1846). The supplement gives the Sanskrit Devanāgarī text and the Latin translation by von Schlegel. Garrett adds, however, a long list of "various readings" (pp. 93-96) collected from Malayalam mss., some commentaries and the Calcutta edition of the *Mahābhārata*. Belvalkar found it worthwhile to select 43 of these variants for his critical edition. Working on his own edition of 1855 J. Cockburn Thomson disagreed with both von Schlegel and Larssen:

> I have now done enough to wary the reader with pedantic niceties, which can interest but a few, and those rather of a German than an English turn of mind. It is, however, the duty of an editor to state and defend the corrections which he makes in the work of his predecessors.[6]

During the twentieth century various editions appeared which questioned the traditional number of 1,400 lines or 700 *ślok*s in the *Saptaśatī Gītā*. The Suddha Dharma Mandalam, Mylapore, Madras, 1917, presented a *Gītā* with 745 *śloks*. Like R. Garbe before him, F.O. Schrader also pointed out interpolations in the *Gītā*, and even tried to give arguments for doing so by referring to the Kashmir Recension of the *Gītā* (Stuttgart, 1930). S.N. Tadpatrikar of the Bhandarkar Oriental Research Institute, edited a *Gītā* with numerous variants from old Kashmiri mss. (Poona, 1934), giving tribute to F.O. Schrader of Kiel University. All this made persons like Rajavaidya Jivaram Kalidas Shastri react strongly, since he believed in the literal origin of the full *Gītā* text on the historic battlefield. He rejected the *Śuddha Dharma Gītā* and produced his own *Gītā*, revised in the light of a rare and ancient ms. claimed to be of CE 1178.[7]

The Belvalkar Critical Edition of The Gītā

In the critical edition of the *Mahābhārata* we find the critical text of

6. J.C. Thomson, *BG or the Sacred Lay*, London, 1855.
7. For more editions and details, see Callewaert & Hemraj, pp. 28ff.

the *Gītā*, as it occurs in the 6th book, Bhīṣmaparvan. The first fascicle of the Bhīṣmaparvan (7th volume) appeared in 1943-45, the second in 1947. The *Gītā* is given in chapters 23 to 40 (pp. 114-88) of this critical edition, while it appears in chapters 25 to 42 of the "Vulgate" edition. After the death of V.S. Sukthankar in 1943, Belvalkar became the chief editor of the *Mahābhārata*. Already in 1935 he had agreed to edit one *parvan* or book of the *Mahābhārata*, because of his love for the *Gītā*:

> My choice fell naturally upon the Bhīṣmaparvan, embodying as it does the world famous *Gītā*, to which I was attracted since my own college days and of which I have been a close student ever since.[8]

The editor soon found out that the text of the Bhīṣmaparvan was better attested than other sections of the *Mahābhārata*. The reason why this text was better preserved was not difficult to find:

> It is evident that the *Bhīṣma* has suffered least at the hands of provincial interpolations. The proximity of the *Gītā*, which was read and adapted as a philosophical textbook throughout India, probably acted as a sort of wholesome check upon the latter-day Vyasaids.[9]

Though there have been also deliberate interpolations in a few cases, the *Gītā* text contains mainly unintentional variants:

> It is easy to see that most of these variations are due to quite normal causes such as the accidental writing of the same letter or letters twice, the accidental omission of an intervening group of letters (or words) owing to the wandering of a scribe's eye from a similar-looking earlier group of letters (or words) to another similar-looking later group, the conscious attempt to smooth over an original metrical or grammatical irregularity, the substitution of a marginal or an interlinear explanatory word for the original words in the text, and in the case of a popular

---

8. S.K. Belvalkar, "The Bhīṣmaparvan", in: *Annals BORI*, Poona, 1947, p. CXXIX.
9. Ibidem, p. CXXVI.

> text like the *Gītā* (which many scribes might have known by heart), the copying from memory rather than from the original before the eye, the last case of it only a little while ago.[10]

In 1941 Belvalkar published the *Gītā,* according to the Śaṅkara Commentary, and in 1959 he brought out his own critical English translation.[11] In fact, Belvalkar expanded the basis for textual criticism of the *Gītā* by adding several mss. for collation to those used for the other chapters of the Bhīṣmaparvan. The main problem regarding the extent of the *Gītā* arises from the *Gītāmāna* which gives as official number "745 *śloks*": 620 verses attributed to Kr̥ṣṇa, 57 to Arjuna, 67 to Sañjaya and 1 to Dhr̥tarāṣṭra.

Different Recensions of The Gītā

Whatever the extent of the verses, and the method of calculating them, the problem cannot be separated from the manner in which the text itself was transmitted. Though one can discuss the terminology used, the clarification brought by Belvalkar is important:

> A 'Version' should mainly embody modifications happening during the course of scribal transmission from a common codex. . . . A "Recension" should connote more deliberate and far-reaching alterations in the text, often changing its tone and emphasis.[12]

Usually, for practical reasons, Śaṅkarācārya's text is considered almost equivalent to the original. His dates are generally accepted as 788-820. Belvalkar concludes:

10. S.K. Belvalkar, "The so-called Kashmir Recension of the *Gītā*", in: *A Volume of Indian and Irianian Studies*, Bombay, 1939, p. 17.
11. Even the Belvalkar critical edition did not remain unchallenged. S.R. Shastri gives in the critical introduction to her translation (1959), a collation of different mss. and texts (pp. 73-78), with 60 variants given in 3 columns, from, e.g. a well-written ms. with 17 miniatures of *c.* 1812 and another small size ms. (12.5 x 7.5 cm) of *c.* 1754.
12. S.K. Belvalkar, "The so-called Kashmir Recension of the *Bhagavadgītā*", in: *Annals BORI*, 19, 1938-39, 17, fn.

> We can accordingly conclude that, except for about a dozen minor variants, the forms of the *Gītā* as preserved in the *Bhāṣya* of Śaṅkarācārya is still the earliest and the most authentic available manuscript evidence.[13]

Still the question must be asked whether there is no pre-Śaṅkara form of the *Gītā* available? Gode gives some quotations from a Jain source and concludes: "Haribhadrasūri (*c*. 750) had before him some text of the *Gītā* which was different from the Vulgate text",[14] unless they are his own making. Schrader's suggestion about a Kashmir recension being closer to the original is refuted by Belvalkar:

> F. Otto Schrader . . . puts forth the view that these Kashmirian sources with their 14 additional stanzas and 4 half-stanzas unknown to the Vulgate, as well as the 282 exclusively Kashmirian *varietas lectionis*, preserve a more authentic, and even an intrinsically superior text of the *Gītā*, which, he claims, was pre-Śaṅkara.[15]

Belvalkar declares all these variants to be of a secondary nature, for they only remedy some grammatical defects, simplify and normalize the syntax, or smoothen difficult passages. One clear example of pious tampering with the original is recorded in the case of a noteworthy Kashmirian writer, the scholiast Bhāskara. T.R. Chintamani was the first to publish excerpts from the fragmentary commentary of Bhāskara, as he is quoted by the great Kashmirian Abhinavagupta. Both knew Śaṅkara, and the new readings they introduce must have been their own inventions. Hence, Belvalkar argues:

> The extra stanzas which are found in the Kashmirian recension

---

13. Ibidem, p. 34. See also T.R. Chintamani, ed., *Śrīmad Bhagavadgītā* (A Kashmirian Recension with the Sarvatobhadra Commentary of Rajanaka Ramakantha), Madras, 1941.
14. P.K. Gode, "The *Bhagavadgītā* in the Pre-Shankaracarya Jain Sources", in: *Annals BORI*, 20 (1938-39): 194.
15. S.K. Belvalkar, *Bhagavad-Gītā*, critic. edn., 1945, editorial note, p. XVI.

> cannot be said to have originally belonged to the *Gītā*, and subsequently omitted from it. In a work like the *Gītā* the tendency rather would be to make additions than omissions. Nor is the Kashmirian recension alone in having extra stanzas. In some of the mss. hailing from the other parts of India, extra stanzas, more than half a dozen, are found.[16]

Belvalkar concludes that he cannot accept the view that the recension was current prior to the eighth century, or that it is more authentic than the recension known to Śaṅkara. Van Buitenen opened the discussion again, stating that "very close to Śaṅkara's date, there existed two variant texts that were equally authoritative".[17] Another ancient witness which could possibly challenge the unicity of Śaṅkara's text is the Old-Javanese version of the *Mahābhārata*, which quotes only 80-3/4 stanzas of the *Gītā* (and 56 in paraphrase) but adds also a few extra stanzas as if belonging to the *Gītā*. Belvalkar has made a thorough study of this tenth-century testimonium (pp. LXXXV till CII, with tabulation in Appendix II, pp. 727-53), and arrived at a negative conclusion:

> It was thought necessary to undertake a detailed examination of the Old-Javanese "version" of the *Gītā* because of the claim made on its behalf that it either constitutes, or at any rate serves as an important fingerpointer on the trail of a Third Recension of the *Gītā* (by the side of the two others, the Vulgate and the Kashmirian Recensions) which, it was hoped, would one day come to light in its entirety.[18]

The only valid critical conclusion is that this old version is not of any great help. The Old-Javanese version does not support an Ur-text or any intervening forms of the current text. What the Old-Javanese translation should teach is to place the *Gītā* again in its total context of the *Mahābhārata*. Textual criticism cannot isolate the *Gītā* apart from the *Mahābhārata*.

---

16. T.R. Chintamani, op. cit., p. 104.
17. J.A. Van Buitenen, "A Contribution to the Critical Edition of the *Bhagavadgītā*", in: *JAOS*, 85, 1965, p. 104.
18. S.K. Belvalkar, *Bhīṣmaparvan*, pp. CI-CII.

Selective Editions of The Gītā

A translator concerned with the transmission of the message rather than with the mere form of the text will naturally have to decide about the size of his text, because for some readers it may be considered irrelevant to have the complete text of the *Gītā*.

The shortest text found is the *Ekaślokī-Gītā* with one verse only: Sacchidananda Svami chose verse 8.7, quoted in Sanskrit and in English translation (1908). The traditional *bījam* or seed-*mantra* is verse 2.11a. In the *Saptaślokī Gītā* (e.g. Gita Bhavan, Gorakhpur edition) the following seven verses are usually published: 8.1; 8.13; 11.36; 13.13; 15.1; 15.15; 18.65. An *Aṭhārahśloki Gītā* of eighteen verses has also been published for use in worship and meditation, e.g. by P.P. Gokhale (Kanhad, 1964) and D.S. Sharma, *Upāsanā Gītā* (1944), which appeared in English, Gujarātī, Marāṭhī and Hindī. A *Gītā* of 40 verses has been published in Sanskrit, Tamil and English, for the Students' Club of Tiruvallur (1961). Ramaṇa Maharṣi made a selection of 42 verses (*Gītā-sāram*), Tiruvanamallai. Dhar Murli (1940) selected 108 verses and Svami Shivananda published even more verses (2nd edn., 1953). A text of 388 verses — more than half of the total *Gītā* — was translated by Keshab Kanto (1966).

Instead of selecting portions, one can also keep the complete *Gītā* but in a different arrangement. In his Quest for the Original *Gītā* (Bombay, 1969) Khair published his *Trikāla-Gītā* using red, blue and black colours for the subsequent layers or authors of the *Gītā*. J.M. Chatterjee (Delhi, 1977), re-arranged the *Gītā* in 15 chapters, adding quotations. V.R.P. Das (formerly Lt. Henry Wahab) compiled a *Śrī Gītāmṛta Bodhinī* in which the translation of A. Besant is re-arranged under 27 headings (Madras, 1908). It has also been argued that the Lord's *viśvarūpadarśana* (ch. 11) should come first, since in the Indian tradition instructions are based on faith and experience.

In order to make the *Gītā* more attractive to devotees, it has also been edited along with other devotional books, like the *Viṣṇusahasranāma*, or in the forms of a *Pañcaratna-Gītā*, which gives five extracts of the *Mahābhārata*, viz. the *Mahābhārata*, the *Gītā* (with *Māhātmya*, *Viṣṇusahasranāma*, *Bhīṣmastavarāja*, *Anusmṛti* and *Gajendra-mokṣa*; e.g. Indore, 1850). In the original Sanskrit the *Gītā* was printed for the first time at the beginning of the nineteenth century. The polyglot edition of Garrett (Bangalore, 1849), with parallel colums in Sanskrit, Kannada and English, with Appendix in Latin and a List of Malayalam variants, was a brilliant achievement, never surpassed afterwards.

In Callewaert & Hemraj (1983, pp. 111-341) we made an extensive survey of the then existing translations of the *Gītā*, in 34 Indian languages and 38 non-Indian languages, with amazing figures like: 30 into Braj, or 273 into English (till 1982!). In the 75 English translations of verse 1.1 (*kurukṣetre dharmakṣetre*) which we compared we found for *dharma* the following translations: "holy", "sacred", or the nouns "right", "righteousness", "religious activity", "law", "righteouos war", "duty", "religious ceremony", "truth", "justice", "morality", "pilgrimage".

6

The "Earliest" Pad of Mīrā (1503-1546)[1]

[1991][2]

If Mīrā died at the age of 43, it is remarkable that at the end of the twentieth century there should be as many as 5,197 *pads*[3] with her name available. It has become a boring expression in studies about Mīrā that it is very difficult, if not impossible to decide which and how many *pads* are most probably by Mīrā. And yet, ever-expanding collections go on appearing. In some editions the question of authenticity is solved on the basis of content, in others on the basis of language. Rarely do authors bother to look at the written material.

Of course, it remains a mystery why the written tradition, in the case of Mīrā, seems to have started so late (*c.* CE 1800), if we compare it with the spate of manuscripts with *nirguṇa* material in

---

1. These dates are only indicative, because there is no evidence to support these or other dates. I copied them from Tivari: 1974 (see further), pp. 127 and 156. [For the problem of translating Mīrā, see Florence Pasche Guignard, "Go West, Mira! Translating Medieval Bhakti Poetry" (with an extensive bibliography, and in Appendix: Translations of the *Padāvalī* into English), in: Maya Burger & Nicola Pozza, *India in Translation through Hindi Literature. A Plurality of Voices*, Peter Lang, Bern, 2010, pp. 195-234.]
2. In: *Orientalia Lovaniensia Periodica*, 22 (1991), 201-14.
3. See further, Tivari: 1974, p. 124. Of these, 3,797 songs are supposed to be in Hindī, 817 in Gujarātī and 583 by Indirā Devī. During his Ph. D. research (1950-62) Tivari supposedly studied 4,614 songs attributed to Mīrā.

Rajasthan, or *saguṇa* material in the Braj area from CE 1600 onwards. Why? Several reasons have been brought forward. The *pad*s of Mīrā very soon became the (exclusive?) property of women in the home. Women did not scribe, as *sādhus* or (male) singers did. Or, the *pad*s of Mīrā were scorned, to such an extent that they never became part of the standard repertoires of singers. We read in a letter of M.L. Menaria (Udaipur, 1 July 1938) to Purohit H. Sharma, Jaipur:

> People here are not interested in Mīrā Bāī as you and I are. Even the Mahārāṇā Sāhib believes that Mīrā has been a black-blot on the fair page of the Mewar History and musicians are not allowed to sing the *pad*s of Mīrā Bāī in the Palace. But this is only for your private information. Please do not make a mention of this anywhere in your book.[4]

With due respect for the oral traditions, my approach to the problem of authenticity has always been through the first manuscripts. Even if that approach, in the case of Mīrā, will not add much certainty about authentic *pad*s, at least it can question the claims made in the numerous editions current now.

Mīrā in The Ādigranth

Although scores of books and editions about Mīrā have appeared since 1900, little attention has been given to the *pad* of Mīrā quoted in the Banno version of the *Gurugranth*. I call it the "earliest *pad*" of Mīrā because there are reasons to believe that the date of the Dakor manuscript (1585; see further) is not correct. The *pad* of Mīrā is not found in the "standard" version of the *Gurugranth*, but only in the Banno version, which was (and still is) banned as dissident in orthodox Sikh circles. Professor Pritam Singh gives a very good description of the "earliest" Banno manuscript, preserved in Kanpur, and of which I was able to make a photographic copy in 1983. He writes:

---

4. This letter is found in the correspondence of P.H. Sharma, preserved in the *विद्याभूषण ग्रंथसंग्रह*, Jaipur. For a detailed description of this correspondence, see N.S. Bati, "मीराप्रकरण", in: परंपरा, 1982, pp. 49-124.

> Banno was deputed by Guru Arjan to get P1 (the autograph) bound by some expert bookbinder of Lahore. Banno's earnest request that he be allowed to have the honour of carrying P1 to his village, was granted by the guru-compiler on the condition that he would not stay there for more than one night. Bhāī Banno was scrupulous in observing this condition but manoeuvred frequent en-route halts, during which he put specially-recruited members of his retinue at work and got P1 copied from one end to the other, before reaching Lahore. Both P1 and B1 (the first Banno copy) were got properly bound at Lahore and brought back. . . .[5]

What we should remember here is that around CE 1604 there were *pad*s with the *chhāp* of Mīrā in Punjab, from which one *pad* was selected to be part of the Sikh repertoire, either in the original version compiled by Arjan himself, or in the (Banno) copy. In an article of 1903 Macauliffe remarks:

> Guru Arjan at first inserted one of Mīrā Bāī's hymns in his collection of the Sikh sacred writings but subsequently drew his pen through it.[6] It is preserved, however, in the *Granth* of Bhāī Banno, which can be seen at Mangat in the Gujrat district of the Punjab. The following is the hymn:
>
> God hath entwined my soul, O mother,
> With His attributes and I have sung of them.
> The sharp arrow of His love hath pierced my body
> through and through, O mother.
> When it struck me I did not know it, now it cannot be
> endured, O mother.
> Though I use charms, incantations and drugs, the
> pain will not depart.

---

5. Pritam Singh, "Bhāī Banno's copy of the Sikh Scripture", in: Monika Thiel-Horstmann, *Bhakti in Current Research, 1979-1982*, Berlin 1983, p. 326. Pritam Singh there enumerates the specific differences between the Banno version and the standard Kartarpur text.
6. C.S. Srinivasachari adds here: ". . . saying that though it was good, still its authoress lived and died an idolater". "Mīrā Bai, the Saint of Rajputana", in: *The Indian Review*, October 1925, pp. 715-20.

> Is there anyone who will treat me? Intense is the agony, O mother.
> Thou, O God, art near, Thou art not distant; come quickly to meet me.
> Saint Mira, the Lord, the Mountain-wielder, who is compassionate, hath quenched the fire of my body, O mother.
> The lotus-eyed hath entwined my soul with the twine of his attributes.

This *pad* is found in the Banno manuscript at Kanpur on folio 369, under *rāg mārū*. This is the last *pad* under this *rāg*. It is preceded by 10 *pad*s of Kabīr, 2 of Nāmdev, 2 of Jaydev and 2 of Raidās. I am very grateful to Prof. Pritam Singh, of Patiala, for the transcription of this *pad* of Mīrā in the Banno manuscript into Devanāgarī:

> मनु हमारो बांधिओ माई कवल नैन आपने गुन । रहाउ ॥
> तीखण तीर बेध सरीर दूरि गयो माई ।
> लागिओ तब जानिओ नही अब न सहिओ जाई री माई । १ ॥
> तंत संत अउखद करउ तउ पीर न जाई ।
> है कोऊ उपकारु करै कठिन दरदु माई री । २ ॥
> निकटि हउ तुम दूरि नही बेगि मिलहु आइी ।
> मीरां गिरधर सुआमी दैआल तान की तप बुझाई री माई ।
> कवल नैन अपने गुन आपने तन बाधिओ माई । ३ ॥

Perhaps the most surprising about this *pad* is that it is *not* found in the Dakor manuscripts, and hardly in any edition. I found it only in the edition of Purohit Hari Narayana Sharma (1944; p. 174; see Shekhavat: 1967; *pad* 368), where it has a specific reference to *Granth-sāhib gāīvande kī bīd*, as follows:

> मन हमारा बाँध्यो माई कँवल नैन अपने गुन ।
> तीखन तीर बेध शरीर दूरि गयो माई ।
> लाग्यो तब जान्यों नहीं अब न सह्यो जाई री माई ।
> तंत संत औषद करउ तऊ पीर न जाई ।
> है कोऊ उपकार करे कठिन दर्द री माई ।
> निकटि हो तुम दूरि नहीं बेगि मिलो आई ।
> मीराँ गिरधर स्वामी दयाल तन की तपति बुझाई री माई ।
> (कँवल नैन आपने गुन बाँध्यो माई ॥)

Why does this *pad* not appear anywhere else? The numerous *nirguṇa pad*s found in the Rājasthānī manuscripts and in the *Gurugranth* justify the hypothesis that singers had quite a mixed repertoire when they travelled to and from Punjab. Mīrā's *pad*(s) were part of some repertoire. But if we find it written down in the *Gurugranth*, why did it not survive in the repertoires which were written down much later, from 1800 onwards, in Rajasthan and elsewhere? The *pad* deals with *virah*, and in the mammoth edition by Anand Svarup (1957), we find 162 *virah pad*s of Mīrā. This theme was certainly not unfamiliar to her.

The Earliest Manuscripts

I have looked at more than 100 books in Hindī, English, Gujarātī and Bengālī[7] and I noted scores of titles of articles in different languages, dealing with Mīrā. It was my experience again[8] that most authors copy from a few standard predecessors, adding often only fancy details without referring to sources. Critical editions have undergone the same fate: editions go on expanding, as authors copy from earlier editions and add *pad*s from contemporary singers' repertoires. Very few bothered to look at the earliest manuscripts. I list below the most important editions of the *pad*s of Mīrā, with the date of publication, the number of *pad*s, and the manuscripts; I give NM (no manuscripts) if there are no manuscript sources mentioned.[9]

Vyas: 1842	43 *pads*; NM
Ramachandra: 1897	20 *pads*; NM
Desai: 1897	113 *pads*; NM
Apte: 1908	157 *pads*; NM
Belvedere: 1909, etc.	38 to 167 *pads*; NM
Kalekar: 1922	352 *pads*; NM

7. Not all titles consulted are listed here.
8. See my study about the sources for Dādū in Callewaert: 1978, pp. 21-75 and about the sources for the biography of Nāmdev, in Callewaert & Lath: 1989.
9. For more early manuscripts, see below, Shekhavat: 1974c.

Narottam: 1930	161 *pads*; NM
Chaturvedi: 1932	202 *pads*; NM
Mishra: 1934	126 to 127 *pads*; NM
Shrivastav: 1934	139 *pads*; NM
Shrivastav: 1938	209 *pads*; NM
Sharma: 1944	662 *pads*; NM
Jain: 1945	176 *pads*; NM
Gahlot: 1945	108 *pads*; NM
Brajratnadas: 1948	506 *pads*; NM
Sharma: 1949	8 *pads*; ms. 1638 69 *pads*; mss. 1585 (?) and 1748, 34 *pads*; manuscript 1748[10]
Majumdar: 1950	185 (480) *pads*; NM
Prabhakar: 1951	246 + 119 *pads*; NM
Padmavati: 1952	590 *pads*; NM
Bhatnagar: 1952	104 *pads* (earliest 1822)
Anand Svarup: 1957	1312 *pads*; NM
Vishnu: 1958	12 *pads*
Bhati: 1962	242 *pads*; NM
Shekhavat: 1967	662 *pads*; see Sharma: 1944
Sharma: 1972	301 *pads*; NM
Shalabh: 1972	34 *pads*; (Nahta); NM
Padmavati: 1973	601 *pads*; NM except for the 6 *pads* from a ms. of 1755
Tivari: 1974	103 *pads*; NM
Shekhavat: 1975	405 *pads*; 236 mss., of which 4 mss. of the eighteenth century.

10. Sukul (see 2a.) also refers to the Kashi and Kanpur mss. of 1670.

The Dakor Manuscripts

Dakor, with the famous Raṇchoḍjī temple, is at a two-hour busride from Baroda in Gujarat. In 1934 Lalit Prasad Sukul, of Calcutta, made a tour of western India in search of manuscripts.[11] He had more success than Bhagvandas Tivari in 1960 and myself in 1988. He saw very old manuscripts, I did not. One manuscript, dated 1585, apparently had 69 *pads* of Mīrā which were also found in later manuscripts (see further) and in later printed editions, albeit in different versions. The second manuscript shown to Sukul in 1934 was dated 1748, and had 103 *pads*. The first 69 *pads* in that second manuscript were identical with those in the first manuscript, although the language was "more Gujarātī".

According to Sukul's informant in Dakor, Bhatt, whose ancestors served in the temple, the manuscript Sukul saw was copied from the autograph by Bhatt's ancestors in 1585. That autograph was written during Mīrā's life by her servant, a lady called Lalitā. No further information is given about the autograph manuscript but the copy was taken away "during the seventeenth century by some Muslim invader, along with all the treasures of the temple" (Sukul, p. च). It came back one day, Sukul copied the 69 *pads* in 1934, but it is not clear what happened to the autograph copy after that. Earlier, both manuscripts had been copied by Bhatt (p. घ) and sent to Shyam Sundardas in Banaras. Sukul had seen that copy (of the manuscript of 1748) with S.S. Das at Banaras, some time before he came to Dakor. The copy of the older manuscript was then with Ramchandra Shukla. Through the courtesy of Bhatt, a copy of both manuscripts was also given to Sukul (p. ङ).

Where are all these copies now? Several people have questioned the authenticity of the earliest manuscript, mainly on linguistic basis.[12] I have my doubts about the authenticity because the date is so early. No manuscript with *bhakti* literature that early is found in

11. I have my information from his detailed account in Sharma: 1949 (see further), pp. 272ff.

12. See further, Shekhavat: 1974c.

Gujarat. If we compare this manuscript with manuscripts in Rajasthan, it would be as early as the Fatehpur manuscript of the City Palace, Jaipur (1582). That Jaipur manuscript gives three repertoires, with mainly the *pad*s of Sūr. Like a thunder in a blue sky, how do we find in Dakor a manuscript with just one repertoire, and only of Mīrā? Even with the spate of scribing of *bhakti* literature from 1600 onwards, we find no other complete repertoire of Mīrā written down until 1800 or later. It is quite likely that a repertoire with Mīrā's *pad*s took shape during her lifetime but are there indications to believe that they were written down by a girl, a maidservant? Why was this manuscript preserved "and venerated" (*pūjā*, p.छ) in the Vallabh temple of Dakor? Mīrā was not a Vallabhite, although tradition says that her *pad*s were sung there.

It is interesting to note that, in the course of time, the number 103 increased to 295.[13] I compared these 103 *pad*s with later versions in printed editions. They are basically the same but at times also quite variant, as is shown in the example below. I give below *pad* 8 in the Dakor manuscripts, and compare it with the version in printed editions. The variants (highlighted) of basically the same *pad* are clearly the result of the singers' creativity.

Pad 8 in Dakor manuscript (1585, as given in Sharma (1949), p. 1):

आली म्हाँणे लागां बृन्दाबण णीकां ।
घर घर तुडसी ठाकर पूजां दरसण गोविंदजी कां ॥
निरमड नीर बह्या जमणा कां भोजण दूध दह्यां कां ।
रतण सिंघासण आप बिराज्यां मुगट धर्‍यां तुडशी कां ॥
कुंजण कुंजण फिर्‍यां सांवरा सबद सुरण्या (सुण्या?) मुरडी कां ।
मीराँ रे प्रभु गिरधर नागर भजण बिणा नर फीकां ॥

Pad 1 in Anand Svarup (1957); section 8: *brajbhāv ke pad*, p. 575:[14]

आली म्हाँने लागे बृन्दाबन नीको ।
घर घर तुलसी ठाकर पूजा दरसण गोविंदजी को । १ ॥
निरमल नीर बहत जमना में भोजन दूध दही को । २ ॥

13. See further, Tivari: 1974b, pp. 127ff.

14. Also found in Padmavati: 1952; *pad* 497, p. 276.

रतन सिंघासन आप बिराजै मुगट धर्‌यो तुलशी को । ३ ॥
कुँजण कुँजण फिरत राधिका सबद सुणत मुरली को । ४ ॥
मीराँ के प्रभु गिरधर नागर भजन बिना नर फीको । ५ ॥

Pad 245 in Anand Svarup (1957); section 8: *brajbhāv ke pad*, p. 658:

राधा म्हांनै लागै बृन्दाबन नीको रे ॥
वृंदाबन में तुलसी का बिडला जाके पान चरी को । १ ॥
वृंदाबन में धेनु बहुत हैं भोजन दूध दही को । २ ॥
वृंदाबन में रास रच्यो है दरसण कृष्णजी को। ३ ॥
मीराँ के प्रभु गिरधर नागर बिना रंग सब फीको । ४ ॥

Pad 253 in Anand Svarup (1957); section 8: *brajbhāv ke pad*, p. 661:[15]

उधो म्हांनै लागै वृन्दाबन नीको रे ॥
वृंदाबन में धेनु बहुत हैं भोजन दूध दही को रे । १ ॥
मोर मुकुट पीतांबर सोहै सिर केसर को टीको रे । २ ॥
घर घर में तुलसी को बिडलो दरसण माधवजी को रे । ३ ॥
मीराँ के प्रभु गिरधर नागर हरी बिना सब फीको रे । ४ ॥

Let us compare the following versions:

8 (Dakor: 1585)

1 (Anand Svarup: 1957)

245 (Anand Svarup: 1957)

253 (Anand Svarup: 1957)

Version 1 and 8:

Except for राधिका in 1, line 4, instead of सांवरा in 8 and the curious spelling ड in 8 for ल in 1, there are no major differences between these two versions of the same *pad*.

Version 1, and 245/253

The comparison between 1 on the one hand and 245 and 253 on the other is more rewarding. If, hypothetically, we accept 1 as the basic text, we note very interesting changes brought about by singers. We read राधा in 245.0 but उधो in 253, instead of आली in 1. Several

15. Also found in Padmavati: 1952; *pad* 498, p. 276.

lines in 245 have nearly the same message as in 1, but are worded differently. *Pads* 245 and 253, which are otherwise quite different, have an identical line (about the cows and the milk in Vrindaban), which is different in 1. Line 1 in *pad* 1, with गोविंदजी, becomes line 3 in 253, with माधवजी. Noteworthy also is the *gey-vikār* रे, which is a filler added by a singer in 253.

Manucripts of 1670

Sukul further reports that he saw a manuscript in the Nagari Pracarini Sabha, Banaras and one in Kanpur which had the same set of songs, and were dated Saṁvat 1727 (CE 1670). Apparently, this text is not available in print.

Selective Bibliography of the Editions of the Pads of Mīrā[16]

1842 Vyas Dev, *Saṅgīt Rāg Kalpadrum*, Bangiy Sahitya Parishad, Calcutta (1842), 1914; 43 *pads* of Mīrā.

1893 K.P. Khatri, *Mīrābāī kī Jīvanī*, Thakur Prasad & Sons, Calcutta.

1897 I.P. Ramacandra, *Mīrābāī ke Bhajan*, Meerut; *pads* of Sūr, Narsī, Tulasī, and 20 *pads* of Mīrā.

1897b I.S. Desai, *Vr̥hat Kāvya Dohan* (Guj.), 10 vols; 7th edn., 1927; 113 *pads* of Mīrā.

1898 Munshi Deviprasad, *Mīrābāī kā Jīvan Caritra*, Bangiy Hindi Parishad, Calcutta (1898), 1962.

1905 Munshi Deviprasad, *Mahilā Mr̥duvāṇī*, Banaras, 1905.

1908 T.H. Apte, *Gāthā Pañcak*, Pune, 1908; repr. in 5 vols. by R.C. Dhere, Pune, 1983. In vol. 5, pp. 114-41, are given 157 *pads* of Mīrā. No sources.

1909 Anonymous, *Mīrābāī kī Śabdāvalī*, Belvedere Press, Allahabad; 38 *pads*; in the 1976 edn. 167 *pads* are given, with alphabetical index.

1922 G. Kalekar, *Mīrābāī Bhajan Bhaṇḍār*, 1922; 352 *pads*.

1930 Narottam Das Svami, *Mīrā Mandākiṇī*, Un. Book Depot, Agra, VS 1987; 161 *pads* (along with *pads* of other poets); based on an unspecified "old manuscript". According to Shekhavat 1974c (p. 11) the editor has tried to make the *pads* conform to "Rājasthānī".

1930b Viyogi Hari, *Mīrābāī, Sahjobāī Dayābāī kā Pad Saṁgraha*; Gandhi Pustak Bhandar, Prayag, 1930; 36 *pads* of Mīrā.

16. For a recent bibliography see Florence Pasche Guignard, "Go West, Mira! Translating Medieval Bhakti Poetry" in: Maya Burger & Nicola Pozza, *India in Translation through Hindi Literature. A Plurality of Voices*, Peter Lang, Bern, 2010, pp. 195-234; bibliography on pp. 223-34.

1931 Viyogi Hari, *Bhajan Saṁgraha*, vol. III; 62 *pads* of Mīrā.

1932 P. Chaturvedi, *Mīrābāī kī Padāvalī*, Allahabad (1932), 17th edn. 1983. The author gives 202 *pads* (pp. 99-158) with alphabetical index and a commentary on words. Chaturvedi himself doubts the authenticity of the 202 *pads* he selected. The edition of 1972 gives a set of selected *pads* which is different from what Chaturvedi gave in earlier editions. No manuscripts are referred to. In his Introduction he points out that three kinds of *pads* are especially subject to questioning about authenticity:

— the *pads* which deal with family quarrels,

— the *pads* which show a Sant influence,

— the *pads* which have a Yog or Nāth connotation.

He does, however, incorporate dubious *pads* about Mīrā's family (pp. 105-10; *pads* 27-38), a *pad* which mentions that Raidās is Mīrā's guru (*pad* 24; p. 104), *yog*-connected *pads*: 115 (pp. 57-58), 121 (p. 60), 127 (p. 88), etc., and a Punjābī *pad*: 165, p. 151. English translation by Alston: 1980 and Pandey & Zide (1964), and Hindī translation by Sambhu Singh (1969).

1934 B. Misra, *Mīrā kī Prem Sādhnā*, (1934: 126 *pads*); 2nd edn., 1946: 216 *pads*; 3rd edn., 1957: 217 *pads*.

1934b M. Shrivastava, *Mīrābāī kā Kāvya*, Sahitya Bhavan, Prayag; 139 *pads*; see further: 1956.

1934c Anathanath Basu, *Mīrā Bai. Saint and Singer of India*. London,

1935 Banke Behari, *The Story of Mira Bai*, Gorakhpur, 1935.

1938 V. Kumari Shrivastav, *Mīrā Padāvalī*, Hindi Bhavan, Lahore; 201 *pads* "taken from earlier pub1ications".

1944 P.H. Sharma; see K.S. Shekhavat (1967).

1945 H.C. Jain, *Mīrā aur Unkī Premavāṇī*, 1945; 176 *pads*.

1945 M. Singh Gahlot, *Mīrā. Jīvanī aur Kāvya*, Banaras 1945; the author gives 108 *pads* of Mīrā, "of which 40 were not published before" but no source is given.

1948 Shri Brajratnadas, *Mīrā Mādhurī*, Varanasi, 1948, (2nd edn. 1967; 3rd edn. 1970); 506 *pads*. No reference to manuscripts.

1949 S.N. Sharma and others, *Mīrā Smr̥ti Grantha*, Bangiy Hindi Parishad, Calcutta 1949 (270, 20, 59 pp.). On pp. 141-52 J.P. Gupta gives 8 "unpublished" *pads* of Mīrā. He found them in the (then Gujarati Vernacular Society, now) Gujarat Vidya Sabha, manuscript No. D 477 K, dated 1638. Four *pads* may have variant readings in other editions but *pads* 2, 4, 5, 7 were, according to the author, then not printed anywhere else. On pp. 27ff. Lalit Prasad Sukul gives 69 *pads* based on the Dakor manuscripts (dated 1585 and 1748) and *pads* 70-103 based on the manuscript of 1748. 18 Articles.

1950 M.R. Majumdar, *Mīrābāī: Ek Manan* (Gujarati), Baroda (1950), 1975; gives on pp. 253-55 a detailed chronological Table; on pp. 187-261 are given 185 *pads* (480 in later editions) under 8 headings, and on pp. 262-97 the *Mīrābāī kī Parcī*, (in 12 *viśrām* and 200 *dohe*). No written sources referred to.

1950b Padmavati Sabnam, *Mīrā: Ek Adhyayan*, Lokasevak Prakashan, Kashi.

1950c Shri Madhur, *Mīrānī Prem-Vāṇī*, (Guj.), 1950; 251 *pads*.

1951... Indira Devi, *Shrutanjali* (1951), *Premanjali* (1953, with rpts), *Sudhanjali* and *Vibhanjali* (1958, rpt), *Deepanjali* and *Bhavanjali* (1960; rpt), *Ushanjali* (1971), Hari Krishna Mandir, Poona; 100 *pads* attributed to Mīrā.

1951b K. Prabhakar & Banke Bihari, *Braj-Chandra Cakori Mīrā*, Vrindavan, 1951; 246 Hindī *pads* and 119 Gujarātī *pads*, with commentary. No sources given.

1951c Shrikrishna Lal, *Mīrābāī: Jīvan-carita aur Ālocanā*, Hindi Sahitya Sammelan, Prayag (1951, 1970), 3rd edn. 1972, 188 pp.

1952 Padmavati Shabnam, *Mīrā. Bṛhat Pad-Saṁgraha*, Kashi, VS 2009; 590 *pads*, selected from earlier editions and from singers' repertoires. The author rejects "as unauthentic the *pads* in which the quarrels of Mīrā with her family are referred to. This issue had become a popular item in the folklore, and *pads* referring to that must be of a later date. On the other hand, those *pads* are most probably authentic in which the themes of the *līlā* of Kṛṣṇa and of *virah* are dealt with. Reason: that is what Nābhā mentions as Mīrā's specific quality and that is what apparently made her popular. This should, then, not prevent us from accepting also as possibly authentic the *pads* which deal with a Sant or Yogic theme. I have tried to bring together in one volume as many *pads* as I could find: published, unpublished and from performers" (Introduction). See also Padmavati (1973).

1952 U.S. Bhatnagar, *Rājasthān meṁ hindī ke hastalikhit granthoṁ kī khoj*, vol. 3, Udaipur 1952; on pp. 17ff. are given 104 *pads* "from Udaipur", and in the appendix the author gives 54 *pads* from different sources, of which one is a dated manuscript of 1822.

1956 M. Shrivastava, *Mīrā Darśan*, (1956); gives the 103 *pads* of the Dakor manuscripts. See above, 1934b.

1957 Svami Anand Svarup, *Mīrā Sudhā Sindhu*, Shri Mira Prakashan Samiti, Bhilwara, VS 2014; 1312 *pads*; no sources given.

1958 Vishnu Kumari Manju, "Bhakta Kavayitrī Mīrā ke Aprakāśit Pad", in: *Hindustānī*, 19, 4, 1958; 12 *pads*.

1962 Desraj Singh Bhati, *Mīrābai aur Unaki Padavali*, Ashok Prakashan, Nai Sarak, Delhi, 1962; 4th edn.; 400 pp.; 242 *pads* with Hindī commentary and alphabetical first-line index. The author also gives variant versions but does not mention any source.

1962 B.V. Trivedi, *Mīrānā Pade* (Guj.), Bombay (1962); 3rd edn. 1986; 252, 58, 103 Gujarati *pads*, with alphabetical first-line index.

1965 L.S. Saktavat, *Mīrā Darśan*, 1965 (10th edn.); 151 *pads*, basically based on the Dakor manuscripts.

1967 Kalyan Singh Shekhavat, ed., *Mīrā Bṛhat Padāvalī*, vol. I, Jodhpur, 1967. Vol. I gives 662 *pads* (with *rāg* and *tāl*) selected by P.H. Sharma and his Introduction (9 pp.) of 1944. The *pads* are classified in the alphabethical order of the first line. There is no reference to the manuscripts, because there is no key to understand the abbreviations Sharmaji used (see vol. II, Shekhavat: 1975, pp. 82f). Apparently, he collected *pads* of Mīrā "from all over Rajasthan" (Introduction). For vol. II, see 1975.

1969 M. Sambhu Singh, *Mīrā Padāvalī*, Jaipur, 1969; on pp. 109-277 he gives 130 *pads* (= P. Chaturvedi, edn.), with commentary and Hindī translation.

1969 B.B. Trivedi, *Mīrābāī Nām Vadhu Gujarātī Pad*, 1969.

1971 N. Sundaram, *Mīrā aur Āṇḍāl kā Tulanātmak Adhyayan* (Ph. D. in Jabalpur University, 1971); "my study is based on the 202 *pads* published by P. Chaturvedi", p. 72.

1972 Krishnadev Sharma, *Mīrā Padāvālī*, 1972; pp. 165-382: commentary; text based on Narottam Das, Bh. Mishra, Braj Ratnadas and *Mīrā Smṛti Grantha*. Alphabetical first-line index of 301 *pads*.

1972b G. Salabh and others (eds.), *Mīrā Smṛti Grantha*, Sahitya Niketan, Ajmer, 1972; 27 articles without footnotes; on pp. 132-44: A. Nahta, "*Mīrābāī ke Aprakaśit Pad*"; 34 *pads*, without reference to the source.

1973 Padmavati Shabnam, *Mīrā: Vyaktitva aur Kṛtitva*, Hindi Pracharak Sansthan, 1973; 601 *pads* but without clear reference to sources. The norm for selecting *pads* is odd: "Those songs are more *prāmāṇik* which have not undergone the handling by singers. Most songs with the name of Mīrā have undergone the influence of the *gey-paramparā*. The authenticity of these songs is doubtful. Those *pads* are probably more authentic which have an identical reading in all the manuscripts" (pp. 404f.). I argue that precisely those *pads* may be less reliable, because they may belong to just one single repertoire. On pp. 43f., App. 1: 6 *pads* based on a Nagari Pracarini Sabha manuscript of 1755. See above, Padmavati (1950 and 1952).

1974 Bhagvandas Tivari, *Mīrā kī Bhakti aur Unkī Kāvya-Sādhanā kā Anuśīlan*, (Ph.D. Thesis, Sagar University, 1963), Sahitya Bhavan, Prayag, 1974. The author refers to two manuscripts which also give the total of 103 *pads* as they are found in the Dakor and Kashi manuscripts (see Sharma: 1949); one is from Kashi (1670), the other from Kanpur (1670).

1974b Bhagvandas Tivari, *Mīrā kī Prāmāṇik Padāvalī*, Sahitya Bhavan, Prayag, 1974. The author discusses the different collections and gives (on pp. 127-272) the 103 *pads* of the Dakor manuscripts, along with variant versions in other editions.

1974c Kalyan Singh Shekhavat, *Mīrābāī kā Jīvanavr̥t evaṁ Kāvya*, Hindi Sahitya Mandir, Ratanada, Jodhpur, 1974. This is a Ph.D. of 1969. In chapter 1 the author gives a survey of publications about Mīrā, and a list of manuscripts. Of interest are manuscripts numbered 9,259 and 12,577 in the Jodhpur collection, both of the eighteenth century VS.[17] He further doubts the authenticity of the *pads* found in the earliest Dakor manuscript (p. 27). For the edition of the *pads*, see Shekhavat (1975).

1974 Shashi Prabha, *Mīrā Kośa*, Allahabad, 1974.

1975 Kalyan Singh Shekhavat (ed.), *Mīrā-Br̥hat-Padāvalī*, II (1975), Jodhpur. This volume gives 405 *pads*, of which 215 were not published earlier. Besides that set of 215 *pads* are given: 50 *pads* from a *rāg-rāginī* illustrated manuscript of the nineteenth century; 49 *pads* "which show great similarity with one of the 215 *pads*"; 42 *pads* "which are similar only in the first two-three lines"; 40 *pads* "which are similar in most lines except in one or two"; 9 *pads* "which are quite variant from a similar one in the set of 215". The editor consulted a total of 236 manuscripts all over Rajasthan, mainly of the nineteenth century VS, with a few exceptions: seventeenth century VS (*c.* CE 1700?), 4 folios, Chaupasani No. 1667; CE 1769, 2 folios, Chaupasani No. 4670; CE 1777, 3 folios, Chaupasani No. 7187/6; CE 1779, 124 folios, Jodhpur 31,077.

1980 L. Bhatnagar, *Dharma Sampradāya aur Mīrā kā Bhaktibhāv*, Delhi 1980; 224 pp.

1980 Raj Nagpal, *Mīrābāī kī Padāvalī*, Delhi, 1980; in the second part is given a commentary on the *pads* edited by Chaturvedi.

1981 Usha Kiran Sharma, *Mīrā kī Abhivyañjanā Śailī*, Ajmer, 1981; 355 pp.: "I based my study on the Chaturvedi edition because that has become a standard textbook in all universities. Further I refer also to the Jodhpur *Mīrā Br̥hat Padāvalī*" (1967 and 1975) (p. 11).

1982 Nilima Simha, *Mīrā: Ek Antaraṅga Paricaya*, Delhi 1982; reprints the 103 *pads* of the Dakor manuscripts.

---

17. The date "seventeenth century VS" for manuscript 1667 in the Chaupasani collection (p. 32) is hopefully not a mistake. The author missed the following interesting manuscripts in the collection of the Jodhpur Oriental Institute: No. 30,346 (CE 1656), colophon not confirmed; one song; No. 1,163 (CE 1783), fo. 32, 33, 35-39; No. 1,247 (eighteenth century VS); No. 2,626 (CE 1784), fo. 849-850; No. 1,177 (eighteenth century VS), fo. 202-203. I have noted a seventeenth-century CE manuscript in a private collection in Jaipur (one song) and one in Vrindaban.

    A careful scrutiny of the hundreds of *pad-saṁgraha* manuscripts of the seventeenth-eighteenth centuries may be very rewarding. Of course, there are hundreds of manuscripts with *pads* of Mīrā, dated nineteenth century VS.

1984 N.S. Bhati (ed.), "Mīrābāī rī paracī va paracī kāvya", in: *Paramparā*, pp. 69-70, 1984, Chaupasani, 124 pp. Hindī edition of the biography of Mīrā by Sukh Saran.

English Translations[18]

1901 U.N. Mukhopadhyay, *Mīrābai of Udaipur*, Calcutta 1901; with English and Bengali translation.

1903 M. Macauliffe, "The Legend of Mīrā Bai, the Rajput Princess", in: *Indian Antiquary*, 32 (1903), pp. 329-35. On p. 335, the author remarks in note 10: "The hymns in this life of Mīrā Bai are taken from Raja Raghuraj Singh's Bhagat Mala".

1923 M. MacNicol, *Poems by Indian Women*, The Heritage of India Series, Calcutta, 1923; 10 *pads* in English are given on pp. 59-66.

1934 R.C. Tandon, *Songs of Mīrābai*, Hindi Mandir, Allahabad 1934; English translation of 50 *pads* of Mīrā.

1956 H. Goetz, "Mīrā Bai, Her Life and Times", in: *Journal of the Gujarat Research Society*, vol. XVIII, April 1956, 2, pp. 87-113; (Bombay Bharatiya Vidya Bhavan, 1966).

(n.d.) T.L. Vaswani, *Saint Mira*, Pune; a few *pads* in English; no sources given.

1961 Banke Behari, *Bhakta Mira*, Bharatiya Vidya Bhavan (1961), 2nd edn. 1971; gives 128 (2nd edn. 184) *pads*; 80 *pads* are quoted from Prabhakar & Behari (1951); 112 *pads* in English translation; Hindī first-line index.

1964 S.M. Pandey and N. Zide, *Poems of Mīrābāī*, Chicago, 1964; based on the 11th edn. of Chaturvedi (1932).

1973 S. Kurl, *The Devotional Poems of Mīrābai*, Calcutta, 1973; 50 *pads* in English translation.

1973 S. Eveland, "Devotional Songs of Mira Bai", in: *Literature East and West*, 2-3-4, June-December 1973, pp. 238-43. No sources given.

1975 P. Nandy, *The Songs of Mīrābai*, Arnold-Heinemann, New Delhi, 1975; poetical translation of 50 *pads*. No source or reference given.

1977 B. Dhingra, *Songs of Meera: Lyrics in Ecstasy*, Orient Paperbacks, New Delhi, 1977; 96 *pads* in English translation; no sources given.

1979 V.K. Sethi (ed.), *Mīrā the Divine Lover*, Soami Satsang Beas, 1979; poems of Mīrā on pp. 55-239: 97 *pads* in English translation based on *Mīrā Bṛhat Padāvalī*, *Mīrā Sudhā Sindhu* and the Belvedere edition.

1978 S. Eveland, *The Divine Lover of Mīrā Bai and Mechthild von Magdeburg: A Study of Two Women's Literary Description of a Mystical Relationship with God*; Ph.D. dissertation, Austin, Texas, 1978.

---

18. For five additional titles before 1988, and 17 publications since 1988, see above n. 16.

1979 Nicole Balbir, *Chants mystiques de Mīrābāī*, Paris 1979.

1980 A.J. Alston, *The Devotional Poems of Mīrābai*, Motilal, Delhi 1980; based on P. Chaturvedi: 15th edn.

Conclusion

There must have been, 450 years ago in Rajasthan, a lady who sang *pads* of devotion. She is mentioned in the Nābhā *Bhaktamāl* and one of her *pads* is preserved in the *Gurugranth*. Unlike her male contemporaries, however, her *pads* were not written down in the form of a repertoire until about CE 1800. If we must find her *pads* in seventeenth-century manuscripts, we have to go through Pad-saṁgraha manuscripts. Similarly, it should be very rewarding to classify the sources "about" Mīrā, starting with Nābhā, and see the ever-increasing number of data.

7

An Early Hindī Databank in the Computer

[1991][1]

FOR the first time in the history of linguistic analysis we now [in 1991!] have available on computer a databank of several megabytes of early Hindī *nirguṇa* poetry. Computer utilities have been developed in our research unit to create this databank, in Devanāgarī, and to consult it in different ways. This has opened a new line of research into the vocabulary and grammar of this literature. Here I limit myself to an analysis of the vocabulary used by six *bhakta*s of the sixteenth and early seventeenth centuries in northern India (see Callewaert & Op de Beeck: 1991, and Callewaert: 1993).

Nearly 400 years ago, singers of *bhakti* songs in the circle around Dādū in Rajasthan stored in their memory the songs of five great saints: Dādū, Kabīr, Nāmdev, Raidās and Hardās.[2] This repertoire, classified in clusters under a particular *rāg*, comprised more than 1,000 *pad*s. Later, scribes wrote the huge repertoire on paper and it became known in Dādūpanthī manuscript collections as *Pañcavāṇī* or "Five Voices". Scores of manuscripts with different versions of the *Pañcavāṇī* were found at the end of the twentieth century, mainly in Rajasthan. The versions differ because, apparently, different singers must have compiled the huge corpus

---

1. In: *South Asia Research* (London), vol. 11, No. 2, November 1991, 189-93.
2. For the discussion about the compiler or compilers of the *Pañcavāṇī*, see above, pp. 83ff.

independently, relying on their own repertoire; they must have committed them to writing independently.

Singers at the end of the sixteenth century found in the *Pañcavāṇī* inspiring material for their performances. I found in these "Five Voices" representative material that is very useful for a literary and linguistic study. Although the manuscript material consulted is generally dated *c.* CE 1600 and later, we have in the manuscripts the *pad*s and *sākhī*s of the five *bhakta*s as they were sung before CE 1600. For, the manuscripts give the version that was popular in the repertoires of the singers. These singers adapted the idiom and the morphology of the language to the needs of the local audiences they performed for, and there is little doubt that the language which we find in published texts is not exactly what Kabīr spoke or Nāmdev sang. Similarly, the literature attributed to Gorakhnāth in the manuscripts is not in the language of the tenth-eleventh centuries when Gorakh may have lived.

I list below the contents of the *Pañcavāṇī*:

	lines	words	bytes
Dādū 2,453 *sākhīs*	2,519	40,278	215.662
443 *pads*	4,112	32,128	186.420
Kabīr 737 *sākhīs*	744	11,964	64.754
200 *pads*	991	14,110	78.036
Nāmdev 258 *pads*	1,384	13,399	77.754
Raidās 94 *pads*	441	7,865	43.138
Hardās 96 *pads*	782	7,470	42.034
Total	10,973	127,214	707.798

This is indeed the very impressive total of lines of a performed repertoire that was written down in the early seventeenth century. Adding to this

Sundardās 1,371 *sākhīs*	2,706	22,914	127.101
Sundardās 210 *pads*	1,101	17,579	94.927

we have as **grand total** nearly one megabyte of *bhakti* texts that can be analysed:

lines	words	bytes
14,780	167,707	929.826

Let us look at these figures in more detail, as calculated by the computer. It is surprising how many words seem to be used by only one poet, even if we take into account the morphological changes that result from the singers' intervention.

Below I compare

A the number of different words used by each poet

B the total number of words used, and

C the unique usage, that means the number of words used only by the particular poet and nowhere else in the total corpus of 167,707 words

	A	B	C
	different words	total	unique usage
Dādū *sākhī*	6,439 (or 16% of)	40,278	2,484
pad	6,182 (or 19% of)	32,128	2,145
Kabīr *sākhī*	3,860 (or 32% of)	11,964	*[3]
pad	4,756 (or 33% of)	14,110	*
Kabīr *Bījak*			
sākhī	2,392 (or 45% of)	5,327	?
pad	3,321 (or 41% of)	7,982	?
Nāmdev *pad*	4,810 (or 36% of)	13,399	1,711
Raidās *pad*	3,143 (or 40% of)	7,865	810
Hardās *pad*	3,105 (or 41% of)	7,470	973

3. In the complete *Kabīr-Granthāvalī* (*sākhīs* and *pads* together), we found 2,933 words used by no other *bhakta*.

Sundardās

sākhī	4,629 (or 23% of)	20,208	**4
pad	5,258 (or 32% of)	16,478	**

We observe the following:

* the greatest variety in vocabulary, i.e. the highest number of different words used, is found in the oeuvre of Hardās and of Raidās, the lowest in the *sākhīs* of Dādū.

** For Dādū, Kabīr and Sundardās I also compared the two genres, i.e. the words which occur only in the *sākhīs* and not in the *pads* of that poet, and only in the *pads* and not in the *sākhīs*.

Dādū

sākhīs: of the 40,278 words, 10 per cent (4,169 words) are not found in his *pads*;

pads: of the 32,128 words, 11 per cent (3,747 words) are not found in his *sākhīs*

Kabīr

sākhīs: of the 11,964 words, 19 per cent (2,319 words) are not found in his *pads*

pads: of the 14,110 words, 22 per cent (3,214 words) are not found in his *sākhīs*

Sundardās

sākhīs: of the 20,208 words, 13 per cent (2,650 words) are not found in his *pads*

pads: of the 16,478 words, 19.5 per cent (3,221 words) are not found in his *sākhīs*.

** It may be that the vocabulary of the *sākhīs* differs from that of the *pads* because they are a different genre. Interestingly, there seems to be a closer similarity between the vocabularies used in the *pads* of the various poets, than between the vocabularies of the *sākhīs* and the *pads* of the same *bhakta*. When we compare the

4. In the complete oeuvre of Sundardās (*sākhīs* and *pads* together), I found 3,389 words used by no other *bhakta*.

sākhī-vocabularies of Dādū and of Kabīr we have the following interesting result:

Kabīr

sākhīs: of the 11,964 words, (only) 19 per cent (2.254 words) are not found in Dādū's *sākhīs*; (vice versa 12%).

pads: of the 14,110 words, 22 per cent (3,108 words) are not found in Dādū's *pads*; (vice versa 15.5%).

The Table below shows in percentage the occurrence of words in each *bhakta*'s work, from four times down to only once.

Dādū *sākhī*	Dādū *pad*	Kabīr *sākhī* + *pad*	Kabīr *Bījak*	Nāmdev *pad*	Raidās *pad*	Hardās *pad*	Sundardās *sākhī* + *pad*
I give first the total number of words:							
40,278	32,128	26,074	18,931	13,399	7,865	7,470	36,686
Now the number of different words:							
6,439	6,182	8,616	5,721	4,810	3,143	3,105	9,950

In the next four lines I give the percentage of words used four, three, two times, or only once:

Dādū *sākhī*	Dādū *pad*	Kabīr *sākhī/pad Bījak*	Nāmdev *pad*	Raidās *pad*	Hardās *pad*	Sundar *sākhī/pad*
Used four times						
4.95%	4.85	4.02/3.92	3.47	2.89	2.8	4.31
Used three times						
7.06%	6.94	7.13/7.17	5.8	5.46	9.6	7.45
Used two times						
14.42%	14.83	15.3/15.12	14.41	14.46	14.27	15
Used only once						
53.38%	55.5	59/61.19	67.09	67.9	68.6	52.89

It is further observed that the occurrence of negations (*na*, *nahī, nāhī, nā, nāhi*) is strikingly high. The Table below gives the total number of words in each work, followed by the number of negations, and the relative number of negations (e.g. Dādū *sākhī*: 1 out of 31 words is a negation):

	total	negations	=
Dādū *sākhī*	40,278	1,217	1 out of 33
pad	32,128	881	1/36
Kabīr *sākhī*	11,964	479	1/25
pad	14,110	866	1/16
Kabīr *Bijak sākhī*	5,327	187	1/28
Kabīr *pad*	7,982	263	1/30
Nāmdev *pad*	13,399	366	1/36
Raidās *pad*	7,865	280	1/28
Hardās *pad*	7,470	164	1/45
Sundardās *sākhī*	20,208	534	1/38
Sundardās *pad*	16,478	473	1/35

Summing Up

The 0.7 megabyte *Pañcavāṇī* of the early seventeenth century in Rajasthan gives a unique sample of *bhakti* songs popular among performers who memorized a total of 1,100 *pad*s and 3,000 *sākhī*s. A few striking features of that poetry have been described here by way of example but we could ask the computer many more questions. When we look at the vocabulary of the *bhakta*s, we notice that each of them uses more than half of the words (between 53 and 68 per cent) in his vocabulary only once. We notice a difference in the number of different words used by each *bhakta*: between 17 per cent (Dādū *sākhī*) and 46 per cent (Hardās) are different words. Corresponding to this number also, there is a large number of words used by one particular *bhakta* only, and found nowhere else.

There is as yet no way to find out to what an extent the editions of the *Kabīr-Granthāvalī* and of the *Bījak* represent the language of Kabīr himself. In any case, there is a striking difference in the vocabulary of both collections, as is demonstrated by the computer counts. At the same time, however, we notice a big difference in vocabulary between, e.g. the *sākhī* collection of Dādū and his *pad* collection. This is not an exception: the same difference between the vocabularies of the two genres is also noticed in Kabīr and in Sundardās. If ever there has been a myth that Kabīr excelled in his use of a varied vocabulary, it is destroyed by the computer count.

And, last but not least, in *each* of these *bhakti* works the word with the highest occurrence is the negation *na* or an equivalent.

8

The "Name" in Nirguṇa Bhakti Literature

[1994][1]

In this article I want to reflect on the holy "Name" in *nirguṇa bhakti* from my own personal perspective. Living in a Christian tradition I often perform the following exercise in order to better understand the inspiring *bhakti* literature with which I have become familiar. Going down to the deep level of my personal search for "the Other One", I try to understand and experience that Reality within the stories, models and terminology commonly used in the *nirguṇa bhakti* tradition. The experiences I study in *bhakti* text-editions, I tell myself, can be clear to me only if I can understand them on the level of my personal search and experience. That approach is even more rewarding than the scholarly endeavour and the publication of scholarly works.

The least difficult way to understand, e.g. the Holy Name is to trace its theological and etymological development from the earliest sources at hand to the period under study and to define the common and unique elements in each *bhakta*'s approach. More difficult, and more demanding, is the search from within: if the "Name" meant something to a *bhakta*, what does it mean to me in my own experience? Addressing that question is my goal while describing the holy Name in *nirguṇa bhakti* literature.

Nirguṇa bhakti literature, as opposed to *saguṇa*, is a handy but not very accurate term. It is only accurate if it refers to the claim of

1. In: *Journal of Vaisnava Studies*, New York, vol. 2, no. 2, 1994, pp. 63-174.

the *nirguṇa bhakta*s — let me henceforth call them Sants — that the Divine should be experienced and worshipped without, they say, the extravagant rituals that often shrouded the worship and devotion in *saguṇa* traditions. *Nirguṇa* is a misleading term if it would suggest that the Sants never used *saguṇa* terms when describing their experience of the divine. McLeod aptly points out that for Guru Nānak God "is both *nirguṇa* and *saguṇa*, both absolute and conditioned, both unmanifest and manifest" but *saguṇa* "in Guru Nānak's usage relates not to anything resembling anthropomorphism but to his concept of divine immanence".[2] Against the background of that immanence, it will be explained further, we have to look for the deep meaning of the "Holy Name".

No doubt, the Sants had much in common with the Vaiṣṇav Bhakti tradition, especially the emphasis on *bhakti* or feelings of love for and of God. The *saguṇa bhakta*s offered their love to an *avatāra* of Viṣṇu, while the Sants gave their love to God beyond form, through strictly inward meditation. Here they tread on the same path as the *saguṇa bhakta*s and the recitation of the Name, too, is an essential part of that path. The recitation of the Name is a prominent feature in the songs of Guru Nānak, and of Dādū, Kabīr, Nāmdev, Raidās and Hardās, the five *bhakta*s of the *Pañcavāṇī* tradition (see above, pp. 83ff.)

Kabīr (c. 1450-1518?)

As modern research goes on, the amount of "authentic" sayings of Kabīr goes on diminishing. In her translation of 1993[3] Vaudeville has rejected quite a few verses which were translated by her in 1974,[4] with the result that the complete oeuvre of Kabīr is rather small.

2. McLeod: 1968, p. 167.
3. Charlotte Vaudeville, *A Weaver Called Kabīr*, (Selected Verses, With A Detailed Biographical and Historical Introduction), Delhi: Oxford Univerity Press, 1993. All the quotations here are from this book. [In 2000 I published *The Millennium Kabīr Vānī: A Collection of Pads*; see below, pp. 206ff.]
4. Ch. Vaudeville, *Kabīr*, I, Oxford, 1974, which is based on the P.N. Tivari's *कबीर ग्रंथावली.*

The thought of Kabīr has to be gleaned from brief and terse sayings and from his lyrical songs. It is not available in a systematic exposé. Looking at the select translation prepared by Vaudeville (1993) we can best illustrate Kabīr's usage of the Name with quotations. Although lengthy studies have been devoted to the "theology" of Kabīr, there is not more to be said about his concept of the Name than what we find in these quotations. It should be clear that Kabīr extols the "Name" (of God) without ever referring to the divinized god Rām of the *Rāmāyaṇa* epic.

My only wealth
 is the Name of Hari:
I don't tie it in my belt
 nor do I sell and spend it. *refrain*

Your Name is my field,
 your Name is my orchard,
the object of my Love,
 my only refuge.

Your Name is my fortune,
 your Name is my capital —
Beside your Name
 I know nothing.

Your Name is my kith and kin,
 your Name is my Brother —
On the last day, your Name will be
 my sole Companion.

I cling to your Name
 as a poor wretch finds a Treasure —
Says Kabīr, as a tramp
 grabs sweetmeats.[5]

At first sight Kabīr seems to believe in the nearly magical power of the recitation of the Name:

---

5. Ch. Vaudeville, *Kabīr*, I, p. 258.

With a garland on my neck
  and the Name of Rām on my tongue,
Repeating the Name a thousand times,
  I offer my *salām*.

Kabīr, for that one who, even in dream,
  keeps muttering the Name of Rām —
Let the skin of my own body
  be shoes for His feet!

Kabīr has given up
  all his weaving,
On his body he has written
  the Name of Rām!

Hari is my spinning-wheel, and I, the little spinner:
  invoking Rām's Name, she's spun, the little wife.

But Kabīr rejects the practice of merely reciting the names mechanically:

O Paṇḍit,
  all your babbling is lies:[6]
If by crying "*rām*" the world is saved,
  then by saying "*sugar*" the mouth is sweetened!
Worship the Name of Rām.

That Sultan alone
  holds universal sway.
The Jogi cries:
  "*gorakh, gorakh*"!
The Hindu utters
  the Name "*rām*",
The Mussalman repeats:
  "God is One"!
But the Lord of Kabīr
  pervades all.

6. Vaudeville (op. cit.) glosses: "The Pandit challenged here is a 'Vaiṣṇav' of kinds — in so far as he believes in the magic efficacy of the Vaiṣṇav Name of God" (p. 226).

There is no doubt that for Kabīr the recitation of the Name has a great salvific power and saves one from the shackles of rebirth:

> Through the Name of Hari,
>   Kabīr became renowned
> And the accounts of his sins
>   of many births were torn up.
>
> They put on dazzling garments
>   and they chew fragrant betel-leaves.
> Yet without the Name of the one Hari
>   they go in chains to the City of Death.
>
> This world is nothing but dirt,
>   only those who invoke Rām are saved:
> Says Kabīr, hold fast to the Name,
>   though you fall and stumble, you'll reach the summit.
>
> Without Hari's Name, there is no salvation
>   so says Kabīr, Rām's servant.
>
> Without Rām's Name, all sank to perdition,
>   see and ponder the fate of the body:
> Yet, without Hari's Name
>   in chains he'll go to Yama's hell.

Our insight into Kabīr's understanding of the Name enters a deeper reality when we look at the following quotations, where Kabīr emphasizes the need to know the Name. These lines suggest that for Kabīr (as for Guru Nānak, see further) the Name stands for God's being, the sum total of all that He is, the focus of all that can be said and thought about Him. This insight is miles away from the mechanical recitation of names of all kinds. Here, the recitation of the Name is a way of meditating on the essence of God's reality.

> Kabīr, he who has known Rām's Name,
>   gets frail of body.
> People have not known the Name of Rām,
>   they have pursued evil ways:
> Man didn't know the Name of Rām,

They never knew the Name of Rām
and they fell a prey to Kāl !

You keep singing the Name of Rām
and exhorting others —
But you know nothing of Hari
and you wander all over.

Carrying your Veda and Purāṇas, O Paṇḍe,
you go along like a donkey
loaded with sandalwood.
The secret of the Name of Rām, you've never known
and so you come to shame.
Offering myself unto thy Name,
wherever I look, Thou art!

If the soul absorbs itself
in the Name of Rām,
Old Age and Death give up
and Error scurries away.

All my attires I've put away, all my companions I've left
through the power of Rām's Name.
Drink the nectar of Rām's Name,
of Him who is the Lord of all joy.[7]

Guru Nānak (1469-1539)

Much vaster than Kabīr's oeuvre, and also more reliable from the textual critic's point of view, is the work of Guru Nānak. It is only natural that we should thus have many more quotations on which to base our study of the holy Name. As with the other Sants, Guru Nānak's thought is not set out systematically but an excellent analysis is given in McLeod's study,[8] from which I have borrowed heavily for the present description. For Nānak, there is a radical

7. For the more than forty occurrences of *sumiraṇ* (to remember, to meditate) in the works of Kabīr, I refer to Callewaert & Op de Beeck: 1991, vol. 2, p. 1046.

8. McLeod: 1968, especially pp. 191-99 and 214-19.

difference between the "Name" of God and the "names" of God: Hari, Rām, Rahīm, etc. While the names of God may help the searching mind to find peace and focus the attention on God, the Name (a term occurring hundreds of times in Guru Nānak's work[9]) stands for the total revelation of God's being, the essence of all His attributes, the deepest of His Reality. Tracing the origin of the term *śabad* or "Word" McLeod emphasizes that *śabad*, closely related to the Name of God, is the vehicle of revelation.

> The function of the Word is that it provides the means whereby man can know both God and the path which leads to Him, the means whereby the individual may secure release from his bonds and so attain union with God.[10]

Without explicitly saying that much, Kabīr expressed each of these elements in his verses about the Name. For Nānak, "all that concerns God, all that relates to the path which leads to Him is the Word".[11] And, "In this and many other extracts "Name" could be replaced by "Word" without altering the sense at all".[12] The Name is synonymous with the Word in Guru Nānak's thought: the Name "is the revelation of God's being, the only proper object of contemplation, the standard to which the individual's life must conform, the essential means of purification and salvation".[13] In the light of such a definition we can with much more devotion sing

> Whatever He has made is an expression of His Name.
> There is no part of creation which is not such an expression.[14]

and grasp the deeper meaning of the numerous lines in which Guru Nānak extols the greatness of the Name and encourages his followers to repeat the Name in their heart. Again, such a meditation

---

9. See Callewaert: 1996, *Śrī Guru Granth Sāhib, With Complete Index*, part II, pp. 464ff.
10. McLeod: 1968, p. 192.
11. Ibid., p. 193.
12. Ibid., p. 195.
13. Ibid.
14. Ibid., p. 196; *Japjī* 19.

is miles away from the mechanical *jap*. It is an entering into the essence of God's presence in this world, through the different manifestations of His Reality, both in the physical world and in the innermost of man's heart. Such a meditation brings about salvation: "If the mind be defiled by sin, it is cleansed with love of the Name".[15] This meditation focuses not on the sound or vibrations of a *mantra* (although that may help) but on the nature and qualities of God. Only if the name is interiorized, can the devotee enter the divine reality of the Name.

Nāmdev (c. 1270-1350)

Although he comes chronologically much before Kabīr and Guru Nānak, I quote Nāmdev here because we can understand him better in the light of the observations made in connection with Guru Nānak. For Nāmdev, too, the Name is God's very essence; it is his orchard, the basis of his life:[16]

> Your Name is the substance
> the rest of the world is hollow. (p. 171)
>
> The Lord's Name is my farm.
> The Lord's Name is my orchard.
> Lord Banvārī is my treasure. (p. 143)
>
> Nāmdev has found the name Hari.
> If death comes now,
> what can it do, crazy one?
> I am now free. (p. 147)
>
> Foolish are the speakers
> and foolish the listeners
> who do not cherish the Name
> of the Lord of Life.
> Mere noise: the Vedas,
> putrid: the Purāṇas,

15. McLeod: 1968, p. 215; *Japjī* 20.
16. All quotations are from Callewaert & Lath: 1989.

They do not know the secret
of the name *rām*. (p. 148)

Ceaselessly I cry *rām rām*,
Loudly shouting his Name. (p. 165)

I have wandered for endless lives
redeemed each time
as I sang your Name. (p. 170)

Sing the name of Rām
the state of *nirvāṇa*.
Your tongue lies idle
what better can it do? (p. 175)

The name Rām redeems
whenever you think of it.
A day has countless minutes
think of Rām for a few of them,
all your sins will turn to ashes. (p. 211)

The name Rām
is my capital, my wealth.
It is a capital dear to my heart.
It is a capital that will never end.
No trader has a capital like it. (p. 218)

Donating thousands of cows
cannot equal the Name.
(*pad* 143, p. 343; also *pad* 196, p. 362)
The name is a boat,
taking you across the ocean. (*pad* 143)

The name of Hari is a rock. (*pads* 163, 166)

Nāmdev also speaks about the "splendour of the Name" (*nām pratāp*, *pads* 174, 178).

Raidās (c. 1450-1520)

The low-caste cobbler of Banaras who attracted huge crowds and shocked the brāhmaṇs is even today a catalyst for low castes in the

Banaras area. His songs are amazingly refined and have, in the original, a rhythm that carries away audiences. Again, a study of the Name in the work of Raidās is limited to a few quotations in which the greatness of the Name is extolled. Interestingly, we find *rām sumiran* instead of *nām sumiran*:

> The remedy for the sickness of the lustful was
> Vedic rituals, chanting, pilgrimage and giving alms.
> Remembering Rām is the true medicine (song 23).[17]

What is in a Name? Both the Judaic and the Christian tradition honour the Name of God with great respect and awe. The "hallowed be Thy Name" is found in Matthew 6.9-13 and in the Jewish antecedents of the Lord's Prayer. In the Judaic tradition the name YHWH is associated with the story of God appearing to Moses and giving him His name, rendered as "I am who is" according to folk etymology. The avoidance of the pronouncing the name of YHWH in the Jewish tradition is generally ascribed to a sense of reverence. It may, however, also have to do with a too orthodox interpretation of the third commandment about not misusing the name of God. In the same tradition, the Name was so important that even committing it to writing was in some cases prohibited, for fear that the paper with the Name may one day be discarded. Clearly, as in the Sant tradition, here, too, the Name stands for the very essence of God.

Why should the Name of God be so important as to make it equal to the very essence of God? Or, on the basis of what human experience have religious seekers in different traditions honoured the Name of God so intensely? This enquiry should help us to understand why the "Name" is more than just the repetition of the names of Hari, Gobind, etc. and why respect for the Name should not be limited to a mere chanting of names. For Nāmdev and Kabīr the Name of God was their "orchard", their very livelihood.

17. Callewaert & Friedlander: 1992. For the references with *nāv* or *nām* in the songs of Raidās and of Dādū (who uses the terms very frequently) I refer to Callewaert & Op de Beeck: 1991 (vol. 2).

Amazingly, an enquiry into "who I am" often results in a reflection about "what do people say that I am?", "what am I in the eyes of the others?" An exaggerated worry about what people say can no doubt lead to frustration but it remains a fact that, to some or to a great extent, a person is what he/she is in relation to the others. I am what "I am for the others". Closely linked to this is my name. My name is given to me by somebody else and in some cultures the real name is only given when the child is one or more years old, when the person is said to really exist. It is through my name that I start to exist for others. Or, for others I exist through my name. If I cannot be fully known as I am, at least my name can be known. In that name is given a definition of what I am. It is not a mere sound or an identification card. For others my name carries a set of good and bad qualities, of representations present and past, of reminiscences, of affection and aversion. The name Winand, for others, is (partly) me and is for others a way to approach me, to remember me, to visualize me, partly to know "who I am".

Since the human mind can approach the divine *only* in human categories and with human analogies, it is natural that the name should play an important role in the relation of man with God, and in the description of the relation of God with man. In the Sants' conception of God, His Name is very important but for them God is not absolutely non-different from His names (as He is in the Vaiṣṇav traditions). By thinking and speaking about God the seeker may reach but cannot really name Him. In fact, with all the names given, the Sants say, God's Name is really nameless (*nām nirnām*). And yet, because the human mind functions in categories of thoughts and words, of concepts and sounds, we like to conceive of God's Name as a separate reality, existing in and by itself. The secret of that Name suggests that God really has to remain unknown, and yet He reveals Himself through His names. As Nānak pointed out, there is a radical difference between the Name of God and the names of God. The names of God, different from His Name (read "real being"?) are given in tradition or through a guru or through personal experience.

My own favourite names for God are "Supreme Bliss (*ānandam*) and Loving compassion (*karuṇā*)", for others it may be *śūnya*, as for Rajab and other Sants, or Allāh, Kr̥ṣṇa, Jesus. The *preferred Name* of God is pregnant with meaning and has the highest potentiality of spiritual energy. It is the *sat nām* of Kabīr, the *sabīj mantra*. Although nameless, that Name can be meditated upon and enables the seeker to experience the Ultimate Reality, the Reality that is beyond all names.

A very significant term, used by the Sants, for this Name is "the Word" or *śabad* (*śabda*). Here again, we describe the divine reality in very human words. As sounds may come before ideas and concepts when writing a poem, so does the Word come before anything else. It stands for the very Reality humans like to describe. That Reality, that Word, that Name is not the external sound imparted by the guru, nor is it chosen out of the innumerable names of God available in traditional works. It is the Name coming from the Divine, full of mystic power.

"My only wealth is the Name of Hari", says Kabīr.

9

The Sarvāṅgī of Gopāldās

A Seventeenth-Century Anthology of Bhakti Literature

[1974; 1993][1]

THIS book is not only a fascinating product of a seventeenth-century memory, or a marvellous synthesis of *bhakti* literature: it is a wonderful experience as well if you can sing it or have someone to sing it for you. As we read the manuscript and automatically chanted it, immediately the good songs stood out, even before we saw the *bhaṇitā*: Sūrdās, Kabīr, Dādū.

When I first discovered this huge manuscript I was baffled by the neatness of its handwriting, the immense variety of the *bhakta*s quoted in it and its size: 1.6 megabyte, or more than half of the size of the *Ādigranth*. Only when the input of the text in the computer was completed,[2] could I grasp the importance of this document:

1. In: *Orientalia Lovaniensia Periodica*, 5, 1974, pp. 187-96.

   Also Callewaert: 1993; I give here only a few quotations from the Introduction. Some information is added, quoting from Winand M. Callewaert, "A 17th C. Anthology of Hindī Poetry", in: *Orientalia Lovaniensia Periodica*, 5, 1974, pp. 187-96. Through a fresh study of the manuscript I have been able to identify not a few errors in my transcript completed in March 1991. This list of errors and corrections is now available on the Electronic Corpus of Bhakti Texts, Leuven.

2. Elated with the completion of the huge work of input and revision, we (Prof. Adeshvar Rao, Visakhapatnam, and myself) added discreetly, in italics, the following line to the end of the colophon, on p. 520: लुवेण विश्वविद्यालये आदेश्वरस्य व विनान्तस्य संयोगात् पाठशोध: संपूर्णो भवेत् ॥ रामनवमी २४ मार्च १९९१ ॥

1,669 *pad*s and 6,568 *sākhī*s of 138 identified *bhakta*s, and *c.* 640 *ślok*s. Of Kabīr only, the compiler Gopāldās quotes, in the year 1627, as many as 358 *pad*s and 609 *sākhī*s, of Dādū 401 *pad*s and 1,452 *sākhī*s.[3] The variety of the quotations makes one wonder how a person could be acquainted with so many repertoires. Of the total of *c.* 26,800 lines in the complete work, *c.* 13,900 lines are with *pad*s of 138 identified *bhakta*s. There are further 4,413 lines with literature of (so far) unidentified poetry (of which some *sākhī*s are no doubt of Dādū and Kabīr but without a *bhaṇitā*).

It has taken me years to discard the notion that Gopāldās compiled his anthology from existing manuscripts lying on the floor in front of him. It was hard to imagine that without manuscripts a person could produce such a wonderful selection of *pad*s and *sākhī*s and classify them according to theme. But slowly, as I made progress in the wonderful world of performers rising before me from the manuscripts, I started to imagine a *bhakta* of the Dādūpanth with a fabulous memory. He must have spent many days of many months listening to travelling singers and storing in his memory whatever he heard. In the colophon of his *Sarvāṅgī* Gopāldās states that he was 37 years of age when he completed the collection and wrote it down on paper, in 1627. He must have been 14 when Dādū died in 1603, and he declares himself to be a disciple of Santdās, a disciple of Dādū. If he does not call himself a disciple of Dādū, we may perhaps presume that Gopāldās was initiated into the Dādūpanth after 1603. Narayandas[4] suggests that Gopāldās may have been "of the family" of his guru Santdās. There is otherwise no information available about Gopāldās.

Classification According to Rāg

It is not only amazing that Gopāldās could store such an amount of literature in his memory. How could he make a selection based on

3. The standard edition by P.N. Tivari of the *कबीर ग्रंथावली* gives 200 *pads* and 737 *sākhīs*. The standard edition of the *दादूदयाल ग्रंथावली* by P. Chaturvedi gives 443 *pads* of Dādū and 2,453 *sākhīs*.

4. Svami Narayandas, *श्रीदादूपंथपरिचय*, vol. 2, p. 399.

126 different themes ? It is clear that he received his material from the singers' repertoires to which a singer would perform the *pad*. With only two exceptions all *pads* have the *rāg* to which a *pad* had to be performed.

We have shown in our studies of Nāmdev and of Raidās[5] that the *rāg* tag was an essential part of the "text" of a *pad*, and that variation in the *rāg* takes the researcher back to the period of oral transmission. In the singers' repertoires *pads* appear to have been classified in *rāg* clusters: in Gopāldās's *Sarvāṅgī*, too, the *rāg* tag is preserved but the *pads* do not appear in clusters of identical *rāgs*. On the contrary, we often find in one chapter as many *rāgs* as there are *bhaktas* quoted. Only towards the end of his work does Gopāldās seem to copy more directly from one singer's repertoire: more songs of a particular *bhakta* are given under the same *rāg*. It is also amazing how the compiler remembered, according to the content, songs which in existing repertoires must have been classified under a different *rāg*. In chapter 61, e.g. Gopāldās quotes 8 *pads* of Sūrdās, and each *pad* has a different *rāg*, which each must originally have belonged to a different *rāg* cluster. It is further to the credit of Gopāldās's memory that — as far as I could see — not a single line is given twice!

Arrangement of the Material

There seems to be a regular pattern in the way Gopāldās arranged the material available to him. The basic frame is a selection of *pads*, interspersed in most chapters with *sākhīs*. However, there are also chapters with only *sākhīs*.

Not all chapters are equally long. Chapter 12 has only 44 lines and chapter 82 has 18 lines, while chapter 17, *Sādh mahimā*, has 33 *pads* and 83 *sākhīs* or *śloks*. Similarly, chapter 35 is very small but chapter 36 is huge. Chapters 62-64 are again huge and chapter 78 has 94 *pads* of 15 *bhaktas*. Often Gopāldās gives first a *pad* of Kabīr, followed by one of Dādū. If Gopāldās was a Dādūpanthī, this would confirm how high the esteem for Kabīr was in the early Panth. In

5. Callewaert & Lath: 1989 and Callewaert & Friedlander: 1992.

not a few chapters Gopāldās gives sub-titles. This is clearly the result of scribal editing as singers would not have used sub-titles during their performances.

There is also the relatively high number (1,300 or 4.8 per cent) of lines in Sanskrit or pseudo-Sanskrit, often at the end of a chapter. No doubt, the presence of Sanskrit quotations (from the *Bhagavad-Gītā* and the *Bhāgvat Purāṇ* mainly?) was meant to enhance the status of an anthology in the vernacular. But it raises questions as well. Who created the numerous lines in Hybrid Sanskrit? Should we have (around 1627, i.e. one generation after Dādū) in the early Panth the traces of Brahmanization as is seen in the enlarged versions of the Biography of Dādū (see below, pp. 173ff.)? In manuscripts of the *Dādūjanmalīlā* (dated CE 1654, 1739, etc.) I noted additions and changes of the text not found in the earlier manuscripts (1653, 1658, 1666): these changes and interpolations were clearly meant to underline the non-Muslim origin, occupation and association of Dādū. From that account it appears that Dādū was several times at loggerheads with the brāhmins. Would Gopāl's generation have tried to soften the rough edges by giving the Dādūpanthī literature a firm footing in Sanskrit? Was that a local trend meant to please the brāhmins, or is it part of a more general phenomenon of looking for authority by adding Sanskrit? It would appear that the person dictating to the scribe of the manuscript consulted for my edition, or that the scribe himself, did not know Sanskrit well. In *aṅga* 25.49 we read in the manuscript पूर्णाहस्त्रिभुवन (in the way one would pronounce it) instead of पूर्णा:स्त्रिभुवन (in the way one would write it).

Mnemonic Devices

Very frequently one can discover a kind of mnemonic device in the fact that a similar keyword occurs in consecutive *pad*s or *sākhī*s of different poets. Without trying to be exhaustive I give a few examples below:

Nāmdev, in 10.9.0	ध्रिगते बकता धृगते सुरता
Mohan, in 10.11.0	ध्रिगते रसनां धृगते ते बांणीं ध्रिगते श्रवनां ध्रिगते प्रांणीं

Kabīr *sākhī* 14.3	कबीर ऊंचा चढि असमांन कूं मेर उलंघी उडि
Dādū *sākhī* 14.4	अनल पंषि आकास कूं माया मेर उलंघि

We see झिलिमिलि in 8 consecutive *pads*: 73.1-8 (Dādū 5, Nāmdev, Garībdās, Aṅgad).[6] Even with these obvious devices, one keeps wondering how Gopāldās could link one *pad* to another. It would appear also that at times the *rāg* is the mnemonic device, especially with a *rāg* otherwise not frequently found; e.g. *rāg sidhūrau* in 58.8-11: Dādū, Sojhā and Bakhanā.

In not a few chapters Gopāldās gives sub-titles. This is clearly the result of scribal editing as singers would not have used sub-titles during their performances. Or did they add them in the scribbled notes used for their performances?

Aṅga 19, त्रिदोष साच अतीत के लष्यनि की पारष has four sub-titles:

नाम माला ग्रंथ
अवलिसिलूक ग्रंथ
नर वैबोध ग्रंथ
चौपई अतीत के अंग की चौपई; अभै मात्रा ग्रंथ.[7]

The Sarvāṅgī of Rajab

During the same period of search for manuscripts in 1973 I managed to copy four manuscripts with the *Sarvāṅgī* of Rajab, who was also a disciple of Dādū (see above, pp. 3ff.). In this work Rajab has grouped thematically, in 144 *aṅgas*, *sākhīs* and *pads* from his own *Vāṇī* and of 88 identified Bhaktas[8] in Hindī, Persian and Sanskrit. About 102 *aṅgas* in the Rajab *Sarvāṅgī* are identical with titles of *aṅgas* in the *Vāṇī* of Rajab.[9] In the colophon the work is said to contain 8,000 verses.

This compilation has been edited by S. Iraqi,[10] but that edition

6. For more examples, see Callewaert: 1993, pp. 8-9.
7. Ibid., pp. 9-10.
8. Not "66 Bhaktas" as is said in P.N. Tivari, *कबीर ग्रंथावली*, p. 143 and in Ch. Vaudeville, *Kabīr*, Clarendon Press, Oxford, 1974, p. 59.
9. Vraj Lal Varma, *रज्जब बानी*, Kanpur, 1963.
10. S. Iraqi, *The Sarbaṅgī of Rajabdās*, Aligarh, 1985. For a few samples from the Iraqi edition, see Callewaert: 1993, pp. 18ff.

is not a faithful or accurate reprint of the manuscripts consulted. It should be noted that the editor also gives *candra-bindu*s, which are totally missing in the manuscripts, and unfortunately there is no detailed index or table of contents.

A comparison of the two *Sarvāṅgī*s, of Rajab and of Gopāldās, confirms that early in the seventeenth century the Dādūpanth was an important nucleus of literary activity in northern India. The results of that activity were rivalled only by the endeavours of Guru Arjan in Punjab but the relevance of both traditions for later generations is equal. In the *Sarvāṅgī*s we find a treasure-trove of, to a great extent, unpublished material; for the material that was already published I found the recension of both *Sarvāṅgī*s to be very accurate and well preserved.[11]

When we look at the structure of the two *Sarvāṅgī*s, we note that both works are independent products of compilation, differing both in the amount and the choice of the material and in the way it has been arranged. Gopāldās has titles for his 121 *aṅga*s which differ generally in wording and length from the 144 *aṅga*s in Rajab's work.[12] Arranging his literature thematically, Gopāldās has much more variety within one *aṅga*, with at times as many as 30 different *bhakta*s in 100 *sākhī*s, a feature which, again, makes one wonder how the memorizing, compilation and copying work was done. Like Rajab, Gopāldās gives plenty of space to the five important gurus of the tradition, quoting extensively from Dādū, Kabīr, Nāmdev, Hardās and Raidās.

It is clear that the *Sarvāṅgī* of Gopāldās is based on sources which are different from those underlying the *Sarvāṅgī* compiled by Rajab. Interestingly, a detailed study of the *pad*s of, e.g. Nāmdev reveals that only 10 out of the 34 *pad*s of Nāmdev common in both *Sarvāṅgī*s, appear under the same thematic heading (*aṅga*) in both *Sarvāṅgī*s.[13]

---

11. See Callewaert & Lath: 1989, p. 125.
12. For the complete comparative list, see Callewaert: 1993, pp. 14-17.
13. For details, see Callewaert & Lath: 1989, pp. 86-87.

Manuscripts

Only two manuscripts of this work, *श्री सर्वांगी सरह चिंतामणि*, came to my notice. One was (November 1973) with Svami Mangaldas, then in Kucaman City, Rajasthan, dated VS 1785 (CE 1728), with 385 folios. Apparently, this is the manuscript consulted by Svami Narayandas, when he refers to it in his *श्रीदादूपंथपरिचय*, vol. 2, p. 400. The *lipikartā* is Sahajarām, disciple of Śivdāsajī. It was written in Sultanpuri, Hariyana. I made three (difficult) journeys to the *āśram* in Kuchaman City (Nagaur Distict) but never managed to see the document. It may well be (still) there, if ever it was. The second manuscript, copied for this edition, was in 1973 in the Dādū Mahāvidyālaya, Jaipur. It is dated VS 1781 (CE 1724), with 364 folios, of *c.* 15X27 cm. Each page has about 32 lines, of *c.* 12 cm long. The scribe is Khānezād Gulām, disciple of Mohan Bābā Kisandār, disciple of Jaitarām.

The early date of the *Sarvāṅgī* (*lipikāl*: १७८१ संबत सत्रा सै इक्यास्या or CE 1627) makes the quotations very important for critical editions. If we accept that a copying tradition may in a "neutral" work of compilation undergo fewer intentional changes than in the complete work of only one particular *bhakta*, it becomes evident that this early anthology (and the one by Rajab) is important for not a few *bhakta*s quoted in it. It is a well-known fact that for modern editions of *bhakti* literature, often only a few and not the oldest manuscripts have been consulted. In the *Sarvāṅgī* anthologies we have (in an eighteenth-century manuscript) a text reflecting a particular set of singers' repertoires written down early in the seventeenth century.

It is not uncommon that the oldest manuscript material was unknown or ignored for several editions of mediaeval Hindī literature produced in the twentieth century. For example, the early standard edition of the *Dādū-vāṇī*[14] is based on five manuscripts, the oldest of which is dated CE 1779, and the most ancient manuscript on which the *Gorakha-bāṇī* (Allahabad, 1950) is based, is dated CE 1658. A study of the quotations in the anthology of Gopāldās may

14. C.P. Tripathi, ed., Ajmer, 1917. Mangaldas: 1951, is a reprint of this work "with the mistakes of the Tripathi-text" (Introduction, p. 3).

help to support the argument made by Maheshvari[15] that several verses attributed to (the legendary) Gorakhnāth are really not his but of another poet. When Dvivedi[16] edited the writings of Rāmānand, he did not consult manuscripts which were dated before 1797.

15. H. Maheshvari, *जाम्भोजी, विस्णोई संप्रदाय और साहित्य,* Calcutta, 1970, p. 422.
16. H.P. Dwivedi, *रामानंद की हिन्दी रचनाएँ* N.P.S. Varanasi, 1955.

10

Bhagatmāls and Parcaīs in Rajasthan

[1994][1]

THE desert and jungles of Rajasthan are full of life, with a great variety of small insects and numerous large animals. Such, too, are the manuscript collections in that dry region, preserving scores of small *Bhagatmāl*s and half a dozen huge works of hagiography, like the *parcaīs* by Anantadās, the *Bhaktamāl* by Nābhādās, the *Dādūjanmalīlā* by Jangopāl, the *Bhaktamāl* by Rāghavdās and other such works.[2] While the extraordinary literary activity of the Dādūpanth has produced the lion's share of this literature, other *sampradāy*s, too, have contributed substantially to the legends and life-stories. From the hagiographical and "biographical" point of view, the larger works are no doubt the most interesting. However, I should initially describe a few small *Bhagatmāl*s, barely more than lists of saints, because of the interesting view inherent in them. The smaller works that originated within the Dādūpanth testify especially to a broadminded, non-sectarian attitude. They list not only the saints of the Dādūpanth but also figures from mythology, Nāthas, Siddhas,

1. In: Winand M. Callewaert & Rupert Snell, eds., *According to Tradition*, Harrassowitz, Wiesbaden, 1994: 87-98.
2. For a fairly exhaustive list of hagiographical works in Hindī, see K.C. Sharma, *भक्तमाल और हिन्दी काव्य में उसकी परंपरा*, Manthana, Rohtak, 1983. Giving much attention to the Nābhādās *Bhaktamāl*, the author gives a list of 85 '*Bhaktamāls*' (composed between *c.* CE 1600 and 1950), 21 "commentaries" and "translations", 5 prose "*Bhaktamāls*", and 26 works "in other languages", stating that many of these works are not available (p. 65).

Rāmānandīs, Vārkarīs, Sheikhs, etc. I enumerate only a few of these works by way of example.

Smaller Bhaktamāls

1. The *Bhaktamāl*[3] by Dādū's disciple Jaggā is a mere enumeration of some 200 saints "from the four *yugas*". Jaggā belongs to the first generation of Dādū's disciples.[4] For a list of saints mentioned in this *Bhagatmāl* and a comparison with the Nābhādās *Bhaktamāl*, see Dube,[5] who states that Jaggā's must be the first *Bhaktamāl* in Hindī literature. It is worth noting that in his list of *bhaktas* Jaggā quotes not only Dādūpanthī saints but also saints of other *sampradāys*, like Sūr, Rāmānand, Raidās, etc. and 24 Muslim saints like Farīd, Bājīd, Qāzī Mahmūd.

In the first 32 *caupāīs* the earlier devotees are enumerated, in order to situate Dādū in an ancient tradition. In verses 33-69 a brief life-story of Dādū and a list of early disciples are given. Interestingly, the foster-father of Dādū is given a name in this account: Lodī (verse 34); in both the early and the later versions of Jangopāl's *Dādūjanmalīlā* (see below, pp. 173ff.), this name is not yet given. Would this indicate that the Jaggā *Bhaktamāl* is of a later date?

The *Bhaktamāl* by Caina (probably a disciple of Dādū's disciple Jangopāl[6]), consisting of 91 *caupāīs*, has another list of names for *c.* 250 saints and seers, including e.g. Nānak and Narsī. In verses 41-91 data are given about the life of Dādū and his disciples. Here too, we find many saints who do not belong to the Dādūpanth. It is likely that the lists compiled by Jaggā and Caina have served as a basis for the vast Dādūpanthī *Bhaktamāl* by Rāghavdās (CE 1660?).

---

3. Nahta: 1965, pp. 275-79.
4. Narayanadas: 1969, pp. 415-16; Nahta: 1965, p. 197.
5. L.P. Dube, *हिन्दी भक्त वार्ता साहित्य*, Sāhitya Sadan, Dehradun, 1968, pp. 18ff.
6. Narayandas: 1975, p. 10. For an edition of the Caia *Bhaktamāl*, see Nahta: 1965, pp. 280-86.

2. The Dādūpanthī Brahmdās composed six *Bhaktamāls* in about 1750.[7] Brahmdās was a disciple of Harnāth (ibidem, p. 36) and a contemporary of King Vijay Singh of Jodhpur ("*c.* vs 1816", p. 7). These six *Bhaktamāls* are the only examples I know of in Rājasthānī. They are remarkable also because Brahmdās quotes "saints" such as Bhuvān Singh, Tilokachand, Cāraṇ Caumukh and others, along with saints from established *sampradāys*. In the first *Bhagatmāl* (of 16 stanzas) the poet emphasizes that God rescues all great devotees; he lists Prahlād, the elephant, Sen (disciple of Rāmānand according to the commentary!), Śabarī, Dādū, Kabīr (in that order), Dhanā, Nāmdev, Trilochan, Narsī, Mīrā and Jaimal.

In the second *Bhagatmāl* (22 stanzas) the Purāṇic stories are told of Narsiṁha, of the potter Siriyāde, Ambarīṣ, Draupadī, Ajāmil, Kabīr, Dādū, Nāmdev, Mīrā, the elephant, the deer, Vibhīṣaṇ, Dhruv, Sen, Govardhan and (the Rāmsanehi) Dariyā. In the eight stanzas of the third *Bhagatmāl* we read about Dhruv, Prahlād, the elephant, the bridge to Laṅkā, the prostitute, Ajāmil and Kabīr. In the last verse Brahmdās mentions his own guru, Harnāth (a follower of Dādū).

Again, in the fourth *Bhagatmāl* (25 stanzas) we read about the saints and Purāṇic events mentioned earlier (among others Sen, Dādū, Dhanā, Mīrā). Interestingly, the descriptions in each stanza are very brief but the Hindī commentary by the editor is a detailed report about miraculous events not given in the *Bhagatmāl*. In the fifth *Bhagatmāl* (54 verses) we find a lengthy account by the commentator about the story of Ghāṭam's theft of a horse. Similarly, in the sixth *Bhagatmāl*, the commentary is more elaborate than the terse lines of the original text. There is for example the well-known story (*gīt* 3, verse 7) of the pious merchant who had become bankrupt but found a treasure and hid it. When he told his wife in

7. Udayaraj Ujjval, ed., *चारण ब्रह्मदास दादूपंथी विरचित भगतमाल*, in: राजस्थान पुरातन ग्रंथमाला, Jodhpur, No. 43, 1959.

the evening about the spot, thieves overheard him and went to dig up the treasure. When they opened the box it was full of snakes. They took the box and placed it in the merchant's house but there it appeared to be full of precious stones again.

The structure and condensed style of these *Bhagatmāls* seem to indicate that most stories were well known to the listeners. The purpose of the compiler seems to have been to bring together in a particular sequence certain inspiring stories, in order to emphasize the fact that God helps those who have trust in Him, that evil is always punished, and so forth.

3. Three hagiographical works of the Rāmsanehī *sampradāy* are mentioned in Nahta (1965), Introduction, p. ड. One was written by Rāmdās (124 *caupāīs*; no date), one by his disciple Dayāldās (VS 1861) and one by Sukhaśāraṇ (VS 1900; 1735 *śloks*). Nahta further refers to a *Bhaktamāl* by Pyārerām of the Nirañjanī Sampradāy, dated VS 1883 (CE 1826).[8] Finally I should mention the *Bhagatviradāvalī* of the Dādūpanthī Haridās, *c.* CE 1700 (41 *chand*)[9] and the *Bhaktamāl* of the Dādūpanthī Parasarām, *c.* CE 1800, which enumerates 335 "saints".[10]

Longer Works

THE PARCAĪS BY ANANTADĀS[11]

Some time before or about 1600 an ascetic of the Rāmānandī order in Rajasthan felt inspired to bring together in a poetic composition the different legends he had heard about the great *bhaktas* of the

8. A long introduction to this *sampradāy* is given in Svami Mangaldas, ed., *श्रीमहाराज हरिदासजी की वाणी*, 267 pp. For a brief mention of these "Rāmsanehi" *Bhaktamāls*, see H. Maheshvari, *History of Rājasthānī Literature*, Sahitya Akademi, New Delhi, 1980, p. 139: Kisandās; 140: Harakhā Rām; 143: Mūldās; 144: Rāmdās and Dayāludās; 145: Pūraṇadās.
9. See K.C. Sharma: 1983, p. 76.
10. Ibidem, p. 91.
11. See below, *The Hagiographies of Anantadās* pp. 198ff.

century. He most probably did not use ink or paper. He narrated and composed as he recited, convinced that he earned great merit by so doing. It is not unlikely that the story he himself narrated a couple of years later was slightly different, because of a particular need or bias in an audience or because he had learnt something more in the meantime. But the purpose was always the same: to sing the praises of the saint and of his *bhakti*. He sang about Nāmdev, Kabīr, Dhanā, Trilochan, Pīpā, Raidās and Aṅgad. Only the *Parcaī* of Nāmdev has an exact date of composition: VS 1645 or CE 1588. He could not have chosen more famous *bhakta*s and four of them (Kabīr, Dhanā, Pīpā and Raidās), he says, were initiated by Rāmānand. Nāmdev, Aṅgad and Trilochan were too remote in the past to be Rāmānand's disciples, even for his perception of historical time. The association with Rāmānand was repeated by Nābhā and Rāghavdās in their *Bhaktamāl*s, and by later tradition but doubted recently by P. Chaturvedi (1964) and other modern scholars.

Anantadās must have heard many legends about the saints. Already in his day dozens of legends about the famed Kabīr and Raidās of Banaras were circulating in Rajasthan; for the other *bhakta*s he had to be satisfied with just a couple of legends. These *Parcaī*s composed by Anantadās became very popular matter for travelling singers and *bhakta*s who drew great inspiration from the conversion of the saints and their miracles, their encounters with brāhmaṇs and *qāzī*s and their unfaltering trust in God who never deserted them. The travelling singers who memorized the *Parcaī*s of Anantadās were themselves also poets, capable of adding or changing a line or two. The result of their genius and creativity is a challenge for the textual critic who looks at manuscripts and tries to restore what Anantadās must have originally narrated.

In earlier editions no old manuscripts were used,[12] nor did the "critical" method take into account the fact that the *Parcaī*s of Anantadās represent an oral tradition. Dikshit[13] listed only one

12. See Callewaert: 2000a.
13. T.N. Dikshit, *परिचयी साहित्य*, Viśvavidyālay Hindī Prakāśan, Lucknow, 1957.

dated manuscript (CE 1833) and more recent or undated manuscripts. Sharma[14] is convinced that he can "reconstruct the original version of the author Anantadās, by collating the different manuscripts at hand" (p. 4). He does refer to manuscript no. 12 in the Dādū Mahāvidyālaya, Jaipur (dated CE 1636), but does not seem to have used it. The main basis for his "edition" is manuscript no. 2 or *DA* 1 (dated CE 1676) in the Dādū Mahāvidyālaya, Jaipur. It is his assumption that this manuscript is "very close to the original *Bhaktaratnāvalī* written down by Anantadās himself" (pp. 1, 9 and 14). I challenge this assumption and suggest that each *Parcaī* had its own path of transmission. That is especially apparent in the different versions of the *Kabīr Parcaī*. It is interesting to note that Sharma observed that "the scribes did not worry much about long or short vowels" (p. 10): is that not precisely what singers would not worry about while singing or while eventually writing down their repertoire?

In 1991 David Lorenzen and his team published an edition and English translation of the *Kabīr Parcaī* of Anantadās, based mainly on what he calls the "Nirañjanī" version found in an India Office Library manuscript of CE 1786. Because of this restriction in "critical text editing" the Lorenzen edition fails to point out the ideological messages found in the different repertoires of the *Kabīr Parcaī*. In my edition I reprint the oldest manuscripts found so far, dated CE 1636, 1665, 1676, 1687, etc.

A comparison between the *Parcaī*s of Anantadās and e.g. the later Priyādās Commentary of the *Nābhā Bhaktamāl* reveals some interesting ideological messages which may indicate a certain sectarian development in the circles where the legends developed. Only a few examples are given here.

14. B.P. Sharma [in: भक्तरत्नावली, (Nāmdev, Trilochan, Aṅgad, Dhanā, Ravidās, Kabīr, Pīpā), Chandigarh: Vishva Bharati Prakashan, 1982] gives the Hindī text (with very few or no critical notes) of the *Parcaī* of Nāmdev (1-5; on pp. 6-7: *Nāmdev kau samvādau*), Trilochan (9-12), Raidās (13-39), Kabīr (40-56), Pīpā (57-112). The *Parcaī* of Dhanā (Dhannā in the *Gurugranth*) is not given because Sharma did not find any manuscript; [it is given in my edition, 2000].

In Priyā's commentary Raidās is said to be reborn in the womb of a Chamār "because in his previous life he was a brāhmaṇ disciple of Rāmānand and he had gone to beg in the house of a merchant". In the *Raidās Parcaī* Raidās is said "to have been a brāhmaṇ in his previous life who committed the grave sin of eating meat". Further, when the "Queen of Jhāli" becomes the disciple of Raidās, there is a fierce debate with the brāhmaṇs. In the Priyādās Commentary there is a "test of the idol in front of a king". In the *Raidās Parcaī* the test is between "Raidās and the brāhmaṇs", no king being mentioned. In section 6 of this *parcaī*, we find the famous debate between Sen, Raidāṣ and Kabīr about the relevance of *saguṇa* and *nirguṇa* worship; that passage is omitted in the Priyā Commentary.

When we look at the *Trilochan Parcaī*, we often find not only similar wordings but even similar lines as in the Priyādās Commentary. However, Priyā states that Nāmdev and Trilochan were companions; this is not said in the *Anantadās Parcaī*. Further details about each of the *parcaī*s of Anantadās, are given in my edition.

THE DĀDŪJANMALĪLĀ BY JANGOPĀL

This mine of sectarian interpolations and variants illustrates a changing ideology in the early group of Dādū's followers. Very soon in the history of the *panth* efforts were made to "explain" Dādū's association with the low caste of the *dhuniyā*s (cotton-carders) and with the Muslims, or to emphasize his celibacy. Jangopāl's *Janmalīlā* is also interesting for another reason: he uses literary devices which sound very familiar to a reader of the Christian gospels and hagiographies. For most Dādūpanthī biographers[15] this *Janmalīlā* has served as the basic source. When trying to find the kernel of historical truth from which later Dādū traditions grew, it is necessary to consider the tendency of hagiographical traditions to conform to certain archetypes for the

15. A detailed list and short description of the sectarian commentaries after Jangopāl's account are given in Callewaert: 1978, pp. 22ff.

behaviour of Sants, telling us how they should have acted. For example: even if it may not be true that Dādū was invited by the emperor Akbar to visit him in Fatehpur Sikri, it was fitting that such an incident be described (and at length), since many saints were said to have been invited by the emperor. Thus, an examination of the sources must not only consider the date of composition but also the sectarian assumptions.

THE SANT GUṆA SĀGAR BY MĀDHAVDĀS

This very interesting document has so far not been edited. Mādhavdās may have been one of Dādū's disciples. The information about this work was given to me for the first time by Shri Sukh Dayāl Dādū (Delhi, 1973), when I was touring north India to copy manuscripts. He had in his possession a manuscript of 237 folios (2,000 *padya*) containing this work which he attributed to Dādū's disciple Mādhavdās.[16] According to Sukh Dayāl the work was written in CE 1604, i.e. one year after Dādū's death.[17] In the Memorial Volume of the Dādū Mahāvidyālaya, Jaipur,[18] the date of composition of this work is given as the "seventeenth-eighteenth century *vikram*", i.e. *c.* CE 1650-1750. Sharma[19] refers to a manuscript in his possession which includes the work *Sant Guṇa Sāgar Siddhānta* composed in CE 1604, scribed in 1910 and copied again in 1934 but expresses his doubts about the authenticity of this date:

> Dādū's disciple Mādhavdās has written a *Dādūjanmalīlā* which he called *Sant Guṇa Sāgar Siddhānta*. It has 24 *taraṅga*. It is said in the manuscript that the work was written in 1604 but if you study it well it appears to be written a little later. Yet, it is a useful work, although it is not as easy (*saral sīdhā*) as Jangopāl's

16. See Narayandas: 1969, *Rāghavadās Bhaktamāl*, pp. 735-36.
17. See Sukh Dayāl Dādū, "आचार्यवर श्रीस्वामीगरीबदासजीमहाराज का आदर्श जीवनचरित्र", in: *श्रीदादूसेवक*, 5, part 4, Jaipur, 1947.
18. Surajandās, ed., *दादूमहाविद्यालय रजत जयंतीग्रंथ*, Jaipur, 1952, p. 78.
19. Sharma: 1936, *सुंदर-ग्रंथावली*, vol. 1:3. I did not find a reference to this work in G.N. Bahura, *विद्याभूषण ग्रंथसंग्रह सूची*, Rājasthān Purātan Granthamālā, Jodhpur, 1961.

> *Dādūjanmalīlāparacī*. Vāsudev Bhaṭṭ borrowed much from this work for his *Dādū Caritra Candrikā*.[20]

His doubts about the date of composition of the *Sant Guṇa Sāgar* are confirmed by Svami Narayandas who writes that "now many manuscripts of this work are found but none of them is dated before CE 1910" and he presumes that "the work was written at the beginning of the twentieth century, consequently not by a disciple of Dādū".[21] Orr refers to this work when he writes:

> A second Janmalīlā on much the same lines is ascribed to another of Dādū's disciples, Madhu Das. This, too, is probably a re-edited version of a genuinely early work. In its present form it can hardly be placed earlier than 1800.[22]

THE BHAKTAMĀL BY RĀGHAVDĀS

This work (1660?), with Commentary (*ṭīkā*) by Chaturdās (1800) is a gigantic work dealing with about 730 saints and devotees, of whom 445 are "historical" *bhaktas*.[23] The *Bhaktamāl* of Nābhādās mentions about 600 saints. Orr gives the following description of this Rosary of Saints:

> The *Bhaktamāl*, completed in 1713, is one of a number of similar works modelled on the more famous *Bhaktamāl* of Nābhājī, written

20. Sharma: 1936, p. 93; see also p. 129. The translation of the Hindī text is by me.

21. Narayandas: 1975, pp. 5-6.

22. Orr: 1947, p. 209.

23. The work was edited by A. Nahta: 1965, pp. 1-248, mainly based on two manuscripts, dated CE 1804 and 1829. The editor gives both the original version of Rāghavdās (in bold type) and the Commentary by Caturdās. In Appendix I, pp. 249-74, he gives the verses of the Commentary which he found in a script of the *Bhaktamāl* text prepared for the press by Svami Mangaldas (Jaipur). Nahta did not find these verses in the manuscripts he consulted.

    Another edition was published by Svami Narayandas: 1969 "because the first edition [of Nahta] appears to be very corrupt (*aśuddha*)". Narayandas used nine manuscripts, dated between 1783 and 1879; he gives no critical apparatus but a very extensive commentary in Hindī.

> about a century earlier. Ragho's poem, like the original, is often concise to the point of obscurity, and assumes on the part of the reader some previous knowledge of the events related. It is in fact, as its name suggests, an aid to memory, being primarily intended as a devotional manual. It has indeed another purpose, namely to give Dādū his rightful place in the roll of saints. The main body of the work is non-sectarian, the bulk of its material being borrowed from Nābhājī; but interest naturally centres in Dādū and his followers, and the subsequent history of the *panth*. The Rosary also resembles the original *Bhaktamāl* in being provided with a Commentary of much later date (1800) which is of the nature of a supplement to, rather than a mere elucidation of the text. The Commentary is the work of Chaturdās of Fatehpur, a fellow disciple of Lal Das, the sixth in succession from Sundardās the Younger. It is now generally incorporated in modern versions of the *Bhaktamāl* but copies of the older without commentary may still be seen.[24]

The *Bhaktamāl* of Rāghavdās was edited by A. Nahta, mainly on the basis of two manuscripts dated CE 1804 and 1829 respectively. The text has both the original version of Rāghavdās and the commentary by Chaturdās.[25] Another edition (Pushkar, 1969) was prepared by Svami Narayandas with his own commentary "because the first edition [of Nahta] appears to be full of mistakes". Narayandas used nine manuscripts, dated between CE 1783 and 1879. In the report on my search for Dādūpanthī manuscripts (p. 157)[26] I have given CE 1720 as the date of compilation of the *Rāghavdās Bhaktamāl* but the date of composition is not clear. The *saṁvat satrah sai satrahotarā* at the end of the work[27] was translated as Saṁvat 1770 (or CE 1713) by P.H. Sharma.[28] However, both editors of the *Bhaktamāl* translate *satrahotarā* not as "seventy-seven" (as P. Chaturvedi does) but as

---

24. Orr: 1947, pp. 213-14.
25. Nahta: 1965, pp. 1-248.
26. "Search for Manuscripts of the Dādūpanthī Literature in Rajasthan", in: *Orientalia Lovaniensia Periodica*, 3, 1973, 155-67.
27. Narayandas: 1969, p. 898; Nahta: 1965, p. 246.
28. Sharma: 1936, I, Introd. p. 2.

seventeen, which would make the work much earlier, i.e. Saṁvat 1717 or CE 1660.[29]

This early date may be dubious; it is contradicted perhaps also by the following degree of discipleship given by Svami Narayandas in *Śrīdādūcaritāmṛt*, p. 8: 1. Dādū, 2. Baḍe Sundardās, 3. Prahlāddās, 4. Haridās jī Hāpā, 5. Rāghavdās.[30]

The date of this huge work is important. In *chappai* 347-348 in the Nahta (1965: 176)[31] Rāghavdās mentions Guru Nānak and his seven successors, including the child Guru Harkrishan, who died in CE 1664 (VS 1722). This would make the date of composition CE 1713 more likely than 1660. However, the two last Sikh Gurus, Tegh Bahādur and Guru Govind, who died in 1675 and 1708 respectively, are not mentioned by Rāghavdās!

An astonishing variety of *sampradāy*s are described in this *Bhaktamāl*: Śrī Sampradāy, Viṣṇu Svāmī Sampradāy, Nimbārka Sampradāy, Mādhva Sampradāy, Rāmānandī Sampradāy, Caitanya Sampradāy, Puṣṭi Mārg, Rādhāvallabh Sampradāy, Rasik Sampradāy, Vārkarī Sampradāy, along with Nānak, Kabīr, Dādū and the Nirañjanī Panth. Nirguṇa Sants, or Muslim saints, are not mentioned in the Nābhādās *Bhaktamāl*. Rāghavdās also mentions Śaṅkarācārya, Tulsī, Pṛthvīrāj, Jaydev, Mīrā, Narsī, Malūkdās, etc. It is interesting to note that Rāghavdās lists Rāmānuja and Rāmānand in the Rāmānuja Sampradāy. In the list of followers of the Viṣṇu Sampradāy he classifies the Puṣṭi Mārg, the Vārkarī Sampradāy, and the Rasik Sampradāy. Even the Gujarātī *bhakta*s are mentioned in that context. The Caitanya Sampradāy appears

---

29. In his *History of Rājasthānī Literature* (p. 126), H.L. Maheshvari seems to take the date CE 1660 for granted.

30. For a detailed description of the data on Dādū in this *Bhaktamāl*, see Callewaert: 1978, pp. 25-28. On pp. 28ff. I list the life-stories of Dādū and other saints, written in the eighteenth century and later. Special mention should be made of the Persian work *Dabistān-i-Mazāhib*, translated by D. Shea and A. Troyer, 3 vols., Paris, 1843; reprint by Khalil and Co., Lahore, 1973.

31. This corresponds to *chappai*s 423-424 in the Narayandas: 1969, pp. 639-41.

within the Mādhava Sampradāy. These "errors" suggest that at the time of Rāghavdās these *bhaktas*, or their *pads*, were popular in Rajasthan but their exact sectarian affiliation was not exactly known.

According to Sharma,[32] who refers to *caupāī* 555 (Nahta: 1965, p. 246) in the *Bhaktamāl*, Rāghavdās was of the Pīpā clan; he was first a Vaiṣṇav who became a Dādūpanthī. Nothing else is known about Rāghavdās.

To Sum Up

In Rajasthan as a region, not necessarily in the Rājasthānī language, we have some fine "Lives of saints" and "Garlands of saints". Most deal with *nirguṇa bhaktas* and not a few are created within the Dādūpanth. The smallest of these *Bhagatmāls* are mere enumerations of saints of different *sampradāys*, composed primarily in order to give Dādū a proper place in the lineage of *bhaktas*. The large *Bhagatmāl* of (the Dādūpanthī) Rāghavdās goes further: composed one or several generations after Dādū, this work also gives the Dādūpanth a proper place among the *sampradāys* of the time.

The *Dādūjanmalīlā* is a particularly interesting hagiography, because we find in it a rather detailed biography of Dādū, along with the typical encomiastic elements of a hagiography, like the "standard" miracles and a long meeting with emperor Akbar. At the same time it is interesting to note that — as a comparison of the earliest manuscripts has revealed — soon after Dādū's death an "enlarged and revised" edition of this *Janmalīlā* started to be circulated. In that revised edition delicate issues such as Dādū's (Muslim) origin, his marital status and so on are described in a subtly different way. It would appear that the generations following Dādū took pains to give Dādū a Brāhmanical origin, and with this bias other Dādūpanthī hagiographies also aimed at giving Dādū his proper place in the tradition of great saints.

32. Sharma: 1936, p. 88.

11

On the Way to Kailās

[1998][1]

If you are looking for research information about pilgrimage to the Kailās, you may not need to continue reading now. This is a personal account of my travel in the Kailās region, as a student of Indian studies since more than 30 years [in 1996]. For that period also the Kailās, mainly as the seat of Śiva in meditation and as a far-away "extraordinary" site for my Hindu friends, has been beckoning me. I had a chance to go there in June 1996, and in this article I like to share some of my experiences, my thrills and my disappointments. I clearly went there as a pilgrim from the Indian perspective. I was well aware of the belief that your sins are expiated if you do the *parikramā* but I had to disappoint my Hindu friends when they asked me what it felt like to be there.

We were a party of eleven Belgians, travelling on the northern route with one passenger-"bus", a supply truck, four Tibetans and one Chinese "companion". You may not travel without that "company" but the fellow himself felt miserable, having to live in Lhasa, without understanding Tibetan and having as much difficulty to breathe as we had. He spoke English well enough, but he became the symbol of the sad side of our pilgrimage: the Chinese presence. Even he stood with bowed head in front of the administrators who once in a while on the road checked our papers. I am sure he sometimes cursed us for wanting to do this tour, because

1. In Alex McKay, *Pilgrimage in Tibet*, Curzon Press, London, 1998, 108-16.

that meant he had to leave Lhasa and sleep in tents. Why on earth do people want to do this?

We travelled from the Bridge of Friendship near Zhangmu for ten days, a total of 2,167 km before we reached Darchen, sitting in a Paris-Dakar truck for more than 80 hours (several times 10 hours a day). We swallowed heaps of dust and after one week, in Shiquanhe we found water in the hotel. A brave lady who could stand the cold water washed her hair and remarked afterwards: "the whole of Tibet went down the sink!". I do a lot of exercise and till now I do not have excessive fat on my thin frame, but on the tour I lost 5 precious kilos, not because of sickness, but because the tour operator was too stingy with the food. And let me not complain anymore now.

It was a pilgrimage of hardship all right but we travelled through the most spectacular scenery I have seen anywhere. For me it was a pilgrimage, but I also had an academic interest. Kailās and Mānsarovar are abundantly mentioned in the Indian scriptures (you can read about this elsewhere in this book). The sixteenth-century "Hindī" poet Tulsīdās describes these sites with great emotion in his *Rāmcaritmānas* but I realized that he did that from hearsay: he has not been there because I did not see all the birds and trees he mentions.

There is more. When I studied the Hindu Vāstu-śāstra or scriptures about architecture, I entered into a way of thinking that was totally alien to me. It is less alien now: the macrocosmic order is to be imitated in the microcosmic world of my environment and of my personal feelings. Central in that relation between the macrocosmic and the microcosmic order is the *axis mundi*, the vertical shaft that links both worlds. This notion of the *axis mundi* is very much present in the plans of buildings, both civil and sacred in India, and I saw it symbolically in all the *chörtens* on the way. That *axis mundi* is Mount Meru in ancient mythology, shaped like a mushroom, on top of which all the Hindu gods, including Brahmā, Indra, Śiva, Viṣṇu, Kuber and so on have their paradises. Agni, the Vedic god of Fire, is the forerunner of the symbolical *axis mundi*, that links our microcosmic world to the macrocosmic harmony. That

Mount Meru, many Hindus will now say, is identical with Kailās, and that is why a pilgrimage there is so auspicious. You can imagine the very strong vibrations of anticipation when I started on this journey. All my indology was focused in one place. I was ripe to go on pilgrimage to Kailās.

Of course, I have been on piligrimages in India, to Paṇḍharpur joining a crowd of half a million Varkaris, or to Banaras, doing the Pañcakrośī *parikramā* that goes around the centre of the universe which is the Viśvanāth (the golden) temple. If that is the centre of the universe, I thought, how much more Kailās should be, where Śiva himself resides.

Those who know me well will testify that I am very committed to my research but when everything is said and published, I consider all my publications only as *līlā*, as a play. It is an exciting *līlā* all right but of little value when compared to the endeavour to search for That which the eye cannot see, in two traditions. For me no doubt the journey to Kailās was a personal pilgrimage but I shall come back to that further when I share some of personal experiences, without any academic pretense.

Let us first look at the itinerary we followed to reach the Kailās. (The A in e.g. 1770A, etc. stands for Altitude).

13 May 1996	Kathmandu (1350A) to Kodari (1770A) 7.30-12.00 a.m.; 117 km to Zhangmu (2300A): 5 p.m.; (12.00 a.m. Nep. = 2.15 p.m. China)
14 May	Zhangmu (2300A) to New Tingri (4200A; *km 255 out of Zhangmu*) 9 a.m.-8 p.m.; 255 km via Nyalam (3600A; km 35), Milarepa cave (3900A), La Lung-la (5010A; km 94) and Old Tingri (4260A; km 195)
15 May	New Tingri (4200A) to "creek campsite" (4310A; km 424) 9.15 a.m.-5.45 p.m.; 169km via Chacho La (5090A; km 310) and Lhatse (3950A; *km 326*) and Brahmaputra ferry (3800A)
16 May	"Creek campsite" (4310A) to lake campsite (*5000A; km 643*) 9.30 a.m.-6.30 p.m.; 119 km via geysers

	(4915A; km 613) and pass (5100A)
17 May	Lake campsite (5000A) to lodge (4920 A; *km 979;* halfway between Tsochen and Gerze) 10 a.m.-9.30 p.m.; 336km, via a pass (5370A at 13.45) and Tsochen (A?; km 832; 16.00)
18 May	From lodge (4920A) to campsite near lake with fresh water spring (4365A; *km 1.228*); 9.15 a.m.-7 p.m.; 249 km, via Gerze (with *chörten*; 4310A; km 1.128)
19 May	From lake campsite (4365A) to Shiquanhe (4135A; km *1.603*; 10 km. East of border with Zamskar); 9.30 a.m.-8.30 p.m.; 375 km
20 May	From Shiquanhe (4135A) to campsite near the Indus River after a vain effort to cut short across the mountains; 4235A; *km 1.685*; 2-6 p.m.; 82 km
21 May	From campsite (4235A) to Thöling (3615A; *km 1.877*); 10 a.m.-6.30 p.m.; 192 km via passes (4875A and 4980A)
22 May	Visiting Thöling and Saparam (Sutlej 3475A; at gate 3585A; highest top 3725A); 40 km
23 May	Thöling (3165A) to Darchen (4480A; *km 2.167*); 8.30 a.m.-9.00 p.m.; 250 km via pass 4800A
24 May	Day One; 9.15 a.m.-4.45 p.m.; 4480A to 4820A
25 May	Day Two; 9.15 a.m.-6.15 p.m.; 4820A via *5350A* (most guidebooks give 5600A or more!) and frozen Gauri Kund lake to 4.580A
26 May	Day Three; 9.15-12.15 (Darchen) and to Mānsarovar (3-4.30 p.m.; 4410A); 35 km at *km 2.202*
27 May	Mānsarovar (4410A) to a lovely campsite (4720A; *km 2.313*); 2.30-6.30 p.m.; 111 km
28 May	Campsite (4.720A) to Paryang (4475A; km 2.484); 10 a.m.-6.30 p.m. via Maryum La Pass (5030A; *km. 2.338)*

29 May	Paryang (4.475A) to Saga (4345A; *km 2.730*); 10 a.m.-8 p.m.; 246 km
30 May	Saga (4345A) to last (and beautiful) campsite near river (4455A; *km 2.886*); 11 a.m.-7.30 p.m.; 156 km (across Brahmaputra at 11.15 and along the Paiku tso)
31 May	Campsite (4455A) to Zhangmu (2.300A; **km 3008**); 12.15-18.00 p.m. (15.45 Nep.); 122 km via La Lung-la (5010A)

One should *not* do what we did on the second day: from Zhangmu at 2300A, across the La Long-la (Pass) at 5010A, go to Tingri at 4260A to spend the night. Half of our party were sick or had a terrible headache when we reached the (rather fine) hotel in New Tingri. On the way there, we stopped in the Milarepa cave and I noted with great interest in the murals the conspicuous presence of Bhairav who is a form of Śiva "as policeman of Banaras, and the patron of Nepal". (Incidentally, Bhairav was also present in the Chiu gompa, near Mānsarovar.)

On the third night — that was even more stupid — we made a detour to see the spectacular geysers but had to spend the night near a lake at 5000A. Manjuśrī, god of wisdom was definitely not in the office of the agency at Lhasa when the beginning of our tour was organized. It was the next day, before reaching Tsochen, that we had an experience that was very disturbing to me (this was my first tour in Tibet). I was in ecstasy contemplating the exquisite beauty of the desolate plateau we were driving through: a desert road with agriculture up to an altitude of 4,500 m, gigantic cloud formations against the backdrop of a dark blue sky and a horizon of snowclad mountains more than 7,000 m high. All of a sudden, in a place of nowhere, we had to stop, for five hitchhikers. Five young Chinese soldiers, hardly having a beard, in green uniform, carrying automatic rifles and electrical batons most probably used to torture people. The elated atmosphere in our bus vanished in the thin air of the Tibetan plateau as they "politely" occupied a seat in our bus.

We realized we were in an occupied land, where even the young Chinese military probably hated to be. This experience was repeated several times on the northern route, and was each time in very strong contract with the jolly character of the Tibetan people we met, or who travelled with us: two cooks and two drivers.

On the fourth day out of Zhangmu we did not find a suitable camping place — no water! — and we drove for a total of eleven hours, 336 km of rough road, through a land of indescribable beauty. The road was very dusty in the month of May, and that is where my personal problem started. My nose got clogged and at night, at an altitude all the time above 4500A, I had no air, because I did not want to breathe through my mouth. It was a frightening experience. After that long day, in a pitchdark night, all of a sudden we found ourselves in front of a Tibetan house (I imagine now that of course the driver knew where he was heading for), somewhere halfway between Tsochen and Gerze; 4920 A. Possibly the only house for more than 100 km in any direction. There we found four generations of people in one room. They put us up for a splendid night. No tents, no wind, no freezing cold.

The northern route is hard but very rewarding. One unique site is the row of about 25 *chörten* just outside Gerze. It is built in an immense open space, and beautifully preserved (on a "low" 4300A). One could see from the trodden path in the sand that pilgrims frequently come here to circumambulate. However, when we did our tour in the month of May 1996, I do not remember having seen one truck with pilgrims on the route from Tingri to Shiquanhe. I saw several such trucks on the southern route from Mānsarovar going west to Tingri (and Lhasa).

Like most townships on the way, Shiquanhe is a Chinese settlement, at about 10 km from the border with Sanskar. Satellite dish, Chinese shops and restaurants lining the filthy square, powdered Chinese prostitutes and plenty of soldiers looking very bored. The Chinese guest house had an unpleasant drunken official but good food. Shiquanhe, a place to fill the petrol tanks and our supply truck and to go away from. Soon we found ourselves on the bank of the Indus River, back in Tibet, 1.685 km out of Zhangmu. Having in me 50 years of Christian and Hindu spirituality, I wrote that evening in my diary:

You, highest in the universe,
  we call on you with many names.
Only with human words,
  with human images
  we stammer to say something about you.
I know that you are full of compassion,
  Lord of the Kailās,
  for every human, for every being.
Where are we going to?
To another body, or
  to an intimate union with you?
Or shall I disappear like one of the
  billion specks of dust on this immense desert road?
I do not know.
Yes I know that I am not a mere speck of dust,
  and that you present yourself to me.

Anticipation increased, as the Kailās was approaching.

The road to Kailās,
  the road of life with all its variety.
I sometimes forget Kailās
  in the intensity of experiences,
  of work, of relations,
  in fatigue and exultations,
  admiring the overwhelming beauty
  along the road of life.
Kailās goes on beckoning, invisible.
On the road to Kailās,
  on the road of life,
  we drive through sand and rivers,
  across the endless plateau and impossible tracks.
We see the yaks in the hot sun of summer
  eating what is not there.

Hundreds of sheep with a lonely shepherd.
Of what does he think in this immense silence?
What happens in his life,
  except for the coming and going of generations?
On the road to Kailās,
  on the road of life,
there is our Tibetan driver
  faultlessly taking us across mountains
  and through rivers,
there are the Tibetan cooks
  ever so friendly and strong,
there are the Chinese officials,
  unfriendly and bored.
We see it all as we spend hours with ourselves,
  on the way to Kailās calling.
Dust, dust, dust.

When finally we approached the mountains we had to cross in order to reach Thöling, somebody (who had travelled in all continents) remarked: "One should not make this (northern) tour at an early age. If you have seen this beauty of nature, you have everything that can be seen on this planet" (except for Antarctica of course). Another said: "Yes, man can never create the pieces of art nature has produced here, but of course it took a very long time to do it". On the last night before Thöling we got stuck again trying to make a short-cut across the mountains. Luckily we got stuck, because it was a beautiful campsite. Hundred yards away there was a tent of nomads, and the fierce dogs really attacked us. We chased them with stones and eventually they agreed on a compromise. Ostentatiously, they passed in front of me, three yards from where I sat on a boulder, writing, and they pissed to mark their and our territory.

During that night I had the first experience of what Kailās would actually mean to me. After all my expectations, it was sheer emptiness. Because of my clogged nose, I had little input of oxygen and frequently I awoke, in panic. I tried to stay awake to control my breathing, and I tried to pray for strength and confidence. I prayed my favourite Sanskrit *mantras* but no peace came. I tried my familiar Christian lines. Total darkness. I prayed to Kṛṣṇa, to the guru of the Sikhs, and to Śiva, Lord of the caves, with all the lines in my memory but He kept not only his third eye closed. All eyes of the divine were closed for me. It was an experience I shall and should never forget. Finally, I concentrated on the mountain I had not yet seen. A piece of rock covered by a glacier, that much I knew. No words, no priests, no traditions. Pure transcendence. I continued to look and fell asleep, solidly. In the morning I awoke with the vision of the Vaisakhi temple in central Bali, dedicated to the Trimūrti, or the three Hindu gods. In the central courtyard of the temple you can see the three seats sculpted from the rock on which the three gods are seated. They are invisible, they have no representation, the seats are empty! When I folded my tent in the morning, it was -8° Celsius.

After 1,877 km we reached Thöling, a major goal of the trek and a very saddening experience. Or were we worn by fatigue? A dusty village without toilets, a couple of temples: that is what remains of the glorious centre of nearly 1,000 years ago. Was it because of lack of rain that the region turned into a near desert from *c.* 1850 onwards? We had glorious predecessors here: the jesuit Father Andrade in 1625, Tucci in 1936 and Lama Govinda in 1948. They left fine descriptions of what was then there.

The once famous White chapel (Lakhang Carpo) with an entrance flanked with two tree trunks (probably carried all the way from Kashmir one day, across high mountain passes), was now a storehouse for wood and stones, on a floor of cobblestones. But the walls are covered with splendid paintings, dating back to the fifteeenth-sixteenth centuries. Those on the right side are in excellent condition: life-size male images of peaceful, tantric yidams. On the left side, slightly damaged, are the female counterparts. Among the most striking images are cemetery scenes that show various stages of sky-burial: improbable figures representing the spirits of the dead, wild beasts devouring corpses, ascetics in meditation, deities presiding over the cemetery. The Yesho ö chapel, dating back to a Guge king of the eleventh century, was now a heap of rubble, destroyed by "young Buddhists at the time of the cultural revolution", we were told! The nice *maṇḍala*-shaped groundplan was the main attraction of the ruin, along with the four elegant *chörten*, shaped like minarets, surviving on top of the perimeter walls.

In sharp contrast with the depressing visit to Thöling, was the sight of Tsaparang, which made our bodies climb to 3725A and our spirits soar even higher. From the top of the "palace" we had an unforgettable eagle's view of the surroundings. In Hall 1, I noticed in the paintings even figures of Gaṇeśa dancing, of Varāha and of Brahmā. The paintings were playful — didn't some of the gods smile at us? — and a section of the exquisite wooden ceiling had been restored. In the wall-paintings of Hall 2, I admired among the Buddhist figures also acrobats and Persian horse-riders. Especially a 5-m high figure of a black Buddha drew my attention: I remained sitting in front of it for 15 minutes and the penetrating eyes and peaceful face have not left me ever since. Excellent reading for the days in Tsaparang and Thöling was the description given by Lama Govinda.

Coming into the vast valley from the east the first view of Kailās is disappointing. Is that all? And why should this one peak among so many have been selected to become so special? I honestly still do not yet have an answer that satisfies me. The trekking around the sacred mountain I personally did not find difficult, except for the lack of air at night but that had to do with my nose again. Most of us were awed or shocked by the sight of the pilgrims who did the *parikramā* kneeling down, for whatever reasons, in twenty days. The atheists in our group remarked: "If God wants this to wash away sins, I do not believe in God". They did not realize that even the Buddhist pilgrims did not believe in God. More striking was the remark of the anticlerics: "If a religion can get people to do this, let this religion disappear!" I thought: "If divine energy is *in* man (and woman), what an amount of energy you gather and you will have access to if you get yourself to do this exercise. Nothing can hurt you anymore in this life, if you go around Kailās with such determination. No doubt, your sins must thus be washed away, not by an external power, but by the sheer divine energy within you". It reminded me of the extreme powers Indian ascetics, in the myths, are said to acquire through *tapasyā* (lit. "heat of ascetic prowess"); it makes them even more powerful than the gods. With that power they even cursed Śiva and made his Liṅgam drop! Asceticism and "divine" energy, a topic neatly avoided in our modern society.

When I came back to Delhi and Belgium, my Hindu friends asked me enthusiastically if I had been to heaven, and back. "Was it a wonderful experience to see Kailās?" I had to disappoint them, saying that it had been a wonderful trekking, in a splendid scenery but that it had been a religious experience of nothingness. Perhaps Kailās had one message for me: "Let go all that you are holding on to".

I should like to conclude with a quotation from my notes a few days after Kailās and Mānsarovar:

We have seen the extraordinary beauty of nature,
  and ruins of once flourishing kingdoms
  with exquisite murals in a setting I saw never before.
We have seen Kailās,
but what will above all stay in my memory is
  the seemingly carefree generosity,
  the readiness to help and
  the lack of complexity
of the Tibetan people.
They are worthy to live in this land.

Part II
Summaries of Published Books
by
Winand M. Callewaert
(from 1989 to 2009)[1]

1. For the complete bibliographical list of Winand M. Callewaert, see http://www.arts.kuleuven.be/caies/wcal.htm

12

The Hindī Biography of Dādūdayāl[1]

[1988]

THE earliest source for the biography of Dādū (1544-1603) is the *Dādū-janmalīlā* written by his disciple Jangopāl, probably soon after Dādū's death. Orr remarks that "the original Life Story may perhaps be dated between 1610 and 1620 and its final revision about 1720-30".[2] I have no arguments to comment on this date, except that the "final revision" means "enlarged version as is seen in later manuscripts". The work was edited "on the basis of seven mss." and published by Sukh Dayāl Dadu (Jaipur, 1947; hereafter referred to as "SDD"). At the end of the *Dādū-janmalīlā* Jangopāl writes about himself:

> I am the devotee Gopāl, an ascetic and a *baniyā*. My true guru is Dādū, the merciful one. It was my great good fortune that I found shelter with him. I sang the praises of that greatest of saints.
>
> — 16.28

When he sat down to write his *Life-story of Dādū Dayāl*, around 1620, he could not have imagined that his text would ever be reproduced by computer, at the end of the twentieth century and the very idea of a critical edition probably never occurred to him: scribes were not supposed to make mistakes while copying; they certainly did not alter the text on purpose or add anything.

His *Janmalīlā* as it is now found in the manuscripts is a goldmine of sectarian interpolations and variants, illustrating the growing

1. Callewaert: 1988.
2. Orr: 1947.

biases in the early group of Dādū's followers. Very soon — one manuscript with the "expanded version" is dated CE 1654 — in the history of the *panth* efforts were made to "explain" Dādū's association with the low caste of *dhuniyās* and with Muslims, or to emphasize his celibacy.

The *Dādū-janmalīlā* is interesting for another reason as well: it uses literary devices which sound very familiar to a reader of the Christian gospels and hagiographies. Is mine the first complete English translation? In his *Memo. on Bhasha Literature*[3] Rev. John Traill wrote from Jaipur, in 1884:

> I must revise the translations of Dādū's Bani of 20,000 lines and his life by Jangopāl of 3,000 lines, for lately I got a very old copy of the Bani. It was written 231 years ago (i.e. CE 1650) and differs slightly from the text I used while translating.

We should remember that in his *Memo.*, Traill gives an outline of the existing religious vernacular literature, in order to be given a grant from the government to collect and copy manuscripts. The manuscripts which I used for the translation of the *Janmalīlā* have only about 850 lines (see further). In consequence, we may presume that Traill knew only of the enlarged version of Jangopāl's story *c.* 1,600 lines) or that he exaggerated the number of lines in order to get a bigger grant. In fact, most figures indicating the amount of literature of each poet he refers to are exaggerated in his *Memo.* The question remains: has Traill translated the *Janmalīlā* into English? Orr remarks that Traill's further work was interrupted by his death in 1909. He was a missionary of the Church of Scotland in Jaipur. These missionaries left Jaipur in 1976 and my enquiries about the archives of the Church (now Church of north India) took me to Delhi, Bangalore, Bombay and Edinburgh (Church of Scotland and The National Library of Scotland). But no trail so far of Traill's translation. [Just before this manuscript went to the press Monika

3. The six sheets of this typewritten document are available in the India Office Library, London, attached to the manuscript of the *Dādūvāṇī* (ref. No. B28).

Horstmann, Heidelberg, sent me this interesting link about Traill: standrewschurchjaipur.org]

A critical edition of this earliest reference to Dādū's life was considered necessary because we find in the SDD edition of 1947, no reference to any of "the seven manuscripts" the editor states to have consulted, and no distinction is made between the texts of the earlier and the later versions. During my search for Dādūpanthī manuscripts in north India,[4] I copied several manuscripts of the *Dādū-janmalīlā*, on the basis of which I prepared the critical edition.[5] The following dates were found in the manuscripts:

A CE 1653, Narainā "private copy"
B CE 1654, Narainā
C CE 1658, Jaipur
D CE 1666, Jaipur
E CE 1739, Narainā
F CE 1700, Narainā
G CE 1711, Jaipur

Without going into detail, I can mention that the number of verses in manuscripts A, C, D and G, in manuscripts B, E and F, and in SDD[6] vary considerably.

	A, C, D, G	B, E, F	SDD
Chapter 1	18	44	67

4. See W.M. Callewaert, "Search for Manuscripts of the Dādūpanthī Literature", in: *Orientalia Lovaniensia Periodica*, 4 (1973), pp. 155-67; 8 (1977), pp. 305-08. Also, "Microfilms of Hindī Literature", in: *Orientalia Lovaniensia Periodica*, 9 (1978), pp. 185-88. A list (with indexes) of the manuscripts available on film with me is published in Winand M. Callewaert and Lieve de Brabandere, "Nirguṇa Literature on Microfilm in Leuven", in: *IAVRI* (International Association of the Vrindavan Research Institute) *Bulletin*, 9 (1980), pp. 28-48.
5. Callewaert: 1988. For more details, see Introduction pp. 11-31; English translation pp. 33-88; Critical edition pp. 89-125; Concordance pp. 127-76.
6. Sukh Dayāl Dadu, ed., *श्रीदादूजन्मलीलापरची* (with a brief commentary, in Hindī), Jaipur, 1947, pp. 2-3.

Chapter 2	18	21	26
Chapter 3	25	29	37
Chapter 4	22	48	59
Chapter 5	28	36	37
Chapter 6	28	28	40
Chapter 7	28	42	53
Chapter 8	24	47	61
Chapter 9	27	43	56
Chapter 10	28	32	40
Chapter 11	21	32	42
Chapter 12	29	34	43
Chapter 13	31	44	56
Chapter 14	34	43	53
Chapter 15	35	73	90
Chapter 16	29	30	36
Total	425	626	796

Important Intentional Variants in the Later Manuscripts of the Dādū-janmalīlā

When we compare the text in mss. ACDG with the text in mss. BEF and in the SDD edition, we notice that the original text has been tampered with, especially with regard to the delicate questions of Dādū's non-Brāhmanic origin and his occupation as a cotton-carder. The earliest version (ACDG) clearly and merely states that Dādū was born in Ahmedabad and that he was working as a cotton-carder (*dhuniyā*). Thus in verse 1.6 of ACDG we read:

> There was great joy in the house of the *dhuniyā* (at his birth).

In BEF and SDD, however, we read instead: "All were overjoyed."

Then follows an interpolation in both BEF and SDD telling the story of the brāhmaṇ merchant in Ahmedabad who found a baby in a river. In SDD, we are told that this merchant's name was Lodīrām. This name is also found in the Rāghavdās *Bhaktamāl*.

In v. 1.16 we read in mss. ACDG: "He carded cotton", for which mss. BEF give: "He entered the state of *sahaj*".

In chapter 2 the encounter with the *qāzī* from Ajmer provokes a discussion which may imply Dādū's affiliation with the Muslims. In v. 11, mss. ACDG, we read: "A Muslim lives by the Divine Word". If this is a definition of the behaviour expected from Dādū, it is neatly avoided in mss. BEF: "without the Divine Word, one cannot go to heaven".

Yet another example of a "correction" is found in the context of a burglary in Dādū's house. In verses 3.9-10 of mss. ACDG we read:

> When the thief found threads (of cotton) the family awoke;
> (Dādū's) mother and wife said. . . .

In mss. BEF and SDD we find instead:

> When the thief found books, the saints awoke; the saints and disciples said. . . .

Verse 4.5b ("he went on carding cotton") in mss. ACDG is missing in both mss. BEF and in SDD. We find hardly any variant in the next chapters, till surprisingly the issue of cotton-carding is raised in the presence of the Emperor Akbar. For "Working hard day and night, there are plenty of cotton-carders in Sīkrī" (in mss. ACDG), we read in mss. BEF: "Roaming around in a holy dress, there are many beggars in Sīkrī" (7.12).

The terms used in the interpolations of mss. BEF to denote Dādū's birth clearly suggest that he was of divine origin:

> He transformed His body and appeared in the form of a child;
> He descended (*avatār līnā*) — v. 1.6.4-5

In verse 1.7 of mss. ACDG we read:

> When he was eleven years old, *bābā būḍhā* appeared to him.

In mss. BEF we read:

> Hari appeared to him in the form of an old man (*būḍhai rūpa*).

The term *būḍhā* may be used in its literal, non-specific sense meaning "an old man"; it may also be an actual name, or it may designate a particular person bearing the name as a title of respect. There is no certainty about the identity of this person but there is definitely a difference between the reading *bābā būḍhā* (in the earliest version, mss. ACDG) and the literal meaning of *būḍhā* (as in the mss. BEF). This difference is emphasized by the fact that Dādū's second-generation disciple Sundardās, when tracing the origin of the Dādūpanth back to Brahmā, calls Dādū's preceptor "Vr̥ddhānanda". Discussing the identity of Dādū's spiritual preceptor, Orr remarks:

> the belief that Buddhan was a historical person is very general among members of the Panth. We have incontrovertible evidence of the presence in Sāmbhar (where Dādū stayed at one time) in the time of Akbar, of a Muhammedan saint of this name, whose lineal descendants still have their home in Sāmbhar.[7]

Variants in v. 10.15 of the *Dādū-janmalīlā* point to a very interesting turn in interpretation in the early *panth*. It looks as if there was very soon a tendency among Dādū's followers to adopt children at an early age. According to the reading in mss. ACDG Dādū sees this custom as a condemnation of child-marriages leading to widowhood (see v. 10.18). "One should not impose marriage on young persons who will get the blame" (mss. ACDG). In the revised version (mss. BEF) the argument is less sharp: "The king listened quietly, with folded hands".

Additions and Omissions in Mss BEF

The additions refer to more miracles or give a special interpretation of a controversial issue. Often the interpolated verses do not fit in the flow of the narrative, or in the numbering of the verses. To the sober report in mss. ACDG about Dādū's birth (v. 1.5), mss. BEF add 3 verses, hinting at the *avatār* aspect of Dādū's appearance:

---

7. Orr: 1947, p. 54.

> He appeared in a body, . . . for the sake of devotion Hari began this *līlā* . . . , the suffering world found new life . . . , holy persons appear at Hari's order, and fulfilling their task of devotion they enter again into Hari.

After v. 1.6 ("there was joy in the house of the cotton-carder"), we find nine additional verses in mss. BEF, with the account of the miraculous adoption by a merchant in Ahmedabad (his name is, however, not given):

> He transformed His body into the form of a child, . . . He became an *avatār*. . .

V. 1.11: The initiation is symbolically described through a roll of *pān*, and mss. BEF add: "He appeared everywhere and all creatures started to sing dādū dādū".

V. 2.22: The encounter with Siddhas is related only in mss. BEF.

In chapter 4 we see the painstaking efforts made in the enlarged version to "explain" Dādū's association with the low-caste *dhuniyā*s. In mss. ACDG we read clearly and unambiguously:

> At first he lived as a cotton-carder but later he accepted food as alms. — v. 4.3b

> He never stopped carding cotton, when ordinary people or even kings came to see him; he went on carding cotton, sitting at the head of his bed, although the *dhuniyā* caste is considered mean. — v. 4.5ab

In mss. BEF great pains are taken to compare Dādū to Kabīr and to suggest that Dādū, too, tried to associate with the lower castes in order to avoid crowds. Apparently very soon in the early *panth*, the relationship with the *dhuniyā*s was considered not fitting to Dādū's status as a guru.

In chapters 5-8 is given the dialogue between Dādū and the Emperor Akbar and people at his court. The additions here are of a different kind, emphasizing Dādū's superiority, even over Akbar.

With folded hands Akbar bowed his head:

Never have I heard such a reply.
I questioned him on the six systems
and nobody ever gave me such an answer. — 5.27:2

From that moment Akbar stopped hurting living beings,
since he had found Dādū, the excellent *pīr*.
He made his decision into a religious law,
that no one should hurt living beings. — 7.25:1

Via a secret road Dādū went to the emperor, who was greatly astonished at what he saw. A strange throne appeared in the sky, radiating bright light and splendid beauty. Svāmījī sat on it, like the Highest-above-all, the Indweller.

Akbar was terrified: "Who can know the ways of Dādū"?
The emperor came down from his throne, bowing low:
"You are the Master, I am your slave". With this miraculous
display, the ignorance of the emperor disappeared:
"I am satisfied, God has appeared, my doubts have gone".
— 7.25:1-11

One day, in the Himalayas, King Bīrbal was caught in an avalanche. It happened in a valley of Kashmir, where one should not make noise.

Not giving attention, the king had shouted and the snow came down with deafening noise. Remembering his promise, Dādū rescued him without delay.

Earlier, King Bīrbal had put his head on Dādū's feet, and had asked for total protection.

If anyone seeks Dādū's protection, he will not fail to find the ultimate state.

An interesting omission in mss. BEF (v. 9.1b) makes an ambiguous context to be understood in a particular (sectarian) way. In the first lines of chapter 9, the account leaves us with the vague impression that Dādū's fatherhood is, like so many events in his life, the result of God's "unknown ways". The addition in mss. BEF of 9.1:2 clearly points to a miraculous intervention and that is precisely the interpretation still current in the modern Dādūpanth.

> Dādū gave (to his wife) two cloves and two pepper-corns. The ways of Svāmījī are not known. A real miracle happened: she became pregnant and four children were born.

The next line (9.1b, missing in mss. BEF: "How were Svāmījī's children born, through a gift or in the human way?") suggests that we cannot know how one "gets" a child. Does the vague, first line of chapter nine suggest that, at the time of composition of the *Dādū-janmalīlā*, two theories were current in the developing *panth*? One: Dādū had children in a human way, and Two: his children were conceived miraculously. I should add that it is not at all surprising that the early followers used the literary device of a "special birth" to emphasize Dādū's greatness. Isn't that a popular device in all religions? Or should we, already at this stage, look for traces of asceticism in the early *panth*?

In the last chapters of the *Dādū-janmalīlā*, we find a few interesting interpolations (in mss. BEF), which emphasize the divine aspect of Dādū's personality:

> Dādūjī said: "Brothers, keep my body and for whatever you ask, you shall get a reply.
> If you fear that my corpse will smell, remember that it is not composed of the five elements.
> If anybody still doubts, let him rub his hand on my body and see.
> My body is not real, like a reflection in a mirror."
> When they rubbed their hand over his body they felt it was like a flame from a lamp.
> They saw his body but could not grasp it with their hands and they were astonished. — 15.18: 4ff.

> When there were no waters and no sun,
> even then Dādūdās already existed. — 15.18: 21

More than 100 disciples, devotees and ascetics are mentioned in *Dādū-janmalīlā* (pp. 25-27) and a summary of Dādū's life is given at the end of Jangopāl's account (16.26f.):

> Dādū spent twelve years as a child.
> Then he met his guru who appeared before him.

In 1573 he came to Sāmbhar and in 1575 Garībdās was born.
In 1585 he met Emperor Akbar and in 1593 he went to Kalyāṇpur.
In 1602 he came to the town of Narainā and in 1603 he became one with Rām.

13

The Hindī Songs of Nāmdev[1]

THIS book does not give the answers some may be looking for. It is not definitive about Nāmdev's date and place of birth (1270-1350?) or of his *samādhi*, about the exact number of *pad*s sung by him (in Hindī), or about "his" language, when and if he travelled through north India. Perhaps we should not even be interested in these facts, convinced that the grapes are sour.

Very illuminating, however, is the historical "exercise" presented in Chapter 1. Starting with a brief enumeration of miracles in the earliest written source (Anantadās: 1588), the hagiographical writings, as time goes on, even mention his exact date of birth (Singh: 1906) and even give a description of his previous birth. Of course, there is one "early" source which cannot be properly classified in our chronological list: the Marathi *abhaṅga*s attributed to Nāmdev and his servant-disciple Janābāī (edited in Avate: 1908, or even earlier in Tatya: 1894). If all the *abhaṅga*s relating to Nāmdev's life were also composed by him, we would be out of the woods. But most *abhaṅga*s probably are not composed by him; quite a few certainly are not. Till we see a critical edition of the Marathi *abhaṅga*s, we cannot date the information found in them. I suggest that there is a relation between the oral tradition from which Mahipati (1762) drew his information and the period when the *Tīrthāvalī* (of Nāmdev?) was written. But that remains a challenging topic for manuscript hunters and text editors.

1. Callewaert & Lath: 1989.

The personality of Nāmdev has constantly eluded us, from the day I started to copy manuscripts with his Hindī *pads* in 1973, through our initiation into the computer age in 1980, up to the present [1985] when 125 *pads* are presented in English translation, selected from our critical edition of 258 *pads*. Seventy-five *pads* are not even critically edited, because they occur only in the *Ādigranth* (36) or only in one manuscript (39).

In Chapters 2 and 3 we describe the Rājasthānī manuscripts in which we found the 258 Hindī *pads* attributed to Nāmdev. Even if we do not go beyond this question of attribution "to Nāmdev", around 1600 when the scribal tradition started, we do get close to early musical repertoires. Relying on our feeling for the way in which musical repertoires were handled and on a mathematical analysis made by the computer, we selected poems which we know were certainly popular around 1550 and probably even before that.

This was only the first thrill in the often dreary task of editing the texts: we caught scribes tampering with the text as well as musicians adjusting the lines to their mood, genius and audience. And in the forest of books about Nāmdev, we know this for certain: the *pads* attributed to Nāmdev in the manuscripts (dated 1582 and later), have not survived unchanged during the possibly 250 years of musical transmission. The variants we find in the manuscripts are to a great extent musical, and often of minor importance. And, the mixture of both musical and scribal variants make all attempts futile to construct a classical stemma.

We give in Chapter 4 a selection of 125 *pads* in English translation. Specialists have read in Nāmdev's Hindī *pads* the experience of a mature mystic, who "must have come to the Punjab at a later age". What we see is some of the earliest Hindī *bhakti pads* sung in Rajasthan and Punjab. These *pads* greatly influenced later trends and *bhaktas*, including Kabīr. When in the Dādūpanth there was a need to go back to the sources and the idea of a *Pañcavāṇī* came up, it was Nāmdev who was presented as the earliest *bhakta*. This mystical poetry is now for the first time available in an English translation, based on a critical edition of the earliest Rājasthānī manuscripts.

In Chapter 5 we give the "critical edition", based on the "musical" and "scribal" versions at hand.

. . .

One sometimes wonders whether looking for manuscripts isn't a waste of time and energy. One peers through catalogues and handwritten lists, corresponds for years, travels in buses, drinks tea again and again, finds temples and institutions open but the person-in-charge absent. Eventually one can copy old manuscripts on film [in the 1980s!] and spend hours at the reading machine. The editors of the *New Oxford Complete Shakespeare* (1986) define the task of editing as "a total waste of time which periodically reconstructs our image of the past". Of course, they did prepare a new edition, leaving out even some very popular passages.

But why bother? Why do we engage in the "waste of time" of re-editing *pad*s sung in the fourteenth-sixteenth centuries and committed to writing after a long period of oral transmission? Certainly, it does no harm to periodically stir up the academic and sectarian complacency and to remind ourselves that the *pad*s we hear and read have been mediated by unknown singers and (usually) known scribes. Very few such transmitters passed on the songs of a *bhakta* without changing them. Musicians adjusted the poetic line to suit the rhythm and adapted the language for the convenience of the audience, as they went from village to village, from one region to another. And then the scribes took over, while the oral tradition, too, continued, adding and changing.

. . .

What do we know about Nāmdev? Rarely have critical questions been asked about the authenticity of the biographical data now so abundantly available in editions of Sant literature. Written material giving information about a Sant results from oral traditions which continue, up to the present day, even after the written tradition had started. The oral traditions kept growing as time went on and were regularly written down in ever more elaborate versions. I do not suggest that these versions are "incorrect". For millions of devotees deriving inspiration from oral traditions the written record is indeed less important. And, "inspiration" is as important a value as "historical authenticity". But when we look at the biography of Nāmdev (and other Sants) from the historical point of view, we have to add that there is very little we know for certain.

. . .

Chapter 1: Do We Know Nāmdev? (pp. 11-54)

It is not our intention to add another biography of Nāmdev to the long list of existing studies. That would be easy but useless. We would then quote all existing (contradictory) opinions and at best we would produce a few concluding remarks to express our own opinion about certain (delicate) issues. Worse still, we could simply make a list of quotations from learned scholars. In most studies about the history of Hindī literature we find many biographies of Sants written in a simple way: biographical information is copied from works published earlier and arranged chronologically. As a result we learn most about a Sant in the most recent works, because nobody has bothered to distinguish the early sources from the later ones, and quite a few data were added as time went on.

It is, however, a very useful exercise to study the sources which mention Nāmdev, to classify them chronologically, and to study the relationships among the data about him. As a result, one notices not only that there are no written sources preserved which antedate the end of the sixteenth century, or roughly 300 years after Nāmdev but also that in the earliest sources very little is said. And what is said is generally of a miraculous order.

. . .

The earliest dated sources — all Hindī (Anantadās: 1588; Nābhādās: 1600 and *Gurugranth*: 1604) — mention only miracles.

. . .

The second wave of biographical *writing* may be roughly placed in the second half of the eighteenth century (Mahipati: 1762, who "wrote from books before him, and from the oral tradition").

. . .

The first mention of Nāmdev's association with Jñāndev is in Mahipati (1762).

Chapter 2: Musicians and Scribes (pp. 55-117)

The *geyavikār* (or "change brought about by a singer") is modelled after the *sāmavikāra* of Vedic times; it was coined in a tradition which gave much attention to textual transformations due to singing.

. . .

We noted several kinds of singer's modifications: inversion of *antarā*s, addition of short phrases or syllables, fillers, "additions" and the diferent approach to the refrain (*ṭek*).

. . .

Orthography in the manuscripts (pp. 111-17). Every scribe of a manuscript had his own particular handwriting. We had the letters in several manuscripts scrupulously copied via a projection of the manuscript films on paper. In some cases the definition of several letters was possible only through induction, comparing the line with the parallel passage in other manuscripts. This list may be helpful for the reading of a difficult letter when parallel manuscripts are not available. For a sample, see p. 188.

. . .

On pp. 119-42 (Chapter 3) we give some computer counts, the Tables with the complete lists of Hindī *pad*s attributed to Nāmdev (with the corresponding numbers in the manuscripts), with the disheartening conclusion that no valid hypothesis can be made as to the "authenticity" of a particular *pad*. With some certainty one may perhaps say that a *pad* found in only one recension was not commonly known/sung at the beginning of the scribal tradition. This may imply that such a *pad* has little chance of belonging to

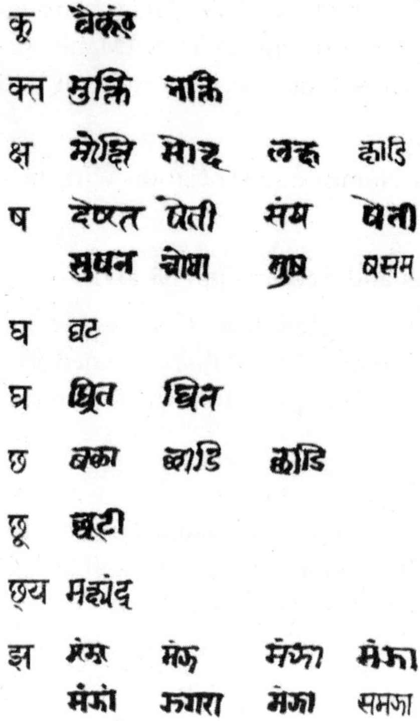

the earliest core of Nāmdev's repertoire. Following this logic, I hypothetically state that those songs which are found in most manuscripts/repertoires have the greatest chance of belonging to the earliest core.

On pp. 143-236 (Chapter 4) we give the English translation of 121 *pads* (see the *pads* marked with "*" on pp. 134-40) and on pp. 237-386 (Chapter 5) the Hindī text (with critical apparatus) of 258 *pads*.

14

The Life and Works of Raidās[1]

BRĀHMAṆS in Banaras were certainly shocked when the low-cast cobbler attracted huge crowds away from their rituals. His message was simple and clear, without arrogance and self-interest. Raidās still is, in the twenty-first century, a catalyst for all who yearns after the "Uplifter of the fallen, the Master of the meek". Humble is his origin and humble is human existence: the voice of Raidās sounds for all, then and now, who identify with that status. The fame of Raidās earned him a place of honour in the prestigious *Pañcavāṇī* in Rajasthan, along with Nāmdev, Kabīr, Dādū and Hardās. In the *Ādigranth* he is quoted as Ravidās.

In Chapter 1 we examine the sources giving data about the life of Raidās. Very little emerges from that analysis as "historical". The only elements in the life-story of Raidās which are almost certainly historical facts are that Raidās was a Chamār from Banaras who became a famous devotee and that he lived some time between *c.* 1450 and 1520.

In order to describe the life of Raidās in greater detail than this, it is necessary to refer to hagiographical sources. Hagiography, however, is a notoriously unreliable source for historical data, as the motivation for its creation is not to give a historical account of a Sant's life but to testify to his greatness. We propose that those data which are common to both the Punjābī and the Hindī hagiographic traditions could perhaps represent authentic traditions about the life of Raidās. The fact that such common

1. Callewaert & Friedlander: 1992.

elements were present in two well-distinguished traditions suggests that they must have sprung from a hypothetical common source. The common core to the major hagiographies of Raidās appears to be based on three main motifs:

One. Raidās became renowned as a devotee after he had a vision of Hari in a dream. The motif of a vision in a dream is of course common in stories of the lives of saints. On the one hand it stands as a metaphor for inspiration; on the other it may represent a psychological truth that ideas often manifest in dreams.

Two. There were contests between Raidās and the brāhmaṇs before the king. This, too, is a common motif in hagiographies and as such could simply be a metaphor for the greatness of Raidās. At the same time, it is rather obvious that Raidās should have come into conflict with the authorities, for the simple reason that brāhmaṇs had to oppose an untouchable Sant becoming famous.

Three. He supposedly initiated a woman from the royal family of Chittor as a disciple. This is not a common hagiographical motif and it is likely that it refers to a historical fact in the life of Raidās.

All these stories magnify his greatness by stressing his transcendent status, which is a common element in hagiographies; they allow even high-caste devotees to accept Raidās into their own pantheons of saints by denying his Chamār origin and granting him a Brāhmanical origin. In fact, Rajab's reference to the miracle of the revelation of the sacred thread (Callewaert & Friedlender: 1882, p. 33) demonstrates that the story of Raidās's "brāhmaṇ" nature must have been accepted in the Dādūpanth in the beginning of the seventeenth century.

In contrast to this, the life-story of Ravidās in the Punjābī *Pothīpremambodh* (Callewaert & Friedlender: 1882, p. 28) does not show such Brāhmanical contextualization, as it contains no references to Rāmānand or to Ravidās's Brāhmanical origin.

Instead, the Sikhs contextualized the figure of Ravidās by assimilating him into the company of *bhagat*s who were the "precursors of Guru Nānak". It is interesting to note that the only miracle referred to in both the Sikh and the Rājasthānī traditions is that of the "coin and the golden bracelet", mentioned by both Bhāī Gurdās and Jangopāl. It is therefore likely that this episode must have formed part of an original hagiographical tradition.

Chapter 2 described the manuscript sources which are the basis for the critical edition: both Dādūpanthī and non-Dādūpanthī manuscripts in Rajasthan (the oldest dated 1582), and the *Ādigranth* in Punjab. Of the total of 111 *pad*s found in these repertoires, 22 are also found in the *Ādigranth,* while 17 are found only in the *Ādigranth.*

In Chapter 3 (pp. 51-80) we discuss the "original" *Vāṇī* of Raidās. When we construct a tentative stemma on the basis of the similarity in the order in which the *pad*s were arranged under the heading of a *rāg*, then our efforts are continually contradicted by the dissimilarity of the oral and scribal variants. The result is a totally blurred and confused pattern, if any pattern appears at all. If we seek to establish an Ur text on the basis of so-called stemmatic clues, we deceive ourselves for the simple reason that an Ur text perhaps never existed. Or, if Raidās one day composed and sang his *pad*s, they very soon became the property of singers who handled them according to their own inspiration, musical genius and particular dialect. Singers may well have combined several versions they had heard and passed on new textual combinations to their disciples or their relatives. We may assume that it was mostly the capable singers, those who were more poetic and creative, who prevailed. We notice the consequences in the stemmatic chaos before us.

If there is not stemma and no justified "critical text", then what do we have? Soon after the year 1500 an enthusiasm for Raidās's songs gripped people in Rajasthan and eventually in Punjab. Poets and musicians sang and recited his verses, adding *pad*s or lines of their own or changing the lines according to their own taste and genius. What then can be the criterion for selecting a particular reading? It is not the stemmatic relation but the best reading. And this best reading is not found throughout in one manuscript/repertoire. But, there may perhaps never be a way to find out to what an extent these *pad*s or particular versions were also created by Raidās.

In Chapter 4 (pp. 81-104) we give a survey of the teachings of Raidās, followed by Chapter 5 (pp. 105-69) with the English translation of 111 *pad*s "of Raidās". Of these, 17 "core *pad*s" have been marked with an asterisk (*).

In Chapter 6 (pp. 171-285) are given the First-line Indexes, the Critical Edition of the *pad*s and the Critical Apparatus. In Chapter 7 (pp. 287-327) we give Index I, with the references to all the words found in the critical edition of the 94 *Pañcavāṇī pad*s and Index II, with the words of the 39 *pad*s found in the *Ādigranth.*

15

Śrī Guru Granth Sāhib, With Complete Index[1]

THE *Ādigranth* is not only the sacred scripture of the Sikhs and a unique document for *bhakti* literature in northern India, it is also a holy book that has an important place in the religious literature of the world. An analysis of the *structure* of the *Ādigranth* in no way suggests a lack of respect for the sacredness of the scripture: human hands and memories were indeed needed to give form to the divine inspiration. Therefore, to describe the genius of the human medium which put that inspiration into writing is a tribute to its inspired origin.

It was with a "mind full of admiration" for the divine inspiration that was committed to writing through the genius of a human medium, that I undertook the very painstaking work that led to the publication of the *Śrī Guru Granth Sāhib, with Complete Index,* in 2 volumes: Vol. I: Text, 1430 pages, Vol. II, Index (1-967, with introductory notes, 1-205), Motilal Banarsidass, Delhi, 1996.

Although Gurmukhī is the sacred script of the *Granth,* I decided to reformat the text and produce an index in Devanāgarī. In that way the result would be accessible to many more people who have a sincere interest in the *Ādigranth.*

The standard reprints of the *Ādigranth,* in both Gurmukhī and Devanāgarī, respect the initial layout of the first manuscript commissioned by Guru Arjan: on each page a standardized number of lines is given and on each line a standardized number of words

1. Callewaert: 1996.

and letters. As a result, the structure of the hymns, the stanzas and the end rhymes cannot easily be observed. It is also very difficult to prepare an index of all the words, along with a workable reference system. In view of such an Index I had to ignore the standard layout and reprint the text in such a way that the structure of the hymns could be visible and at the same time a reference system could be created.

Why did I undertake this job. The main reason is that the *Ādigranth* is the biggest and most comprehensive compendium of *bhakti* literature in northern India. Not only do we find in it a reflection of the high peaks of mystical experience of the Sikh gurus but also a very representative anthology of the *nirguṇa bhakti* period, of over 300 years.

Secondly, I found that the available printed editions (both in Gurmukhi and Devanāgarī) were not useful tools for research. Either they were printed in the way each manuscript has been written, respecting the page layout of the original; that layout does not make it an easy job for a scholar to study even the structure of the text. Or, the editions were printed with a layout that makes the structure visible but then no tools were given to enter into the text. In the printed text of my edition I have added a reference system in the left margin, clearly separating it with a vertical line from the text on the right side, thus respecting the sacredness of the text. As a sample, I print page 1, the beginning of the Japu (that vertical line is not here):

1 ओ सतिनामु करता पुरखु निरभउ निरवैरु
अकाल मूरति अजूनि सैभं गुर प्रसादि ॥

॥ जपु ॥

1ज०1-1 आदि सचु जुगादि सचु॥ है भी सचु नानक होसी भी सचु ॥ 1 ॥
1ज०1-2 सोचै सोचि न होवई जे सोची लख वार ॥
1ज०1-3 चुपै चुप न होवई जे लाइ रहा लिव तार ॥
1ज०1-4 भुखिआ भुख न उतरी जे बंना पुरीआ भार ॥
1ज०1-5 सहस सिआणपा लख होहि त इक न चलै नालि ॥
1ज०1-6 किव सचिआरा होईऐ किव कूड़ै तुटै पालि ॥

1ज०1-7 हुकमि रजाई चलणा नानक लिखिआ नालि ॥ 1 ॥
1ज०2-1 हुकमी होवनि आकार हुकमु न कहिआ जाई ॥
1ज०2-2 हुकमी होवनि जीअ हुकमि मिलै वडिआई ॥
1ज०2-3 हुकमी उतमु नीचु हुकमि लिखि दुख सुख पाईअहि ॥
1ज०2-4 इकना हुकमी बखसीस इकि हुकमी सदा भवाईअहि ॥
1ज०2-5 हुकमै अंदरि सभु को बाहरि हुकम न कोइ ॥
1ज०2-6 नानक हुकमै जे बुझै त हउमै कहै न कोइ ॥ 2 ॥
1ज०3-1 गावै को ताणु होवै किसै ताणु॥ गावै को दाति जाणै नीसाणु॥
1ज०3-2 गावै को गुण वडिआईआ चार॥ गावै को विदिआ विखमु वीचारु॥
1ज०3-3 गावै को साजि करे तनु खेह॥ गावै को जीअ लै फिरि देह॥
1ज०3-4 गावै

Part II (Complete Alphabetical Index, pp. 1-967)

The main output is an Index of all words in the *Ādigranth*. That should allow theologians to trace all possible references in the text and it should enable a translator to make his translation uniform. The linguist, too, will find useful material because the morphological forms classified here reflect the linguistic landscape of northern India in the sixteenth-seventeenth centuries.

. . .

In the Introduction (pp. 1-203) of Part II the following sections are given:

9-12 Contents, discussing (1) the thirteen Sants before Guru Nānak, (2) the seven Sikh gurus quoted in the *Ādigranth*, and fifteen "contemporaries" of the gurus.

12-13 Counting the lines and words, the "unique words", etc. in the *Ādigranth*: e.g. Japu 237 lines, Guru Nānak 8,352 and Guru Arjan 14,880 lines.

15-24 Structure of the *Ādigranth*: the vast bulk of the scripture is a collection of *pad*s and *salok*s classified according to *rāg* (pp. 14-1353), preceded by a liturgical prologue (Japu, pp. 1-13) and followed by an epilogue with various closing compositions (pp.

	1354-1430). An analysis is also given of the intricate numbering system in the *Ādigranth*.
25-28	Glossary of terms in the titles and sub-titles; e.g. *alāhaṇīā*: a composition of Guru Nānak, sung at the moment of death (*Ādigranth*, pp. 578-582).
29-160	Alphabetical first-line indexes. Exactly 2.978 first lines are listed, first in the order in which they occur in the *Ādigranth*, and then in alphabetical order.
161-198	List of "titles" and "sub-titles", illustrating the complex, varied and yet consistent structure of the *Ādigranth*. In view of a better understanding of the musical sub-divisons according to *gharu*, it is interesting to look at the succession of the *gharus*. Also noteworthy is that the sacred formula *1 Oṁkār* occurs 562 times in the *Ādigranth*.

The computer also did some interesting counting. For example, the compositions of the gurus have 37,254 lines or 333,584 words, or roughly 90 per cent of the complete *Ādigranth*. Nearly one-third of the text consists of the compositions of the compiler Guru Arjan.

16

Rāmcaritmānas Word-Index[1]

TILL the end of the twentieth century, no practical index was available for the very popular *Mānas* of Tulsīdās. In 1937, with great care, Dr. Suryakant prepared an index but unfortunately the *Mānas* edition on which he based it has been virtually unavailable for a long time. It remains rather surprising that so influential and beloved a text as the *Mānas* has yet to appear in a truly critical edition. Nevertheless, there are at least three editions currently available that we may characterize as "semi-critical" and that show only fairly minor variations among them: that of the N.P.S., edited by M.P. Gupta; of the Kashiraj Trust, edited by V.P. Mishra; and of the Gita Press of Gorakhpur, edited by Hanuman Prasad Poddar, which first appeared in 1938 in a special issue of its popular journal *Kalyāṇ*. Since then the Gita Press edition has appeared in numerous reprints and formats, large and small, and has been printed in hundreds of thousands of copies.

To suit the convenience of our readers we have decided to base our word index on the text as presented in the Gita Press edition, and utilizing also the numbering system contained therein. Index pp. 17-336.

---

1. Callewaert & Lutgendorf: 1997.

17

The Hagiographies of Anantadās
The Bhakti Poets of North India[1]

SOME time before or around 1600 an ascetic of the Rāmānandī order in Rajasthan felt inspired to bring together in a poetic composition the different legends he had heard about the great *bhakta*s of his times. He most probably did not use ink or paper but sang and composed as he recited, convinced that he earned great merit doing that. It is not unlikely that the story he himself composed, was slightly different a couple of years later, because of a particular need or bias in an audience or because he had learnt something more in the meantime. But the purpose was always the same: to sing the praises of the saint and proclaim the supremacy of devotion (*bhakti*) to God (called Hari, or Rām).

He sang about Nāmdev, Kabīr, Raidās, Dhanā, Aṅgad, Trilochan and Pīpā. More famous *bhakta*s he could not have chosen and four of them (Kabīr, Dhanā, Pīpā and Raidās), he says, were initiated by Rāmānand. Nāmdev, Aṅgad and Trilochan were too far away in the past, even for his sense of history, to call them disciples of Rāmānand. The association with Rāmānand was repeated by Nābhā and Rāghavdās in their *Bhaktamāl*s, and by later tradition but doubted recently by Parshuram Chaturvedi (1964) and modern scholarship. In fact, it may have been Anantadās who was responsible for this association, possibly along with the growing tradition of fashioning Rāmānand, in the seventeenth century, as the founder of the Rāmānandī sect.

1. Callewaert: 2000a.

Many legends about the saints must have been at the disposal of Anantadās. Already in his days dozens of legends about the famed Kabīr and Raidās of Banaras were circulating in Rajasthan. For the other *bhakta*s he had to be satisfied with just a couple of legends. These *parcaī*s composed by Anantadās became very popular matter for travelling singers and *bhakta*s who drew great inspiration from the miracles, the encounters of the Sants with brāhmaṇs and *qāzī*s, their unfaltering trust in God never deserting them. The travelling singers who memorized the *parcaī*s of Anantadās were themselves also poets, capable of adding or changing a line or two. The result of their genius and creativity is a headache and a challenge for the textual critic who looks at manuscripts and tries to restore what Anantadās originally must have recited. A study of the *parcaī*s of Anantadās gives not only an insight in a very creative period of oral transmission. These *parcaī*s are also like a video of late sixteenth-century social and religious thinking.

I

By far the longest and in fact also the most interesting *parcaī* is the one about Pīpā. With its 756 double verses in 35 chapters, it is longer than the *Bhagavad-Gītā*.[2] It is easy to see the basic purpose of Anantadās when looking at this account: through the medium of stories he brings home the basic ideas of the *bhakti* movement. What the devotional singers tried to achieve with their performances of *pad* singing and the commentaries (*pravacan*) on those *pad*s, Anantadās tries to achieve through the stories. His *parcaī*s are a big patchwork of stories, with a few colourful threads running through all of them: the lesson or the moral of the stories. Of course, the purpose of hagiography is not historical but with Anantadās one has the impression that the saint is less important than the sermon the author wants to give with each story told. These hagiographies must have brought about sincere feelings of devotion in devotees but they may perhaps also be called texts of subtle indoctrination.

2. For comparison, Anantadās wrote about Nāmdev 46 double verses (2 chapters), Kabīr 207 (12/13 ch.), Dhanā 68 (7 ch.), Trilochan 31 (1 ch.), Raidās 230 (12 ch.) and Aṅgad 144 (6 ch.).

Even for a devotee of Rām (who is of course not the Rāmcandra of the *Rāmāyaṇa* epic), the Mother Goddess Bhavānī must have been awe-inspiring. If Anantadās uses her authority to say that "only the worship of Rām brings salvation", one can imagine that the villagers listening to Anantadās's account must have been very impressed.

There are several miracles mentioned in the Pīpā *parcaī but* they are less prominent than in the *parcaī* of Nāmdev, who is much more remote in history than Pīpā. In the *Pīpā parcaī* — and in that of Trilochan — a woman plays an important role. I cannot get rid of the feeling that this woman, the youngest queen of Pīpā, called Sītā, is perhaps the more important personality in the story. Although she has to perform a striptease in public with the consent of her husband in the beginning of the story, she emerges at the end — at least in the words of Anantadās — as a very impressive personality. Again — and this is no doubt part of the role model of an ideal woman in Indian tradition — her final fulfilment lies in the service of Rām, and of her husband!

II

The saint Nāmdev lived around 1270-1350 (?) or about 300 years before Anantadās wrote or sang about his life. In our book *The Hindī Songs of Nāmdev* (Callewaert & Lath: 1989) I have devoted a complete chapter to the discussion of the hagiographies of Nāmdev, from the very earliest (the *parcaī* by Anantadās), to publications at the end of the twentieth century. From that survey it appears, as one would expect, that specific details about Nāmdev start to grow in number as time goes on, along with the more miraculous nature of the events. Of the ninety different "data" about Nāmdev in all these "biographies", as few as twelve are referred to in the *parcaī*. These are mainly miracles performed by Nāmdev. The story of the *ekādaśī* fast and the reviving of the brāhmaṇ takes 17 verses of the total of 49, while the weighing of gold against half the name of Rām takes 22 verses (together 39 out of 49!).

III

A refined jewel is the *Trilochan parcaī.* It gives basically only one, simple story (in 31 double verses) but with a neat double meaning. It is the story of Trilochan and his faithful wife, who are so busy serving God that they have no time for their material needs. God visits them one day in the person of a servant, who says:

> I come from nowhere, I am going nowhere.
> I stay with the person who puts me up.
> . . .
> I have no father and no mother,
> no family and no brothers.
> I become a servant when people employ me,
> I serve them as they order me. — vv. 5-7

That is no problem for Trilochan but the servant (God!) has one condition:

> I am always hungry, never satisfied.
> Grinding wheat and preparing bread for me,
> where I live the housewife despairs.
> I do not ask wages, I only want to live:
> where people show me love, there I stay forever. — vv. 8-9

He even tells them his name, "indweller" or one who stays in the family. *Antaryāmī* or indweller is of course a very common name for God as well. The servant also promises that he will always be faithful to them but

> "if your love diminishes I shall have to go", he warns. — v. 12

Anantadās cannot help "explaining" the meaning of the story, as he does in other *parcaī*s as well, possibly for the less intelligent persons in his audience:

> Neither gods nor men know His essence,
> but He is always dependent on His devotees. — v. 17

Very soon the servant appears to be an expert in all trades, and every wish of Trilochan is immediately fulfilled but his wife grows thin because she has to go on and on preparing food for that servant! He "is never satisfied". And at the very moment when the wife goes to complain about this to a neighbour, the servant [God!] vanishes. Trilochan is very sad (Anantadās says nothing about the feelings of his wife!), till God appears to him in a dream and says:

> If you insist I shall come back,
> I shall stay all your life and never go again. — v. 27

Trilochan explains to his wife Haridāsī and to the audience:

> Like a servant He wanders from door to door.
> We have sinned, not knowing His true nature.
> Why, Hari, if You were prepared to appear before me,
> did You not come in your four-armed form? — vv. 27-28

IV

Dhanā, too, was a popular Sant in mediaeval hagiographies,[3] although he often figures in a list of saints, ending with ". . . and Dhanā". Four hymns are ascribed to him in the *Ādigranth*. Macauliffe, most probably relying on Punjābī informants at the end of the nineteenth century, mentions that Dhanā was born near Tonk (Rajasthan) in 1415. Interestingly, the two main events in Dhanā's life are associated with agriculture: God eats the offered food, while Dhanā grazes his father's cows; seeds for sowing are all given to an ascetic (= God) and yet an abundant harvest is reaped; gourds are found to be full of wheat. The moral of the stories is clear:

> Whatever comes in your hands, first consider it as not your own.
> This attitude is dear to Hari. — v. 5.9

V

THE RAIDĀS PARCAĪ

When around 1600 a Rājasthānī writes or sings about Banaras, what stereotypes does he have about the city and what does he

3. See Winand M. Callewaert & Rupert Snell, *According to Tradition: Hagiographical Writing in India*, Harrassowitz, 1994, pp. 88ff.

emphasize? I cannot help imagining that in the *parcaī* of Raidās (and of Kabīr) the focus seems to be on the interaction with the brāhmaṇs. Most incidents in the *Raidās parcaī* are in fact confrontations between the *bhaktas* of Hari and the ritualistic brāhmaṇs. Of course, the lives of other Sants, too, in the Anantadās *parcaī* were not spared from such confrontations.

In the *parcaī* of Raidās in Banaras the brāhmaṇs get a bad press, and in each encounter they are defeated. Their behaviour in defeat can hardly be called an example of religious surrender. Because in a previous birth Raidās was a "brāhmaṇ who ate meat" (v. 1.3) or "did not know Hari" (v. 12.6), he is punished to be born as a śūdra and all his life he will confront the brāhmaṇs as a śūdra. Because of his excellent preaching and singing, the brāhmaṇs were angry (4.11) and advise him that he

> should remain content just remembering Hari's name,
> but never must you worship the *śāligrām*. — v. 4.15

All of chapter 5 is devoted to this confrontation. As in a traditional debate, the brāhmaṇs produce arguments quoted from the scriptures to prove that low caste people should stay away from rituals (5.14f.) but Raidās gives equally compelling examples to prove his point. This reaches a climax when eventually the *śāligrām* comes to Raidās, and not to the brāhmaṇs (v. 6.16).

Five years later comes the episode with the queen of Chittor. There again the brāhmaṇs propose themselves as sole initiators (7.8), eager to get a free ride to Banaras. The queen even has to play hide-and-seek with them. The brāhmaṇs are especially furious because she received initiation from a low caste person (v. 8.2). Verses 8.3ff. are a pathetic litany of hysterical Brāhmaṇic behaviour. Another low caste, Kabīr, is called upon to settle the dispute. After this tumultuous confrontation the *parcaī* continues smoothly, until the queen arrives back home and there has again to face her brāhmaṇs "who died of jealousy" (v. 11.8). The queen does not hesitate to tell them, and everyone in Rajasthan:

> One is mean if one's actions are mean,

one is excellent if one performs meritorious deeds.
Excellence and meanness are in one's actions,
in the human body alone there is no excellence at all.
Desire, anger, greed and the nine gates,
through these all are Chamārs.
. . .
Caste and family have no importance —
one who sings of Rām is dear to Rām. — vv. 11.9-11

However, Raidās advises the queen "to make them happy, . . . , and grudgingly she decided to feed the brāhmaṇs" (v. 11.14), who eventually are converted and admit that Raidās is a saint and "we are sinners" (v. 11.22). Does one often hear such a statement from the mouth of a brāhmaṇ? At the end of the *parcaī* they even throw away their sacred threads and become the disciples of Raidās (v. 12.9).

VI

In the six chapters of his Aṅgad *parcaī* Anantadās tells us the story of Aṅgad who was converted to *bhakti* by his wife and experienced only one major event in his life: he found a precious crown with diamonds while looting a castle and donated it to Hari, even though his nephew Salaihdī wanted it very badly and threatened to kill him. Aṅgad's sister (aunt?) was persuaded to poison him but Aṅgad was saved by God "because the food had already been offered as *prasād*". Eventually Aṅgad leaves the country but is chased by Salaihdī. Under pressure he throws the diamond in a river, and a short while later that diamond surfaces "on the chest of Jagannāth" (v. 5.13).

On pp. 8-29 of *The Hagiographies of Anantadās* are further discussed the historical and "biographical" data in the *parcaī*s, the main stories and their moral lesson, the miracles, the attitudes promoted in the *parcaī*s (e.g. "Anantadās and women" — he doesn't have a good word for women! — ; the place of the guru and the unity of Hari and the devotees), the manuscripts used for the edition, the earlier editions of *parcaī* literature, the editorial methods applied to this edition, and finally a Note on the Rāghavdās *Bhaktamāl*.

Further, the English translation and critical edition of the Hindī text of: pp. 31-42 Nāmdev *parcaī*, 43-97 Kabīr *parcaī* (only Hindī text, with an analysis of the Lorenzen translation), 99-121 Dhanā *parcaī*, 123-140 Trilochan *parcaī*, 141-301 Pīpā *parcaī*, 303-56 Raidās *parcaī*, 357-97 Aṅgad *parcaī*. 399-403 I give the Hindī text of the Seū Saman *parcaī*, and on pp. 405-08 the Hindī text of six *pads* of Rāmānand.

18

The Millennium Kabīr Vāṇī
A Collection of Pads[1]

WHEN around 1500 the Muslim weaver Kabīr sang his songs in Banaras, nobody could imagine that at the end of the twentieth century he would be the most frequently quoted *bhakti* saint in north India. Even south Indians pride themselves in having memorized some of his lines. Rabindranath Tagore translated 100 of his songs and made him known all over the world. Having now prepared a critical edition of the songs of Kabīr, based on the earliest available manuscript material, it is my guess that hardly any of the Tagore songs was ever composed by Kabīr. When Bahadur Singh of Hamburg, in the 1990s, taped about 500 songs of Kabīr now commonly sung during performances by travelling singers in Rajasthan, he noted that hardly any of these are found in the earliest manuscripts I studied. When David Lorenzen, specialist of the Kabīrpanth and its literature, made a survey of the twenty most popular songs of Kabīr in the Kabīrpanth, he noticed that only one of these is found in the earliest manuscripts published in the present edition.

I can understand that a translator of Kabīr may look for a nice song and does not bother about its authenticity. But let us not start writing commentaries on Kabīr and fifteenth-century Banaras quoting those songs.

. . .

1. Callewaert: 2000b.

Interaction in the oral tradition and corruption in the scribal tradition act like fog and pollution, creating a nebulous environment wherein it becomes very difficult to find the original version of the songs of fifteenth-seventeenth-century Sants. Five hundred years after Kabīr was born in Banaras and after at least 80 years of scholarship, do we have any certainty that the songs attributed to him and published in critical and uncritical editions and translations, are by Kabīr? I doubt it more and more. Between Kabīr and our computer age lie 150 years of oral transmission (which never stopped) and 400 years of scribal transmission. We have no oral recordings of Kabīr scolding his audiences and I take it for granted that he did not write down his compositions. What we have are manuscripts in which his popular repertoire was written down, first by travelling singers, and later, in a more respectful and professional way, by devoted scribes. But what do we have of Kabīr in those repertoires?

. . .

There is no consensus among scholars about the authenticity of any of the songs attributed to Kabīr. With due respect for the oral traditions which survive till the present day, my approach to the problem of authenticity starts with a search for the earliest manuscripts. Even if that approach, in the case of Kabīr, may not give us 100 per cent certainty about which songs are authentic and which are definitely not, at least it can question the claims made in the current editions. I argue that with certainty we can only say that the version of Kabīr's songs found in the seventeenth-century manuscripts is the version commonly used and sung by singers at that moment. And secondly, the *pad*s which occur in most repertoires, in different regions, have a better chance of having been composed by Kabīr.

The first attested written document with Kabīr's sayings is dated 1572, written no doubt within the ongoing oral tradition. I argue that

One. Kabīr very soon was "appropriated" by interested parties (from the Gorakhnāthīs and the Rāmānandīs in the seventeenth century to the brāhmaṇs like Hazari P. Dwivedi or other social groups in the twentieth century) for their own ideological purpose or benefit. The corpus of songs with Kabīr's name increased accordingly. This may be compared to the situation of Mīrābāī (*c.* 1503-46) who may have composed 100 songs but at the end of the twentieth century there should be as many as 5,197 songs with her name available (see above, pp. 104ff.).

Two. Among the *pad*s in the *Vāṇī* of Kabīr we can earmark those that may have been popular in the repertoires around 1550, that is possibly two generations after the death of Kabīr and one generation before the first manuscripts still preserved now were written. The norm is "occurrence" in Punjab and/or Rajasthan.

When everything is said and done, one question remains: how could Kabīr become so charismatic that many devotees, possibly during his lifetime and definitely after his death, were happy to insert his name as *bhaṇitā* in their own compositions and let those songs circulate with his name, not their own? What was his genius that eventually was changed into a social consciousness strongly influencing later generations? If in the twentieth century many singers may perhaps not even know who the original Kabīr was, why are they, too, happy to include their own compositions in the repertoires that are performed in his name? What we have here is a social strategy by which certain ideas are promoted using the charismatic name of a person who as such ceased to exist long ago, who may not even have supported the ideas that are now spread in his name. If the singers in Rajasthan recorded by Bahadur Singh are sponsored by brāhmaṇs, as they are, their songs will not be as outspoken in their criticism of brāhmaṇs as Kabīr was. It is the search for that charisma that keeps haunting me and encourages me to look for a "Kabīr" we may still be able to define, that is the person who was popular in 1550. The only way to do that is to look at the songs that were popular in 1550 and may have a chance of having been composed and sung by him. This exercise, of course, in no way shows disrespect for the translators of Kabīr who find inspiration and esthetic joy in what "he" wrote.

. . .

On pp. 3-23 I give a detailed survey of the existing editions of Kabīr, and a list and description of the manuscripts I used for the *Millennium Kabīr Vāṇī* (*pads*).

. . .

In the manuscripts/repertoires dated between 1570 and 1681 I found a total of 593 *pads* with the name of Kabīr. Of these only one is found among the "Twenty popular songs" recorded by David Lorenzen in Banaras in 1991.[2] He states that "with only a few exceptions, the songs attributed to Kabīr that are most popular today are not those found in" the *Kabīr Granthāvalī*, the *Kabīr Bījak* and the *Guru Granth Sāhib*. It is in fact doubtful that Kabīr himself composed these songs, usually called *bhajans*, except perhaps for the few that are also found in the older collections" (p. 205). My study revealed that of the 20 songs labelled as "Kabīr's Greatest Hits" by Lorenzen, only one is found in my critical edition, in only two repertoires: Ms. *J* and the *Gopāldās Sarvāṅgī*. It is song 14, *rām nirañjan nyārā re*, which corresponds to *pad* 430 in my Millennium edition.

— Only 32 *pads* (or at least some lines) are found in the Shukdev edition of the *Bījak*. Of course, there may be more *pads* of this kind not yet identified by me.

— Of the total of 403 *pads* in the Sabhā edition (of 1928), as many as 396 are found in "my" manuscripts. The authenticity of the date ascribed by S.S. Das to his first manuscript (1504) is doubted by most scholars but it is an important manuscript clearly belonging to the Rājasthānī tradition (*c.* 1620?).

— Of the 200 *pads* selected by P.N. Tivari for his edition only 151 are found in the manuscripts consulted by me. In his

2. *Praises to a Formless God*, 1996 (pp. 205-23).

zeal to copy as many versions as possible, Tivari collected also the verses of Kabīr found in printed (uncritical) editions. Of the 11 "kinds" of sources consulted by him only four are manuscript "recensions".

— Of the 221 *pads* found in the *Ādigranth,* only 132 are found in the manuscripts I consulted (some are similar only with half lines). Of these 132, as many as 45 *pads* are classified under a different *rāg* when compared with the (Rājasthānī) manuscripts which I consulted. Of these 45 *pads*, 19 have also a different *rāg* in one or more Rājasthānī manuscripts. Earlier, I was inclined to suggest that these 19 *pads* may be a little more suspect as they possibly travelled along more obscure ways of transmission. But now, it appears from a detailed comparison that all these 19 *pads* with a varying *rāg* also occur in several repertoires: 1 *pad* in 9 repertoires (the highest score!); 2 *pads* in 8 repertoires; 4 *pads* in 7 repertoires; 8 *pads* in 6 repertoires and 4 *pads* in 5 repertoires! This occurrence makes the *pads* with a varying *rāg* in the different manuscript less suspect.

— In her *Kabīr-Vāṇī* of 1982 Charlotte Vaudeville writes: "The second volume, in preparation, includes the annotated English translation of 165 *pads* out of the 200 included in the P.N. Tivari edition. The remaining 35 *pads* had to be eliminated on grounds of doubtful authenticity, since none of them are found in any of the more ancient and reliable collections" (Vaudeville: 1982, Introduction, p. xxv, n. 29). Eventually, in *A Weaver called Kabīr* (1993) only 85 *pads* [and not 165!] are translated. Of these 85 *pads* selected, some are found only in Tivari and/or the *Bījak*, others are found in the *Ādigranth* as well. As the *Bījak* often differs from the other recensions, Vaudeville frequently gives two translations of "the same *pad*". Of these 85 *pads* selected by Vaudeville, only 73 are found in my Millennium edition.

Depending on the occurrence in a number of repertoires, I

have marked *pads* as more or less "popular" around 1550, that is, possibly two generations after the death of Kabīr.

Three *** indicate a high probability of belonging to a very early core, because these songs are found in

— the *Ādigranth* and/or *Mohan Pothī* [1]

— at least one *Pañcavāṇī* manuscript [2]

— at least one *Sarvāṅgī* [3]

— at least manuscript C and/or J [4]

Two ** are given if only in 3 of [1] [2] [3] [4] but including the *Ādigranth* and/or *Mohan Pothī,* while one * is given if the song is found only in 3 of [1] [2] [3] [4] but not including the *Ādigranth* and/or *Mohan Pothī.* Thus looking at the occurrence of a *pad* in repertoires of both Rajasthan and Punjab, we have

— 48 *pads* with ***: found in Punjab and in most Rājasthānī repertoires

— 51 *pads* with **: found in Punjab and in some Rājasthānī repertoires

— 141 *pads* with *: found only in Rajasthan.

. . .

On pp. 81-94 I give the lists with the numbering of the *pads* in the Sabhā edition (S.S. Das, 1928), M.P. Gupta (1969) and P.N. Tivari (1961) and on pp. 95-102 I give the lists with the numbering of the *pads* in the *Ādigranth,* my edition and the Tivari edition.

. . .

Conclusion (p. 111)

Writing about Kabīr's theology, literary qualities or unique language is a quick way to produce an outdated article. With the manuscript material now at hand we can no longer rely on the existing editions. Very wisely C. Vaudeville reduced the number of *sākhīs* she quoted in her 1993 translation (when compared with the 1974 edition) but I suggest we have to be even more severe.

19

Devotional Literature in South Asia
Current Research 1997-2000[1]

AFTER the "Bhakti Conferences" organized in Leuven (1979), Bonn (1982), Leiden (1985), Cambridge (1988), Paris (1991), Seattle (1994), Venice (1997), with corresponding Proceedings published, *bhakti* scholars convened again in Leuven in 2000, and the Proceedings were published in 2002 (Callewaert & Taillieu: 2002).

Much has changed since 1979. The Proceedings then were printed by lead letter setting and sold for Rs. 60. Now we send usb-sticks to the publisher!. Fourteen participants came to Leuven in 1979. At the Seattle conference there were more than 100. And the research, too, has gained immensely in both quantity and quality.

The list of publications in part II of the Proceedings of the Leuven 2000 Conference (pp. 233-314) has 1,162 entries. Forty scholars came to Leuven in 2000, from 14 different countries and 56 Reports were selected for publication (pp. 1-232). Each paper is followed by the relevant points of the ensuing discussion. Index on pp. 315-24.

1. Callewaert & Taillieu: 2002.

20

Dictionary of Bhakti

North Indian Bhakti Texts into Kharī Bolī Hindī and English[1]

"If you do not have the proper tools, make them yourself", said Michelangelo and he prepared his own chisels for carving the exquisite marble statues we still admire. If you do not have a good dictionary to render *bhakti* texts into English, make one yourself. That was the motivation that started to grow in my research unit since 1980. Focusing on text-editions for the following twenty years I managed to find funding to actually start the dictionary in 1996, for four years! The project eventually kept me fully occupied till 2009. Of the *c.* 40,000 words in this dictionary, I give not only the Kharī Bolī Hindī meaning or "equivalent", and the English meanings, the references to Hindī, to Sanskrit or Persian. In many cases I also give the "philosophical" background of the word. In order to illustrate the specific meanings I give abundant quotations from a representative selection of texts of *c.* 1600 onwards in northern India.

The language of this *bhakti* literature is a mixed medium that until now has not been described in detailed grammars and dictionaries, as was the case with Sanskrit. The vocabulary of this medium was borrowed, not only from Sanskrit and Persian but also from local idioms and dialects, and travelling singers adopted many terms and expressions as they travelled from one region to another. Consequently, each fresh edition in this field requires new grammars and glossaries. The language of this vernacular *bhakti*

1. Callewaert: 2009.

literature was mixed, for the reasons mentioned, and a student of this literature has to be acquainted with different linguistic areas in order to produce a translation.

The challenge in this area of research is the fact that this literature is, to a great extent, only accessible in manuscripts and little has been critically edited. Secondly, the language in which these hymns were sung has been studied only imperfectly, although a lot of progress has been made in the last thirty years. It is important that the tools needed to make the texts available to a wider readership should be made available. It is here that we should situate the importance of the *Dictionary of Bhakti.*

List of works in the database:

Input 6 megabyte; Kwic-index (or alphabetical KeyWordInContext: 61 megabyte (*c.* 20,000 pp.). In view of a representative selection of sixteenth-seventeenth-century texts in north India, I included the following —traditionally not very correctly called—

(1) *nirguṇa bhakti*: the *bhagat*s in the *Ādigranth*, the five *bhakta*s quoted in the *Pañcavāṇī* (Dādū, Kabīr, Nāmdev, Raidās, Hardās), the *Bījak* of Kabīr, the *Sarvāṅgī* by Gopāldās, the *pad*s and *sākhī*s of Sundardās,

(2) *saguṇa bhakti*: Gadādhar Bhaṭṭ, the *Caurāsī pads* of *Hit Harivaṁśa*, Haridāsa, Kevalarām, the *Rās Pañcādhyāyī* of Nandadāsa, the *Rāmcaritmānas* of Tulsīdās, the *pad*s of Sūrdās, the *pad*s of Vyās, and further,

(3) the *Prahlād caritra* of Jangopāl, the *Padmāvat* of Jāyasī, *pads* and *sākhī*s of Gorakhnāth, and the *Parcaī*s by Anantadās.

Ādigranth

AB	Benī
ABh	Bhīkhan
AD	Dhannā
AK	Kabīr
AN	Nāmdev

AP Paramānand

APh Pharīd

APi Pīpā

ARa Rāmānand

AR Ravidās

ASū Sūrdās

ASa Sainu

Asad Sadhnā

AT Trilochan

Dp Dādū 443 *pad*s
Ds 2,453 *sākhī*s
[repr. in Callewaert & Op de Beeck: 1991]

G Gadādhar Bhaṭṭ, 68 *pad*s

Gc Gadādhar Bhaṭṭ, 57 *caupāī*

Gp Gorakhnāth, 62 *pads*
Gs 275 *sākhī*s
[repr. in Callewaert & Op de Beeck: 1991]

H Hit Harivaṁśa, *Caurāsī pada*s (84)
[Snell: 1991]

HA Haridās, *Aṣṭadaśa Siddhānta* 18 *pad*s

HK Haridās, *Kelimāl* 110 *pad*s

[Rosenstein: 1997]

Hp Hardās, 96 *pads*

[repr. in Callewaert & Op de Beeck: 1991]

J Jangopāl, *Prahlād caritra*
[Lorenzen: 1991]

KBp Kabīr *Bījak*, 115 *pads*

KBr 84 *ramainī*s

KBs 353 *sākhī*s

[repr. in Callewaert & Op de Beeck: 1991]

Kp	*Kabīr-granthāvalī*, 501 *pads* [Callewaert: 2000b]
Ks	737 *sākhīs*
	[repr. in Callewaert & Op de Beeck: 1991]
Ke	Kevalarām, 128 *pads* [Entwistle: 1993]
N	Nandadās, *Rāsa Pañcādhyāyī* [Vrajratnadās: 1958, pp. 1-327]
Np	Nāmdev, 258 *pads* [Callewaert: 1989]
P	Jāyasī, *Padmāvata*, 653 *pads* [Agravāl: 1998]
	Parcaī by Anantadās [Callewaert: 2000a]
PA	of Aṅgad
PD	of Dhanā
PK	of Kabīr
PN	of Nāmdev
PP	of Pīpā
PR	of Raidās
PT	of Trilochan
T	Tulsīdās, *Rāmcaritmānas* [Gita Press; see also Callewaert: 1997]
R	Raidās, 94 *pads* [Callewaert: 1992]
S	Gopāldās, *Sarvāṅgī* [Callewaert: 1993]
Su	Sūrdās, *pads* [Hawley & Bryant]
Sup	Sundardās 210 *pads*
Sus	Sundardās 1,371 *sākhīs* [repr. in Callewaert-Op de Beeck: 1991]
V	Harirām Vyās, 30 *pads* [Pauwels: 1996]

Part III
Summaries of Published Articles
(from 1996 to 2011)

21

Translating Sant Literature
(North India, 1400-1700 AD)

[1996]*

A GOOD translation of Sant literature is not only a contribution to a better understanding and appreciation of another culture, or personally a satisfying enterprise: it is also a challenge that requires skills of different kinds. The songs of Nāmdev, Kabīr, Raidās, Dādū and other Sants in northern India were written down from 1600 onwards and had been passed on during longer or shorter periods of oral transmission, with a great influence on the life of the masses. In their songs and aphorisms the Sants preached their reaction against the Brāhmanical ritual beliefs and the caste system, and advocated a pure, monotheistic faith. The language they used was no longer Sanskrit but the vernacular.

I see mainly three obstacles to be overcome in the scenic mountains of this lyrical-mystical literature. The challenge of research in this area is first the fact that little of this literature has been critically edited and is only accessible in manuscripts. Second, the "classical" stemmatic approach for a critical edition has to be modified, and third, the language in which these songs were composed and sung has been studied only imperfectly — although a lot of progress has been made in the last twenty years. The result of my research has not only been the preservation of decaying manuscripts (on film) and the critical editions; my study has also

* In E. Garzilli, (ed.) *Translation, Translating, Translators. From India to the West*, Harvard Oriental Series, Opera Minora, March 1996; 1-10.

made possible an innovation in the handling of texts preserved in manuscripts. It has done this by emphasizing the oral aspect of the variants found in manuscripts. With this approach one can — for this literature — abandon the traditional "stemmatic" method and look for variants introduced into the repertoires during the period of oral transmission. As a result critical editing is no longer only a reconstruction of an "archetype". The distinction between "oral" recensions allows the scholar to go back further in history than what a scribal stemma would allow.

. . .

In 1971 I came back from India, after six years of study, and had a clear picture of what my research would consist of: the copying of manuscripts and preparation of critical editions of original texts, and translation. I also saw that my work would necessarily include going to faraway places in Rajasthan and to important institutions in the cities. On the basis of the manuscripts found, I would *reconstruct*, I thought, the archetype of the *pad*s I wanted to edit. Since scribes committed errors, intentionally or unknowingly, these variant readings should enable researchers to establish the relationship between the manuscripts. On the basis of these relationships the stemma should allow one to reconstruct the "critical" text: as classical, scholarly approach to manuscripts leading to the Archetype!

Indian scholars have applied this method to the *bhakti* literature they found in seventeenth-century manuscripts. For example, Professor Shukdev Singh, Banaras, editor of the *Bījak*, told me that "Kabīr wrote down his own *pad*s, and if we find a sufficient number of manuscripts we should be able to reconstruct what Kabīr wrote"! Parasnath Tivari took it for granted that we should be able to reconstruct the original text of Kabīr, if we put together all the little pieces that have survived in the manuscripts. I translate from his critical edition a metaphor about the reconstruction of the text of Kabīr, which can be compared to the piling up of bricks from a wall that has collapsed:

> Today the original design of the house is changed and distorted but the bricks which built it are still there. We have to collect them, and after looking at their original cuttings carefully, to replace them in their original position as far as possible. In this way, we can reconstruct the house.[1]

It all looked very simple and easy but wrong; it became an even more exciting adventure, when I started to discover the singers in the manuscripts. Let me illustrate this growing insight by giving a description of the method of transmission of the songs of the Sants.

. . .

The language of this *bhakti* literature is a mixed medium, that was borrowed, not only from Sanskrit and Persian but also from the local idioms and dialects. The travelling singers adopted many terms and expressions as they travelled from one region to another, often in linguistic styles unfamiliar to some of the singers. This is particularly evident where the songs were in the Perso-Arabic style or where they incorporated Sanskritic diction. In some instances this leads to obscure meanings of the text, while in others it simply leads to the substitution of similar New Indo-Aryan terms for Perso-Arabic terms. Such changes are indicative of the influence of oral transmission. Such linguistic muddling is a type of change which could be expected if a song had been learnt by listening to it at an assembly of devotees, rather than directly to Kabīr or another Sant and their followers. Such changes point to the fact that the performance texts often became altered during transmission because of the limitations in the abilities of the performers. If all these factors are taken together it is no wonder that the versions of the songs found vary to the extent they do. In fact, it is remarkable that they are as consistent as they are.

. . .

This language was not until now described in exhaustive grammars and detailed dictionaries, as was the case with Sanskrit. Consequently, each fresh edition in this field requires a new

1. P.N. Tivari, *कबीर ग्रंथावली*, Allahabad, 1961, Introd., p. 54.

grammar and fresh glossaries and a student of this literature has to be acquainted with different linguistic areas in order to produce a translation. Here again new tools have to be made. Often a parallel passage can be useful to compare forms not found in any dictionary.[2] These publications may be useful both for philologists engaged in translation of parallel texts, and for linguists studying the language of the sixteenth and seventeenth centuries in north-west India. At the same time the abundance of material made available here can help in studying the language and its development.

...

Conclusion

The result of the singers' listening and composing, travelling and camping in different regions was not only that the songs changed their form: the language, too, was adjusted to the capacity of the audiences. Words were changed because they were understood better, or appealed more. In the temple or monastery of a particular sect, or in a village where certain sectarian traditions were predominant, the singers may have adapted even a particular imagery in a particular song. Above all, both the composing *bhakta* and the travelling singers borrowed from previous or contemporary poets. In this stemmatic chaos the translator, I would suggest, has to choose the meaning which makes most sense, even if thus there are several meanings. The translator may have to be satisfied with the fact that (s)he is not even certain that the choosen meaning is really what the original Sant meant.

A result of the stemmatic chaos is also that certain words are morphologically so corrupt that only a comparison with parallel strings of words — often formulaic expressions were borrowed as a whole — can help to find the meaning. Here again the Databanks of *bhakti* literature are useful.

---

2. In view of such a comparison I published Callewaert: 1991, 1996, 1997 and 2009.

22

Kabīr: Scholarly Commentaries on Uncritical Texts

[1996]*

ARE we writing scholarly commentaries on uncritical *bhakti* texts? It is a good exercise at times to ask the following question: if I could start again, would I do what I am doing now?

Of course, situations change and we may acquire more wisdom as we progress in life but I at times ask that question about the research I am doing, which since 1973 has been focused on searching for manuscripts in view of critical editions and an English translation of *bhakti* texts. These texts were created by the mystic-reformers in northern India in the fifteenth-sixteenth centuries.

If I could start again, would I do what I have been doing? The answer is definitely yes, for several reasons. That research has given me some good friends, all over the globe, it has given me the opportunity — when I was young — to make adventurous tours all over Rajasthan, using all available diplomatic skill in order to have access to the manuscripts but most importantly with that research I have contributed to the preservation and critical text-editions of old texts threatened with destruction.

In this paper I hope to illustrate the urgent need — in the area of *bhakti* literature but possibly also in other areas of Indological research — the urgent need to work on texts, according to the

* In *Annali*, Napoli: Istituto universitario Orientale, vol. 56,1, 1996; 88-98.

principle: "Let the commentator say what might be and what ought to be, and let the text-editor say what there is!".

Indological research on the North American continent has contributed immensely to the better understanding of Indian culture, with a mass of well-trained brains, plenty of enthusiasm and with what seems to us in Europe endless resources. But it appears to me that there is an unhealthy dominance here of the religious studies approach at the expense of text-based analytical scholarship.

. . .

It is only to be expected that many students will enter the subject through interest in religion rather than classical Indology, and it is desirable that they should be able to make this sort of move but it is critical that it be understood that this transition into the study of Indian phenomena is of little value unless it takes place through a rigorous training in Indology. This is not just a matter of picking up a language or two. They must also feel the necessity of getting themselves into a position in which they are able to interpret Indian texts within their own cultural context.

. . .

The songs of the *bhakti* mystic reformers were sung, and only around CE 1600 they were written down. Hence, since we have no recordings of the period, our only way to the original "sung" version is through a comparison of manuscripts now scattered all over the region, often in remote villages. For the last twenty years I have travelled extensively all over Rajasthan, as well as to Delhi, Banaras, Punjab, Pune and even Thanjavur. Every year I discovered new — often private — collections with ancient material, and along with my increasing databank of *bhakti* literature on film grew also the conviction that preservation of manuscripts and critical text-editions are a first priority for a student of Indian culture. The economic situation in India is such that the preservation of manuscripts is not the highest priority, although serious efforts are being made. Yet, thousands of manuscripts disappear every year, either through decay or lack of care, or because they are sold to tourists. Steps have to be taken to avert the catastrophy already underway as the result of the neglect of the vast collections of manuscripts. If these collections are allowed to rot away unconserved and are not even microfilmed, there will be little left with which to study Indian contributions to the world.

Do we write scholarly commentaries on uncritical texts? I address question with examples from the the studies on Mīrābāī, the Biography of Dādū, and three *bhakta*s of the *Pañcavāṇī*: Nāmdev, Raidās, and finally Kabīr.

23

The Ādigranth of the Sikhs: A Canon?

[2000]*

AN analysis of the method by which the *Ādigranth* of the Sikhs was compiled in 1604 in no way suggests a lack of respect for the sacredness of the scripture. Human hands and memories were indeed needed to give a form to the divine inspiration and in this article I try to describe the genius of the human medium which put that inspiration into writing. It was not only an inspiration of a moment or of a few months but of several centuries, as is testified by the numerous songs of *bhagat*s prior or contemporary to Guru Nānak. Drawing from my experience when studying huge anthologies of the same period in Rajasthan, I try to analyse the methods Guru Arjan applied to bring all the songs — nearly 6,000! — together, and I ask the following questions: were the songs of the gurus copied from existing written material, or dictated by Guru Arjan or by someone else, or were they written straight from the memory of the secretary Bhāī Gurdās? I wonder whether the canonical status attributed to the *Granth* was indeed part of the project in 1604, or could it have to do with a newly-defined identity of the Sikhs at the end of the eighteenth century?

Let us first see what tradition says about the redaction of the *Ādigranth* (called *Guru Granth* when it was installed as such by Guru Govind Singh). It is often taken for granted that, as early as 1550,

* In Mariola Offredi, *The Banyan Tree. Essays on Early Literatures in New Indo-Aryan Languages*, II, (Proceedings of the Seventh International Conference on Early Literature in New Indo-Aryan Languages, Venice, 1997); Delhi: Manohar, 1999, 457-468.

writing down songs was a common and ordinary enterprise in the Sikh environment. *It was not* in Rājasthānī Sant circles or in Banaras! The conviction about writing by the early Sikhs is evident in the publications of recent Sikh scholars. I quote only a few examples:

. . .

Some sources suggest that written collections of Nānak's songs were produced as early as during the lifetime of Aṅgad, the second guru.

. . .

Guru Nānak died in CE 1538 and in 1581 Arjan became the fifth guru. More than twenty years later it was decided that songs be brought together and written down in a canonical edition. We note 1604, a landmark in Sikh history and in the history of Sant literature in north India. Traditionally the following reason is given why Arjan decided to compile "orthodox" literature. Guru Arjan's enemies (the Minas lead by his elder brother Prithi Chand) were circulating copies of songs not acceptable to the "orthodox" branch led by Arjan.

If that was the reason, it is not clear — and that has been pointed out by even Sikh authors — why the songs of the non-Sikh *bhagat*s were included in the *Granth*, if the purpose was to standardize the Sikh songs! According to tradition, all available manuscripts were brought before Arjan. He examined every single song and instructed his secretary to write whatever was in agreement with orthodoxy. Some manuscripts had even to be brought from Sri Lanka, where Guru Nānak is supposed to have been.

. . .

Finally, I should mention the account which attributes the compilation of an important collection of songs to Mohan or to somebody in his family. This is the famous *Mohan-Pothī*.

. . .

So much for tradition. But what literary evidence do we have to support this description of the event of compilation and to corroborate the reasons why the *Granth* was compiled. In what source do we read for the first time about Nānak carrying a book with him? Here we enter the mine-field of hagiographical writing about the early Sikh Panth. I quote extensively from the earliest attested source, the *Gur Nānak Prakāś* by Santokh Singh. Many of the "traditional" theories current now are clearly formulated in it. In this account we read the dialogue which supposedly led to the decision to compile the *Ādigranth*:

. . .

If, with respect due to oral traditions, we try to argue only from evidence available in literary sources, I should point out that the *Gur Nānak Prakāś* — and the earliest description of the compilation — was written by Santokh Singh in 1823.

. . .

One could — hypothetically — suggest that accounts about the early Sikh Panth not only describe certain events but also add nuances of interpretation due to sectarian developments some time before Santokh Singh, that is, at the end of the eighteenth century or 200 years after Guru Arjan and his compilation of the *Granth*. As a result, what is given in Santokh Singh's dialogue may reflect a sectarian interpretation meant to give more importance to the redaction of the *Ādigranth* by Arjan Dev. Was there any political reason for that, around 1780? With due respect for oral traditions, it would appear that the "first" (?) literary evidence about the redaction of the *Ādigranth* — and the scribal claims about it — was written 219 years after 1604, relying to a great extent on an ever expanding version of the *Bālā Janm Sākhī*.

. . .

The compilation of a huge corpus like the *Ādigranth* was in no way a unique phenomenon around 1600. We have several Rājasthānī collections of enormous size and, like the *Ādigranth*, all are closely connected to the singing tradition. Even more, in early copies of these anthologies we find clear traces of scribes tampering with the text because of a link with the ongoing oral tradition. Looking at what happened to similar huge repertoires in Rajasthan, it should not amaze us if the text of the *Ādigranth* was not as sacrosanct as tradition wants us to believe; that it also was much more in close contact with an ongoing oral tradition than is generally accepted.

Summing up

Compilations of huge collections of Sant literature became quite a fashion in the early seventeenth century in north-west India. In Rajasthan these collections were to a great extent written from memory or from unorganized notes of musicians. The pattern of classification of the songs also points to a close link with the musical tradition.

If we argue that the *Ādigranth* was (to a great extent) written from memory and not (only) from written documents compiled earlier, we may ask the following questions. Is the reason for compilation necessarily as sectarian as later accounts seem to suggest? Even if the original copy prepared under the direction of Guru Arjan is still available, we know that copies were soon made. Was the collection "canonical" from the very start, making changes and additions by early copyists impossible? Many scribes often were singers. They knew the songs by heart. Have they left traces of their interference in the early manuscripts? Can we accept the hypothesis of oral contamination during the first scribal days of the *Ādigranth*? In the Rājasthānī manuscripts of the *Pañcavāṇī* and the *Sarvāṅgī*s we clearly see the interference of singers changing their repertoires and of scribes copying earlier collections.

24

The "Early Hindī" Hagiographies by Anantadās

[2003a]*

SOME time before or around 1600 an ascetic of the Rāmānandī order in Rajasthan felt inspired to bring together in a poetic composition the different legends he had heard about the great *bhaktas* of his times. He most probably did not use ink or paper but sang and composed as he recited, convinced that he earned great merit doing that. It is not unlikely that the story he himself sang a couple of years later was slightly different, because of a particular need or bias in an audience or because he had learnt something more in the meantime. But the purpose was always the same: to sing the praises of the saint and proclaim the supremacy of devotion (*bhakti*) to God (called Hari, or Rām).

He sang about Nāmdev, Kabīr, Raidās, Dhanā, Aṅgad, Trilochan and Pīpā. More famous *bhaktas* he could not have chosen and four of them (Kabīr, Dhanā, Pīpā and Raidās), he says, were initiated by Rāmānand. Nāmdev, Aṅgad and Trilochan were too faraway in the past, even for his sense of history to call them disciples of Rāmānand. The association with Rāmānand was repeated by Nābhā and Rāghavdās in their *Bhaktmāls*, and by later tradition but doubted recently by Parshuram Chaturvedi (1964) and modern scholarship. Many legends about the saints must have

* In Phyllis Granoff & Koichi Shinohara (eds.) *Pilgrims, Patrons and Place: Localizing Sanctity in Asian Religions*, UBC Press Vancouver/Toronto, 2003, 203-23.

been at the disposal of Anantadās. Already in his days dozens of legends about the famed Kabīr and Raidās of Banaras were circulating in Rajasthan. For the other *bhaktas* he had to be satisfied with just a couple of legends.

These *parcaīs* composed by Anantadās became very popular matter for travelling singers and *bhaktas* who drew great inspiration from the miracles, the encounters of the saints with brāhmaṇs and *qāzīs*, their unfaltering trust in God never deserting them. The travelling singers who memorized the *parcaīs* of Anantadās were themselves also poets, capable of adding or changing a line or two. The result of their genius and creativity is a headache and a challenge for the textual critic who looks at manuscripts and tries to restore what Anantadās originally must have recited.

A study of the *parcaīs* of Anantadās gives not only an insight in a very creative period of oral transmission. These *parcaīs* are also like a video of late sixteenth-century social and religious thinking. In the essay I briefly summarize some of the *parcaīs* (pp. 204-10) and then I discuss the following topics:

. . .

Pīpā parcaī: historical and "biographical" data, main stories and their lessons, miracles (pp. 210-20), and further: attitudes promoted in the *parcaīs*.

. . .

Conclusion

The *bhakti* poets in north India (sixteenth-seventeenth centuries) appear before us through different channels. Their songs were written down in manuscripts at a particular time (and copied by scribes later on); or, their songs were transmitted in a continuous oral tradition in which the number of songs was increased and the variant lines were added even more generously than in the scribal tradition; or, commentaries started to appear and finally the poets come to life in their "biographies". These "biographies" could be voluminous *Bhaktmāls* on one side of the spectrum with brief notes on a big number of *bhaktas*, or could be lengthy descriptions of a particular poet on the other side. The *parcaīs* by Anantadās belong to the latter category, which was often scorned as mere legendary accounts, eulogizing and promoting a particular saint. We now know better. Even in the miraculous and quasi-historical accounts a vivid picture of the times of the poet emerges, as is evident in the lengthy *Pīpā parcaī* discussed here. The critical edition and complete English translation of these *parcaīs* I refer to Callewaert 2000a (see above, pp. 198ff.).

25

Bhakti Literature
An Oral-Scribal Archetype

[2003b]*

THIS essay deals with the *bhakti* literature in north-west India between 1400 and 1700. This literature consists mainly of religious songs and hagiographical narratives. The songs were most often not written down by the original poets and were orally transmitted for a period varying from three centuries to fifty years before being written down. The first manuscripts now available are dated around 1600. I propose to describe a method that may enable the textual critic to go beyond the "written archetype" and approach the "oral archetype" of some of these texts.

. . .

Singers changed texts to suit their musical purposes or to adjust to their audiences. Scribes may have changed texts because of laziness, or because they no longer understood the texts, or because they had sectarian or theological interests to defend (as when the values important to a guru who initiated a new trend were quickly overturned by different, often contrary, priorities). A clear example is the *Life-story of Dadu* (see above, pp. 173ff.) that exposed such changing attitudes, apparently creating displeasure within the Dādū sect. More dangerous still is the notion that it

---

* In Ramona Modiano, Leroy F. Searle and Peter Shillingsburg (eds.) *Voice, Text, Hypertext*, Seattle and London: University of Washington Press, 2003, 115-24.

may be worthwhile to look at the earliest manuscripts of the *Ādigranth* of the Sikhs and to consider whether there, too, scribal alterations reflect changing attitudes.

Changing attitudes reflected in a fresh text edition are of historical interest but they also have a theological and devotional importance. Religious insights need constant rethinking if they are not to become obsolete. One way to rethink them is to go back to the earliest sources and to scratch from existing editions the layers of interpretation — and possibly also of manipulation — that the passage of time has seen added to the text. The textual critic's enterprise, therefore, has a social importance as well, especially in living *bhakti* traditions.

Further, for the history of religions, fresh critical editions are needed that are not only based on new "ancient" material but also made with a new methodology. Otherwise, scholars and students will make studies of the influence of Kabīr of about 1500 on the Dādū sect of about 1600, using Kabīr texts of 1700! Studies of this kind, often with titles like "A Comparative Study of . . . (. . . *tulnātmak adhyayan*)", are abundantly available but do not necessarily reach correct conclusions. Finally, linguists and philologists, too, are often misled by wrong chronologies, which are based on editions that have relied on manuscripts from later periods.

In the different editions that I have prepared, I did not apply the same method to all the *bhakti* texts, although what I call the method of "oral-scribal archetypes" gave very good results for at least two texts. Even though the so-called *bhakti* literature is in many ways uniform in its purposes and common elements, a single method could not be applied.

. . .

For the "scribal archetype" method, see *Dādū-janmalīlā* (above, pp. 173ff.)

. . .

For the "oral-scribal archetypes" method, see the editions of the *pad*s of Nāmdev and of Raidās (pp. 183ff. and 189ff.)

It was in the course of research on the *pad*s of Nāmdev that I developed and tested my hypothesis about relationships among manuscripts representing singers' repertoires. With this hypothesis, much *bhakti* literature and its transmission during the oral and the scribal periods can now be studied in a different light.

. . .

If Nāmdev once composed his songs, very soon they became the property of singers who handled them according to their own inspiration, musical genius and particular dialect. Singers may well have combined several versions they had heard. We may also assume that it was mostly the capable singers, those who were more poetic and creative, who prevailed. And we notice the consequences of that creativity in the stemmatic chaos before us.

What then are we looking for in these *bhakti* songs? We are looking for a text which is found in many musical traditions.

. . .

26

The Holy Book of the Sikhs (India)

Sacred Scripture as a Canon

[2004]*

IN this essay I should like to discuss revelation and sacred scripture as a canon, applied to the Sikh religion in India (and abroad). It is rewarding to try to understand the process of canon formation in the Sikh tradition, because of its relevance to other scriptures as well.

If one studies a text as a scripture, one cannot be only concerned with textual problems or contextual meanings: one has to be aware also of the ongoing role of the text in the tradition of the religious community, especially if the text has become a normative source of authority. The reason is that *scripture is a human activity in which people make a text into a scripture by treating it in a certain way*. This view will, in any religious tradition, not be pleasing to believers who see their text as a result of a "direct revelation", whatever that means.

If as a textual critic one is not able to define the nature of "revelation" as basis for the authority of a text, one may ask what the historical developments were/are that eventually did bring a community to define that authority in the way we see it

---

* In D. De Smet, G. de Callatay and J. Van Reeth (eds.) *Al-Kitāb. La sacralité du texte dans le monde de l'Islam*, (Actes du Symposium International tenu à Leuven et Louvain-la-Neuve du 29 mai au 1 juin 2002), Acta orientalia Belgica. Subsidia III, 2004, 425-34.

functioning today. This approach does not lack respect for the feelings of the believer: it studies the human hands that were used by the Divine to bring about a text.

My argument is based on the development of the *Ādigranth* (the Holy Book of the Sikhs, India) in its process of compilation and in the first stages of its scribal transmission. Very clearly the attentive student sees there elements that clarify the growing status of authority. But there is more: a study also singles out the elements that show *how* the *Granth* gradually adopted an authoritative and revealed status in its early development.

Statements

- The sacredness of the Holy Book of the Sikhs lies not in the text but in the minds and hearts of the Sikhs.
- The study of a text as a scripture is not only concerned with its textual problems but also with its ongoing role in the tradition of a religious community.
- Scripture is a *human* activity in which people make a text into scripture by treating it in a certain way.
- It is evident from the works of the Sikh gurus that they were self-consciously involved in the creation of a new scripture *parallel to* both the Hindu Vedas and the Islamic Quran.
- The primary intention of the compiler Guru Arjan was to create an authoritative text for the Sikh community through which it could understand and assert its unique identity.
- We notice that very early in the Sikh tradition the Scripture is portrayed as existing *prior* to the revelation.
- A text is canonical not by virtue of being the final, correct and official version but because it becomes binding on a religious community.

. . .

Conclusion

When studying the Sikh Scripture as an ongoing process of variant readings, one is interested in the history of a text, not just in order to decide what the original reading was but to see how the tradition dealt with the same concerns that people have today. It is a fact that the Sikh scripture cannot be considered as a once-for-always standardized text. There are enough variant readings in the early manuscripts to contradict such a position. It is interesting to observe from the examination of old manuscripts that the later scribes who failed to understand tradition struggled with problematic texts and responded to this problem by tampering with the text of the Sikh scripture. Variations in the early manuscripts must not be regarded simply as scribal errors in the usual sense but rather as examples of *regional or dialectical forms used in the oral transmission of a singing tradition.*

I take it for granted that in order to be sacred a text does *not* have to be correct, or free of scribal errors, which in fact are mainly due to regional divergencies and misunderstandings by the scribes. An examination of the early manuscripts reveals the *evolution of the text* of the Sikh Scipture through different historical phases.

A careful survey of the early manuscript material reveals that there was no unity of this sacred text to be found among its different versions around 1675. There was no one version of the Sikh Scripture that was accepted by all the Sikhs from 1700 onwards, and by the beginning of the nineteenth century they were using more than four different versions of their Scripture.

To conclude, I argue that the issue of canon formation should be treated according to the more radical *power criteria* rather than literary criteria.

27

Kabīr, Do We Sing His Songs or Someone Else's?

[2005]*

THERE may be several reasons why one has interest in the mystics-reformers of the fourteenth-seventeenth centuries in northern India. Besides the scholarly interest, I have been attracted by their inspiring and very modern message. Finding such a message in another culture (too) is not a threat to one's own tradition. On the contrary, it is a gift — in this period of increased communication, and of growing openness in the West — that reveals other aspects of the Divine, or puts renewed accents.

In this essay I should like to address the following questions: Is there a similarity between the times in which these poets flourished, and our times? How did their songs and verses address the contemporary problems, and can they have a message for us? What is the essence of that message? Finally, and most importantly, do we sing the songs as they were created by a particular poet, or are they added by the later tradition?

. . .

I address these questions with a study of Mīrā, Jangopāl's *Lifestory of Dādū*, Nāmdev, Raidās and Kabīr.

. . .

---

* In Anne S. King & John Brockington (eds.) *The Intimate Other: Love Divine in Indic Religions*, Orient Longman, 2005, 129-52.

Regarding Kabīr, I should like to conclude with a consideration about authorship. All the songs composed by the mediaeval saints (Kabīr, Sūrdās, Mīrā and hundreds of others) have the name of the composing saint-poet, usually in the last line. But it is evident from the analysis made above that hundreds of songs created by someone else, sometimes by very good poets, were included in the repertoire of, e.g. Kabīr and were given the name (or *bhaṇitā*) of Kabīr.

In the West this would probably be called "voluntary plagiarism" and I do not know how the copyright laws can deal with this. What are we to make of a situation where, for instance, a good scholar produces a wonderful piece of research on Kabīr and publishes it in an outstanding journal under the name of another famous author? The first author gladly gives up the honour of publishing in his or her own name because — and this is one explanation for the phenomenon I have discussed — it is more important for him/her to belong to the tradition of the second, more famous, author. This would give the first author more satisfaction then if he published under his own name.

Something like this definitely happened in the sixteenth and seventeenth centuries, when good poet-mystics composed a good song and circulated it in the singing tradition with the name of, e.g. Kabīr. In this respect the mediaeval Indian psyche is different from our modern Western attitude. It is essential for an Indian to have a grounding in an authoritative past, to be part of a living memory, to be inscribed in an ongoing social subconsciousness, to be linked to what Indians call a *paramparā*, an authoritative tradition. A similar phenomenon is noticed in the guru-disciple relationship, or in the *gotra* awareness in the caste system. This need to be linked to a glorious past may help to explain why individual authorship may have become less relevant.

28

Pads of Guru Nānak in Rājasthānī Manuscripts

[2006]*

"THIS is dynamite", Hew McLeod wrote to me about [now] 30 years ago and Sikh scholars in Delhi who had agreed to help me to identify the *pads* in the *Ādigranth* politely discontinued the collaboration when they saw the material. Five "Bhakti conferences" passed till eventually I decided to bring the material to the Ninth Conference in Heidelberg [2003] and tell, not what I think but what the manuscripts tell us. At this moment two basic questions are not satisfactorily answered: *when* did these *pads* come to Rajasthan, and *how*? I attempt to give an answer and I am convinced and hopeful that Sikh scholars will be better equipped to speculate about this, looking at what the manuscripts tell us about the beginning of the seventeenth century in northern India

This, however, is certain: the manuscript material leads the student into the very fascinating world of the study of manuscripts and back to the times when we hear devotee-singers who travelled from one village to another in the neighbouring regions of Punjab and Rajasthan, possibly even before 1600.

---

* In Monika Horstmann (ed.) *Bhakti in Current Research, 2001-2003.* (Proceedings of the Ninth International Conference on Early Devotional Literature in New Indo-Aryan Languages, Heidelberg, 23-26 July 2003); with a DVD by Daniel Gold, South Asia Institute, University of Heidelberg, South Asian Studies 43, New Delhi, Manohar Publishers, 2006, 49-113.

Why, of the 974 compositions of Guru Nānak and the 2,218 compositions of Guru Arjan in the *Ādigranth*, were 26 *pads* and *c.* 200 *sākhīs* with the *bhaṇitā "nānak"* circulated in the oral transmission in Rajasthan and were scribed there in Dādūpanthī manuscripts, dated 1614 till 1676? And why precisely these *pads* and *sākhīs*? What are the changes that occurred in that transmission and is there a pattern in these changes? As the *Ādigranth* was compiled in 1604, is it possible that these *pads* were circulating outside Punjab even before that date?

In the Rājasthānī manuscripts all these *pads* are listed as *nānak ke pad*.

- 10 of these *pads* are in the *Ādigranth* attributed to *mahalā* 1 or Nānak.
- 13 *pads* with the *bhaṇitā "nānak"* in the Rājasthānī manuscripts have in the *Ādigranth* the *bhaṇitā "nānak"* (as is customary) but are attributed to *mahalā* 5 or the fifth Guru, Arjan, the compiler.
- 2 *pads* are so far not found in the *Ādigranth*.

. . .

Do these *pads* with the *bhaṇitā "nānak"* published here derive from one archetypal source, either a travelling singer or a written document? They may have entered Rajasthan along different paths and through different villages. Do they rely on different sources in Punjab? Keeping these questions in mind let us look at the variants, in the text and in the *rāgs*.

. . .

It is generally accepted that the *bhagat* literature (e.g. Kabīr) started to be incorporated into the pre-*Ādigranth* singing (or written?) repertoires in Punjab. Taking Kabīr as a test example, we clearly see that the *structure* of the *pads* of Kabīr in the Rājasthānī manuscripts is uniformly different from the structure of those *pads* in the *Ādigranth*. The refrain (called *ṭek* in the Rājasthānī manuscripts) was most probably sung after each stanza but in the manuscripts the *ṭek* line is written at the beginning of the *pad*. In the *Ādigranth* that refrain (called *rahāu*) is usually or often given after the first stanza.

. . .

As can be seen in the 26 compositions published in the article, the *rahāu* lines in the "*nānak pads*" are often given in different places (see e.g. *pad* 9). As for my research I took the Rājasthānī manuscripts as basic text, I also give the lines in the order found in those manuscripts (see sample below).

This, then, is the tricky question. When we examine the structure of the "*nānak pads*" found in the Rājasthānī manuscripts, we note that without one exception, the "Punjab" structure of the compositions is changed into the "Rājasthānī" structure. By whom and why? Did the travelling singers going south to Rajasthan change the structure? Or did the Dādūpanthī scribes separately compiling the *Sarvāṅgīs* and *Pañcavāṇīs* (in the plural: i.e. not following one single archetype!; see above pp. 83ff.)? If we accept that the "*nānak pads*" (of Guru Nānak or Guru Arjan) were originally composed and sung in the "Punjab" structure, *why* was that order changed in Rajasthan?

Why, by whom and at what time? The compositions of the first five gurus of the Sikh tradition and of the north-Indian *bhagats* were brought together in one huge volume in 1604. That immense effort by Guru Arjan was most probably based on already existing manuscript collections predating 1604. Did the compositions quoted below find a basis in the **pre**-1604 texts, or are they based on what Guru Arjan compiled? If we accept that the *Pañcavāṇīs* — the earliest manuscript used here is dated 1614 — are not copies of one single archetype but were produced independently by different *Pañcavāṇī* compilers in the Dādūpanth, it is not unlikely that the first so-called "*nānak* compositions" entered Punjab before Guru Arjan commissioned the compilation of the *Ādigranth*.

There is no doubt that the versions quoted in this article are *not* going back to one single archetype, in Rajasthan or Punjab. If one singer or singers' family would have brought this collection to Rajasthan during their evening singing sessions under a tree or in a temple in Rājasthānī villages, we might be able to construct a kind of stemma. There is no sensible stemma, not of the variant readings and not of the *rāgs*. As a sample, I quote a few lines from *Ādigranth*, pp. 1035 न15; 1-2 in *rāg mārū*; mss. A, C, D, E, F *rāg mārū*; E *bhairū*. Interestingly, ना तदि is found at the beginning of line न15;3 in the *Ādigranth*. For more details I refer to the complete article.

. . .

For endless aeons, there was only utter darkness.

There was no earth or sky; there was only the infinite *Hukam*.

न15	1a	अरबद नरबद धुंधूकारा ॥ धरणि न गगना हुकमु अपारा ॥
A	1	अरबद नरबद धुंधूकार ॥ धरंणि न गगन न अंगेस अपार ॥
C	1	अरबद नरबद धूंधूंकार ॥ धरणि न गगन न हुकम अपार ।
D	0	अरबद त्रबद धूंधूकार । धरणि गूगन न हुकम अपार ।
E	0	अरबद नरबद धुंधुंकार । धूंरणि न गगन न हुकम अपार ।
F	1	अर्वद नर्वद धूंधूंकार । धरणि न गगन न हुकंम पसार ।

There was no day or night, moon or sun; God sat in profound samādhi. | | 1 | |

न15	1b	ना दिनु रैनि न चंदु न सूरजु सुंन समाधि लगाइदा ॥
A	1	ना तदि रैंणी चंदन सूर ॥ सुंनि समाधि लगांईदा ॥
C	1	ना तदि रैंणीं चंद न सूरिज । सुनि समाधि लगांईंदा ॥
D	0	ना तदि रैंणि न चंद न सूरज संन समाधि लगांईदा ॥
E	0	नां तदि रैंणीं चंद सूरिज । सुंनि संमाधि लगांईदा ॥
F	1	नां तदि रैंणीं चंद न सूर । शुंनि समाधि लगांइंदा ॥

Bibliography

Note: The bibliographical references, in the context of Mīrā (pp. 104ff.), are not given in this list. Books referred to in the footnotes with an abbreviation (e.g. **Barathval: 1936**) are here printed in bold.

Avate, T.H., ed., *सकलसंतगाथा*, Poona, 1924, No. 3964.

Bahura, G.N., *विद्याभूषण ग्रंथसंग्रह सूची*, Rājasthān Purātan Granthamālā, Jodhpur, 1961.

Banerji, S.C., *A Companion to Sanskrit Literature*, Delhi, 1971.

Barathval: 1936 = Barathval, P.D., *The Nirguṇa School of Hindī Poetry*, Banaras, 1936.

Barathval, P.D., *Gorakha-bāṇī*, Allahabad, 3rd edn., 1950.

Bati, N. S., "Mīrā Prakaraṇ", in: *Paramparā* (Hindī), 1982.

Belvalkar, S.K., "The so-called Kashmir Recension of the *Gītā*", in: *A Volume of Indian and Irianian Studies*, Bombay, 1939.

Callewaert, W.M., "A 17th c. Anthology of Hindī Poetry", in: *Orientalia Lovaniensia Periodica*, 5, 1974, 163-85 (see also below, Callewaert: 1993).

Callewaert: 1978[1] = Callewaert, Winand M., *The Sarvāṅgī of the Dādūpanthī Rajab*, 1978, 446 pp.

Callewaert, Winand M., "Search for Manuscripts of the Dādūpanthī Literature", in: *Orientalia Lovaniensia Periodica*, 4, 1973, 155-67; and Ibidem, in: *cit.*, 8, 1977, 305-08; also "Nirguṇ Literature on Microfilm in Leuven, Belgium", in: *IAVRI Bulletin*, London, IX (Dec. 1981) 24-48.

Callewaert & Hemraj: 1983 = Callewaert, W.M. & Shilanda Hemraj, *Bhagavadgītānuvāda: A Study in Transcultural Translation*, Ranchi, 1983, distributed by Biblia Impex, New Delhi, 399 pp.

Callewaert, W.M., "The Leuven Text Composition System in Indian Alphabets", in: *ALLC Bulletin*, vol. 12, 1 (1984) 5-8.

Callewaert, W.M., "Indian Manuscripts without Autograph? : A Computer Analysis", in: *The Indo-Iranian Journal*, 30 (1987), 65-71.

1. See http://www.arts.kuleuven.be/caies/wcal.htm for the complete bibliographical list of Winand M. Callewaert.

Callewaert: 1988 = Callewaert, Winand M., *The Hindī Biography of Dādū Dayāl*, (Introduction; critical edition; English translation), Motilal Banarsidass, Delhi, 1988, 179 pp.

Callewaert & Lath: 1989 = Callewaert, Winand M. & Mukund Lath, *The Hindī Songs of Nāmdev*, Orientalia Lovaniensia Analecta, Leuven (and Motilal Banarsidass, *The Hindī Padāvalī of Nāmdev*, Delhi), 1989, 429 pp.

Callewaert & Op de Beeck: 1991 = Callewaert, Winand M. & Bart Op de Beeck, *Devotional Hindī Literature*, 2 vols, Manohar, New Delhi, 1991, 1175 pp.

Callewaert & Friedlander: 1992 = Callewaert, Winand M. & Peter Friedlander, *The Life and Works of Raidās*, Manohar, Delhi, 1992, 335 pp.

Callewaert: 1993 = Callewaert, Winand M., *The Sarvāṅgī of Gopāldās: A 17th Century Anthology of Bhakti Literature*, Manohar, New Delhi, 1993.

Callewaert & Snell: 1994 = Callewaert, Winand M. & Rupert Snell, eds., *According to Tradition: Hagiographical Writing in India*, Harrassowitz, Wiesbaden, 1994, 271pp.

Callewaert: 1996 = Callewaert, Winand M., *Śrī Guru Granth Sāhib, With Complete Index*, Motilal Banarsidass, 1996, vol. 1 (complete text), 1430pp.; vol. 2 (contents and index), 967pp.

Callewaert & Lutgendorf: 1997 = Callewaert, Winand M. & Philip Lutgendorf, *Rāmcaritmānas Word-Index*, Manohar, New Delhi, 1997.

Callewaert: 2000a = Callewaert, Winand M., *The Hagiographies of Anantadās: The Bhakti Poets of North India* (in collaboration with Swapna Sharma), Curzon, London, 2000.

Callewaert: 2000b = Callewaert, Winand M., *The Millennium Kabīr Vāṇī: A Collection of Pad*s (in collaboration with Swapna Sharma and Dieter Taillieu), Manohar, New Delhi, 2000.

Callewaert & Taillieu: 2002 = Callewaert, Winand M. & Dieter Taillieu, eds., *Devotional Literature in South Asia: Current Research 1997-2000* (Proceedings of the Eighth International Conference on Early Literature in New Indo-Aryan Languages, Leuven, 23-26 August 2000); Manohar, New Delhi, 2002 (with extensive bibliography, pp. 233-314).

Callewaert: 2009 = Callewaert, Winand M., *Dictionary of Bhakti: North-Indian Bhakti Texts into Khaṛī Bolī Hindī and English* (with the assistance of Swapna Sharma), D.K. Printworld, New Delhi, 2009 (3 vols., 2187 pp.).

Callewaert, Winand M., "Sants", in: *Brill's Encyclopedia of Hinduism*, vol. III, 2011, 532-45.

Chaturvedi: 1964 = Chaturvedi, P., *उत्तरी भारत की संत-परंपरा*, 2nd edn., Allahabad, 1964.

Chaturvedi, P., *दादूदयाल ग्रंथावली*, Varanasi, VS 2023 (= CE 1966-67).

Chintamani, T.R., ed., *Śrīmad Bhagavadgītā* (A Kashmirian Recension with the Sarvatobhadra Commentary of Rajanaka Ramakantha), Madras, 1941.

Dikshit, T.N., *परिचयी साहित्य*, Viśvavidyālay Hindī Prakāśan, Lucknow, 1957.

Dube, L.P., *हिन्दी भक्त वार्ता साहित्य*, Sāhitya Sadan, Dehradun, 1968.

Dwivedi, H.P., *रामानंद की हिन्दी रचनाएँ* Nagari Pracarini Sabha, Varanasi, 1955.

Eliade, M., *Le Yoga*, Paris, 1954.

Gode, P.K., "The *Bhagavadgītā* in the Pre-Shankaracarya Jain Sources", in: *Annals BORI*, 20 (1938-39) 194.

Griffith, John G., "Non-stemmatic Classification of Manuscripts by Computer Methods", in: Jean Irigoin and Gian Piero Zarri, eds., *La Pratique des ordinateurs dans la critique des textes*, Paris, CNRS, 1979, 73-86.

Guignard, Florence Pasche, "Go West, Mīrā! Translating Medieval Bhakti Poetry" (with an extensive bibliography, and in Appendix: Translations of the *Padāvalī* into English), in: Maya Burger & Nicola Pozza, *India in Translation through Hindī Literature: A Plurality of Voices*, Peter Lang, Bern, 2010, 195-234.

Iraqi, S., *The Sarbaṅgī of Rajabdās*, Aligarh, 1985.

Sitaram, Lalas, *राजाथांनी सबद कोस*, vols. 1-10, Jodhpur, 1962-78.

Maheshvari, H., *राजस्थानी भाषा और साहित्य*, 1960.

Maheshvari, H., *जाम्भोजी. विस्णोई संप्रदाय और साहित्य*, Calcutta, 1970.

Maheshvari, H., *History of Rājasthānī Literature*, Sahitya Akademi, New Delhi, 1980.

Mangaldas: 1947 = Mangaldas, Svami, *गरीबदासजी की वाणी*, Jaipur, 1947.

Mangaldas, Svami, *श्रीदादूदयालजी की वाणी सटीक*, Jaipur, n.d. (1951).

Mangaldas, Svami, ed., *श्रीमहाराज हरिदासजी की वाणी*, Jaipur, 1962.

McLeod: 1968 = McLeod, W.H., *Guru Nānak and the Sikh Religion*, Oxford, 1968.

McLeod, W.H., *The Evolution of the Sikh Community* (Delhi, Oxford University Press, 1975, Oxford, The Clarendon Press), 1976.

Nahta: 1965 = Nahta, Agarchand, ed., *राघवदासकृत भक्तमाल*, Jodhpur, Rājasthān Prācya Pratiṣṭhān, 1965.

Narayandas, Svami, *श्रीरज्जबवाणी*, Ajmer, 1967.

Narayandas, Svami, *श्रीदादूदयालजी की वाणी*, Jaipur, n.d. (c. 1969).

Narayandas: 1969 = Narayandas, Svami, *राघवदासजीविरचित भक्तमाल*, Pushkar, 1969.

Narayandas: 1975 = Narayandas, Svami, *श्रीदादूचरितामृत*, 2 vols, Mantri, Svāmī Jayarāmadās Smṛti Granthamālā, Jaipur, 1975.

Narayandas, Svami, *श्रीदादूपंथपरिचय*, 3 vols., Śrī Dādū Mahāsabhā, Jaipur; Pushkar, 1979.

Orr: 1947 = Orr, W.G., *A Sixteenth-Century Indian Mystic*, London: Lutterworth Press, 1947.

Platts, J.T., *A Dictionary of Urdū, Classical Hindī and English*, Oxford University

Press, (1884) 1968.

Sharma, B.P., *भक्तरत्नावली,* Viśva Bhāratī Prakāśan, Chandigarh, 1982.

Sharma, K.C., *भक्तमाल और हिन्दी काव्य में उसकी परंपरा,* Manthana, Rohtak, 1983.

Sharma: 1936 = Sharma, P.H., *सुंदर-ग्रंथावली,* Rajasthan Research Society, Calcutta, VS 1993 (= CE 1936-37).

Sharma, Vasudev, *संत कवि दादू और उनका पंथ,* New Delhi, Śodhaprabandha Prakāśan, 1969.

Shea, D. and A. Troyer, eds., *Dabistān-i-mazāhib*, 3 vols., Paris, 1843.

Siddons, G.R., "Extract and Translation of one of the Granthas, or Sacred Books, of the Dadupanthi Sect", in: *Journal of the Asiatic Society of Bengal*, 6, 1837 (pp. 481-87 and pp. 751-56).

Simha, K.P., *दादूपंथ एवं उसके साहित्य का समीक्षात्मक अध्ययन,* Banaras, Kashi Vidyāpīṭha, 1971.

Singh, Pritam, "Bhāī Banno's copy of the Sikh Scripture", in: Monika Thiel-Horstmann, *Bhakti in Current Research, 1979-1982*, Berlin, 1983.

Singhal, B.K., *रज्जब की सरबंगी,* Raigarh, 2010.

Dādū, Sukh Dayāl, "आचार्यवर श्रीस्वामीगरीबदासजीमहाराज का आदर्श जीवनचरित्र", in: *श्रीदादूसेवक,* 5, part 4, Jaipur, 1947.

Surajandas, ed., *दादूमहाविद्यालय रजत जयंतीग्रंथ,* Jaipur, 1952.

Thomson, J.C., *BG or the Sacred Lay*, London, 1855.

Tivari, P.N., *कबीर ग्रंथावली,* Allahabad, 1961.

Traill, John, *Memo. on Bhasha Literature*, Jeypore, 1884 (India Office Library, London, manuscript B 28a).

Tripathi, C.P., *दादूवाणी,* Ajmer, 1917.

Tukārām, *श्रीतुकारामाञ्छागाथा,* 2 vols., Bombay: Government Central Press, 1950, 1:594.

Ujjval, Udayaraj, ed., "चारण ब्रह्मदास दादूपंथी विरचित भगतमाल", in: *Rajasthan Purātan Granthamālā*, Jodhpur, no. 43, 1959.

Van Buitenen, J.A., "A Contribution to the Critical Edition of the *Bhagavadgītā*", in: *JAOS*, 85, 1965.

Varma, Vraj Lal, *रज्जब बानी,* Kanpur, 1963.

Varma, Vraj Lal, *संत कवि रज्जब,* Jodhpur, 1965.

Vaudeville, Ch., *Kabīr-Granthāvalī*, Pondicherry, 1957.

Vaudeville, Ch., *Kabīr*, I, Oxford, 1974.

Vaudeville, Charlotte, *A Weaver Called Kabīr* (Selected Verses, With A Detailed Biographical and Historical Introduction), Delhi, Oxford University Press, 1993.

von, Schlegel, A.-W., "Letter to the Honorable Court of Directors of the

Honorable East-India Company", in: *Réflexions sur l'Etude des langues asiatiques*, London, 1828.

Wilson, H.H., *Religious Sects of the Hindus* (London, 1861; reprinted, Calcutta: Sushil Gupta, 1958).

Wilson, H.H., "A Sketch of the Religious Sects of the Hindus," in: *Asiatic Researches*, 16, 1828.

Index